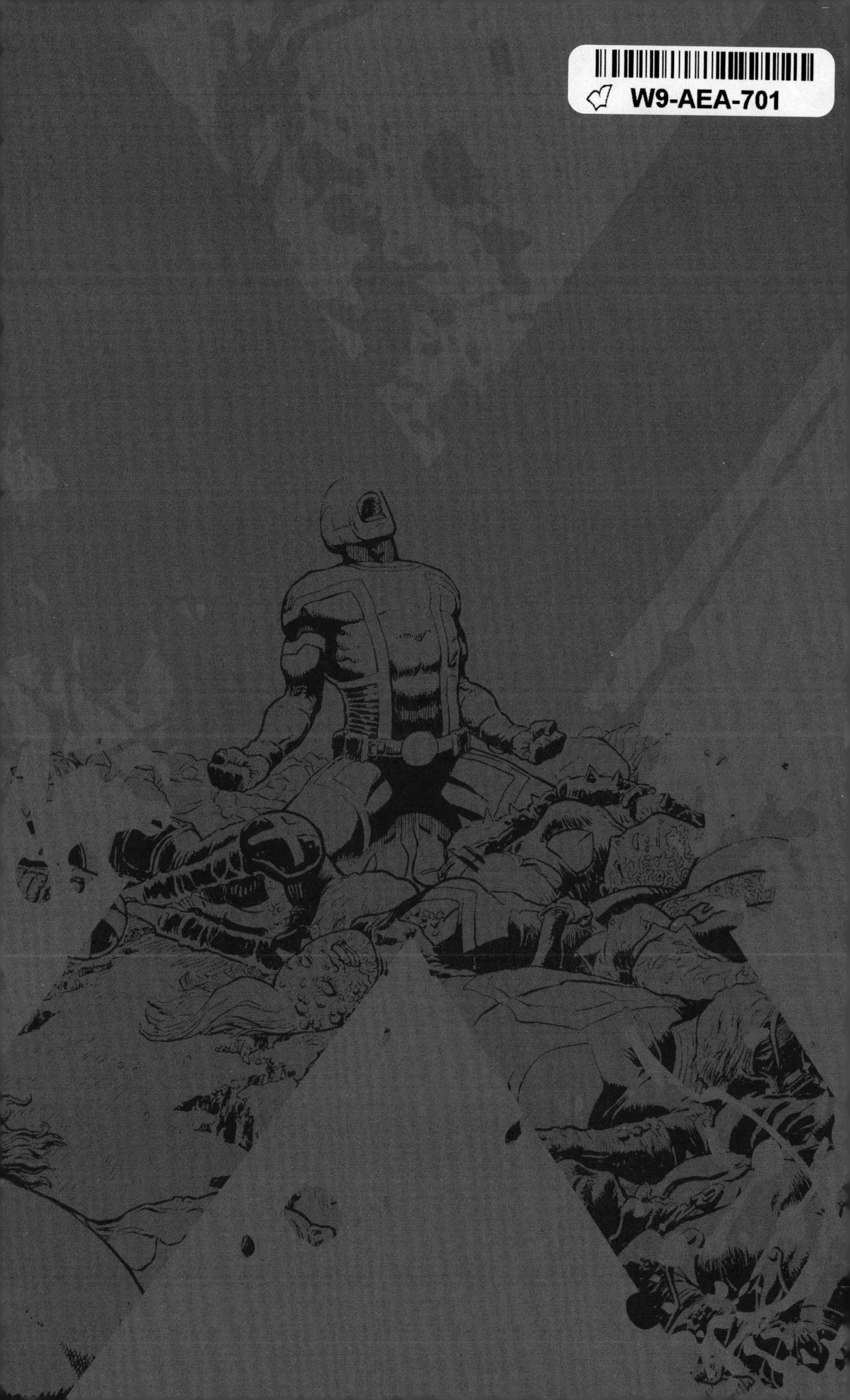

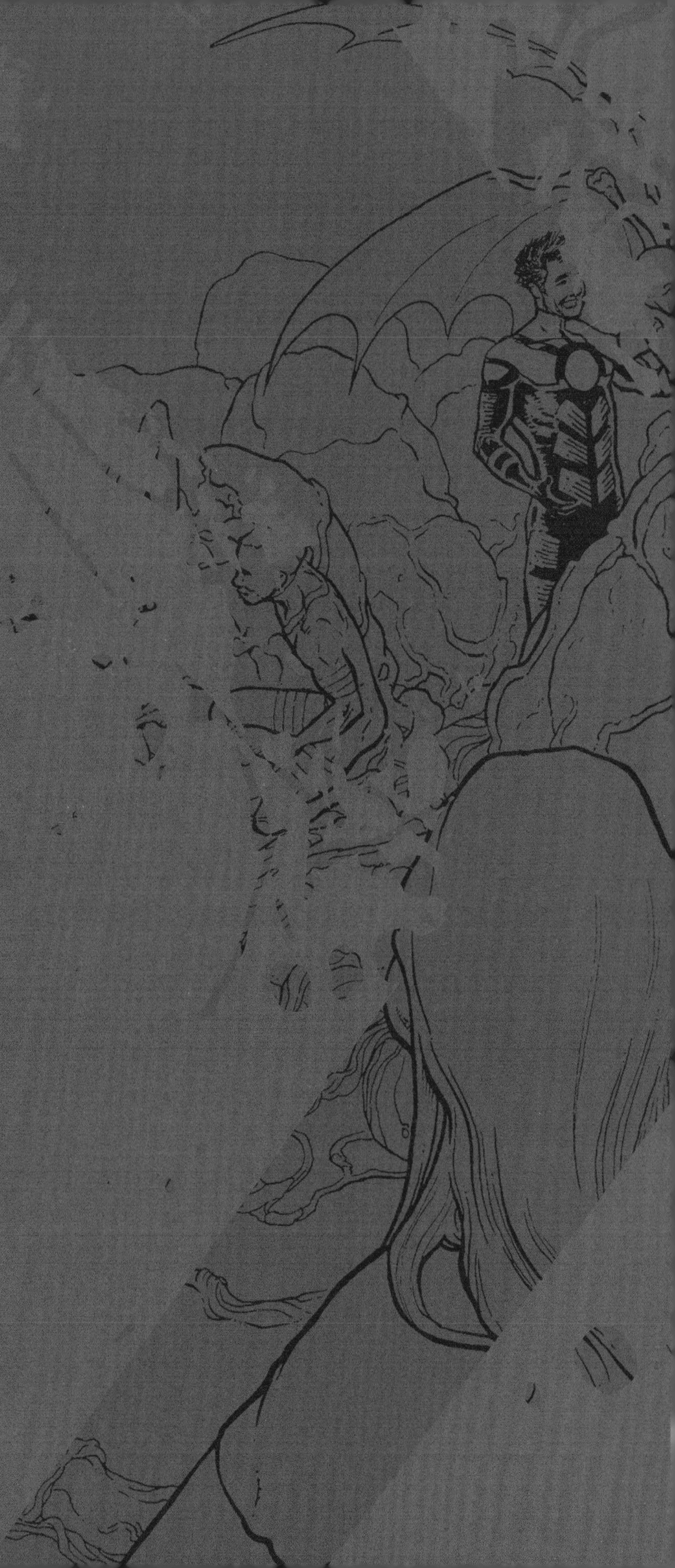

X-Men created by Stan Lee & Jack Kirby

collection editor: Jennifer Grünwald
assistant editor: Caitlin O'Connell
associate managing editor: Kateri Woody
editor, special projects: Mark D. Beazley
vp production & special projects: Jeff Youngquist
svp print, sales & marketing: David Gabriel
book designer: Adam Del Re

editor in chief: Axel Alonso
chief creative officer: Joe Quesada
publisher: Dan Buckley
executive producer: Alan Fine

DEATH OF X. Contains material originally published in magazine form as DEATH OF X #1-4. First printing 2017. ISBN# 978-1-302-90337-4. Published by MARVEL WORLDWIDE, INC., a subsidiary of MARVEL ENTERTAINMENT, LLC. OFFICE OF PUBLICATION: 135 West 50th Street, New York, NY 10020. **Printed in Canada.** ALAN FINE, President, Marvel Entertainment; DAN BUCKLEY, President, TV, Publishing & Brand Management; JOE QUESADA, Chief Creative Officer; TOM BREVOORT, SVP of Publishing; DAVID BOGART, SVP of Business Affairs & Operations, Publishing & Partnership; C.B. CEBULSKI, VP of Brand Management & Development, Asia; DAVID GABRIEL, SVP of Sales & Marketing, Publishing; JEFF YOUNGQUIST, VP of Production & Special Projects; DAN CARR, Executive Director of Publishing Technology; ALEX MORALES, Director of Publishing Operations; SUSAN CRESPI, Production Manager; STAN LEE, Chairman Emeritus. For information regarding advertising in Marvel Comics or on Marvel.com, please contact VC DeBellis, Integrated Sales Manager, at vdebellis@marvel.com. For Marvel subscription inquiries, please call 888-511-5480. **Manufactured between 1/6/2017 and 2/7/2017 by SOLISCO PRINTERS, SCOTT, QC, CANADA.**

10 9 8 7 6 5 4 3 2 1

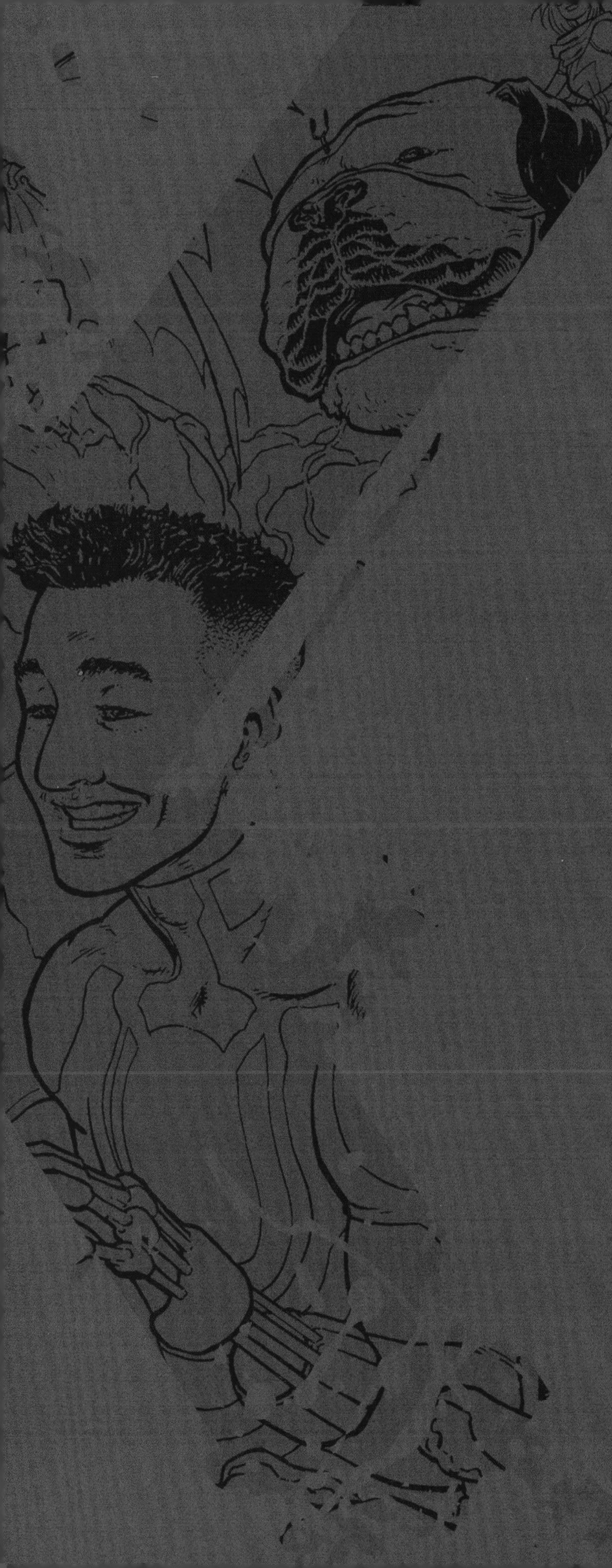

DEATH OF X

WRITERS:
Jeff Lemire & Charles Soule

PENCILERS:
Aaron Kuder (#1-4) &
Javier Garrón (#3-4)

INKERS:
Aaron Kuder (#1), Jay Leisten (#2-4) &
Javier Garrón (#3-4) with
Cam Smith (#2) & Scott Hanna (#2)

COLORISTS:
Morry Hollowell (#1-4) &
Jay David Ramos (#2, #4) with
Jason Keith (#2), Wil Quintana (#2),
Matt Milla (#2) & Andrew Crossley (#2)

LETTERER:
VC's Joe Sabino

COVER ART:
Aaron Kuder & Morry Hollowell

ASSISTANT EDITORS:
Chris Robinson & Charles Beacham

EDITORS:
Daniel Ketchum & Wil Moss

X-MEN GROUP EDITOR:
Mark Paniccia

EXECUTIVE EDITOR:
Nick Lowe

MUTANTS

Considered to be the next step in human evolution,
mutants discover their heritage at puberty,
when they manifest superhuman powers and abilities.
But rather than being celebrated for their gifts,
mutants are hated and feared.

CYCLOPS

EMMA FROST

MAGIK

ICEMAN

STEPFORD CUCKOOS

GOLDBALLS

INHUMANS

Thousands of years ago aliens experimented on cavemen,
supercharging their evolution, and then mysteriously left
their experiments behind. These men and women — called
"Inhumans" — built the city of Attilan and discovered
a chemical called Terrigen that unlocks secret super-powers
in their modified DNA. Black Bolt unleashed the Terrigen
Mists across the planet in the hope of awakening
latent Inhumans worldwide.

CRYSTAL

GORGON

GRID

FLINT

NAJA

ISO

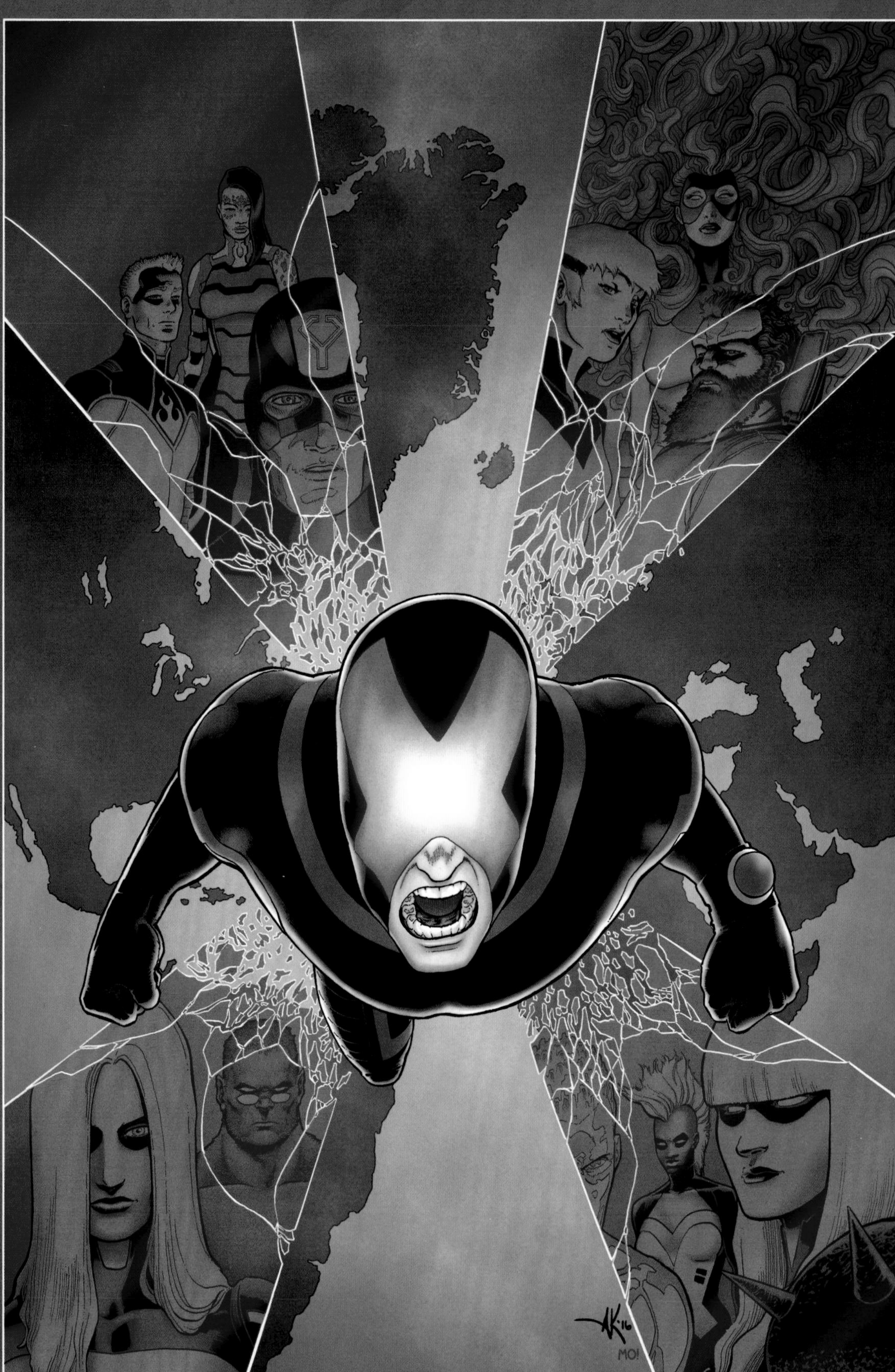

1

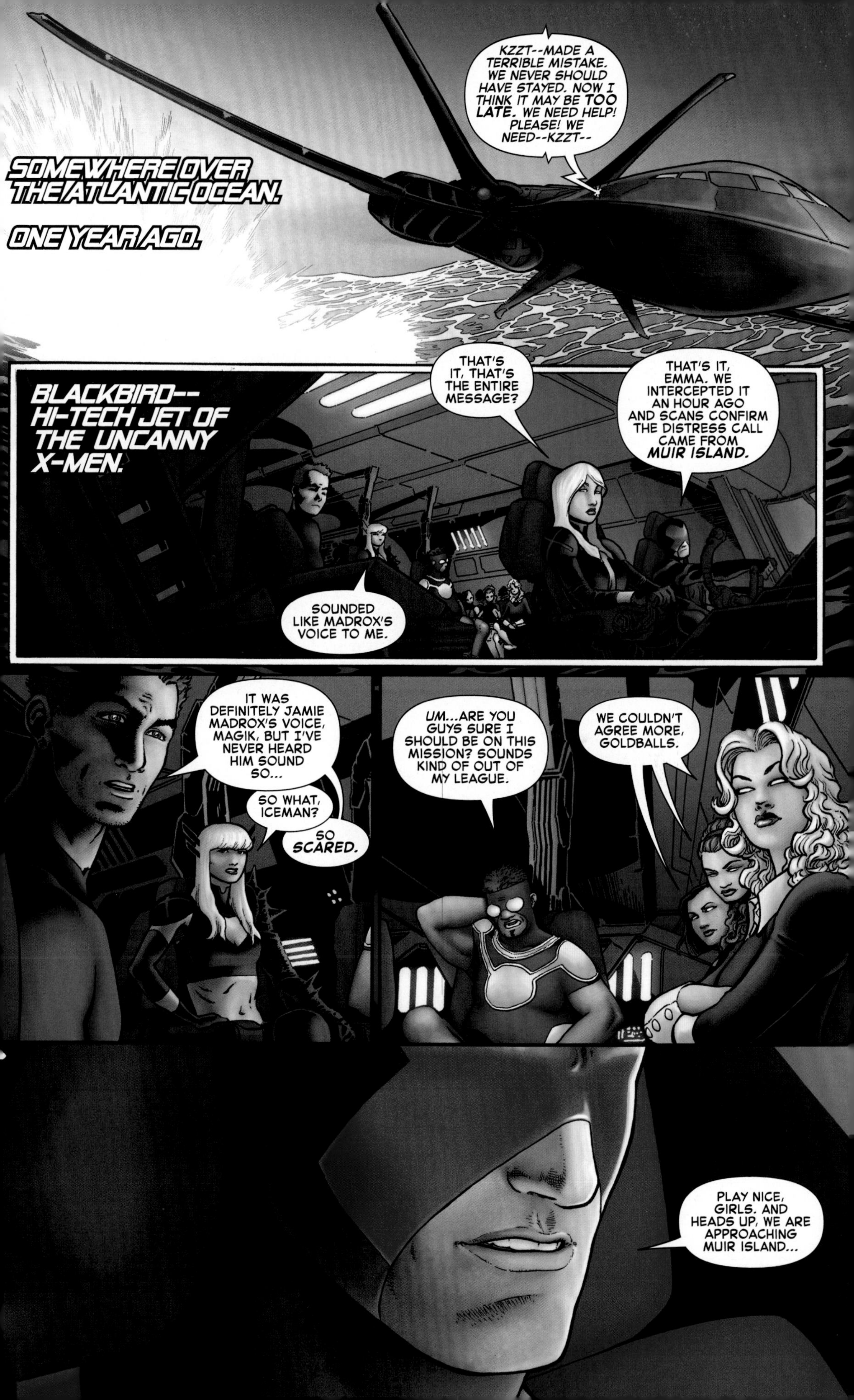
SOMEWHERE OVER THE ATLANTIC OCEAN.
ONE YEAR AGO.
KZZT--MADE A TERRIBLE MISTAKE. WE NEVER SHOULD HAVE STAYED. NOW I THINK IT MAY BE TOO LATE. WE NEED HELP! PLEASE! WE NEED--KZZT--
BLACKBIRD-- HI-TECH JET OF THE UNCANNY X-MEN.
THAT'S IT, THAT'S THE ENTIRE MESSAGE?
THAT'S IT, EMMA. WE INTERCEPTED IT AN HOUR AGO AND SCANS CONFIRM THE DISTRESS CALL CAME FROM MUIR ISLAND.
SOUNDED LIKE MADROX'S VOICE TO ME.
IT WAS DEFINITELY JAMIE MADROX'S VOICE, MAGIK, BUT I'VE NEVER HEARD HIM SOUND SO...
SO WHAT, ICEMAN?
SO SCARED.
UM...ARE YOU GUYS SURE I SHOULD BE ON THIS MISSION? SOUNDS KIND OF OUT OF MY LEAGUE.
WE COULDN'T AGREE MORE, GOLDBALLS.
PLAY NICE, GIRLS. AND HEADS UP, WE ARE APPROACHING MUIR ISLAND...

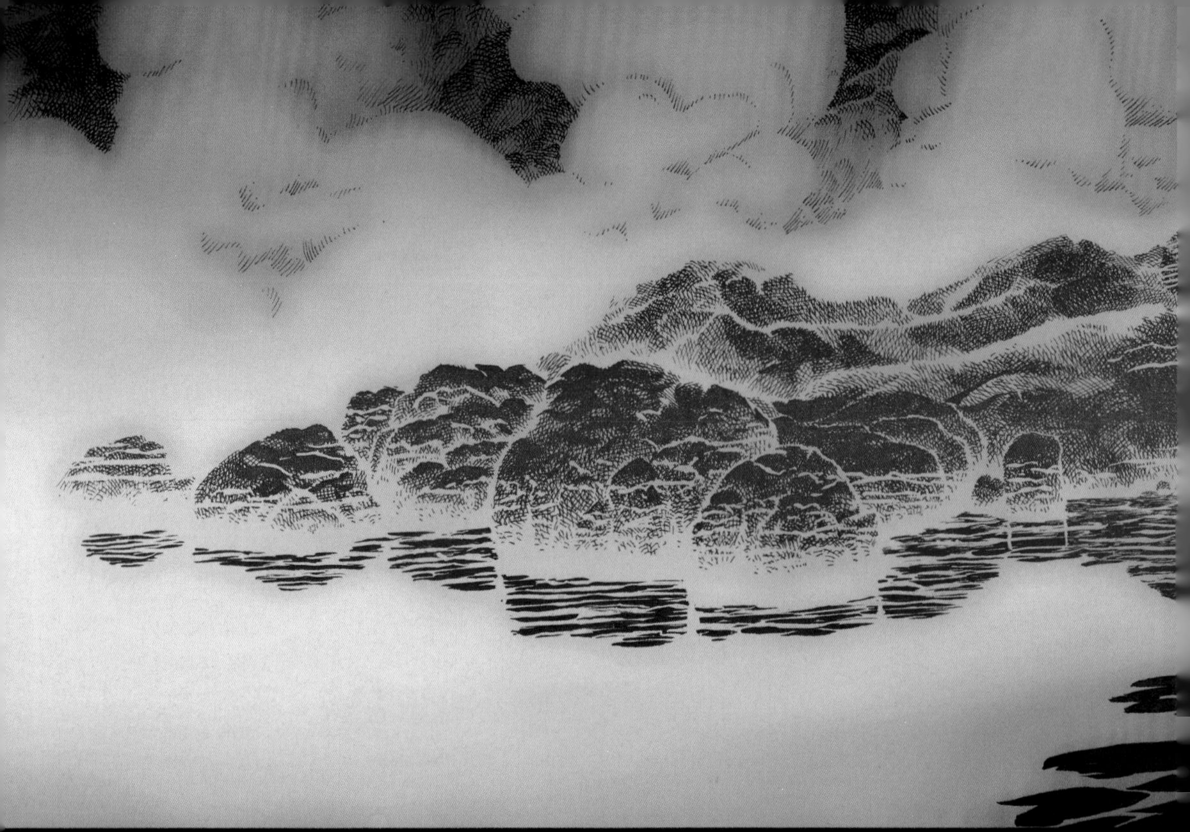

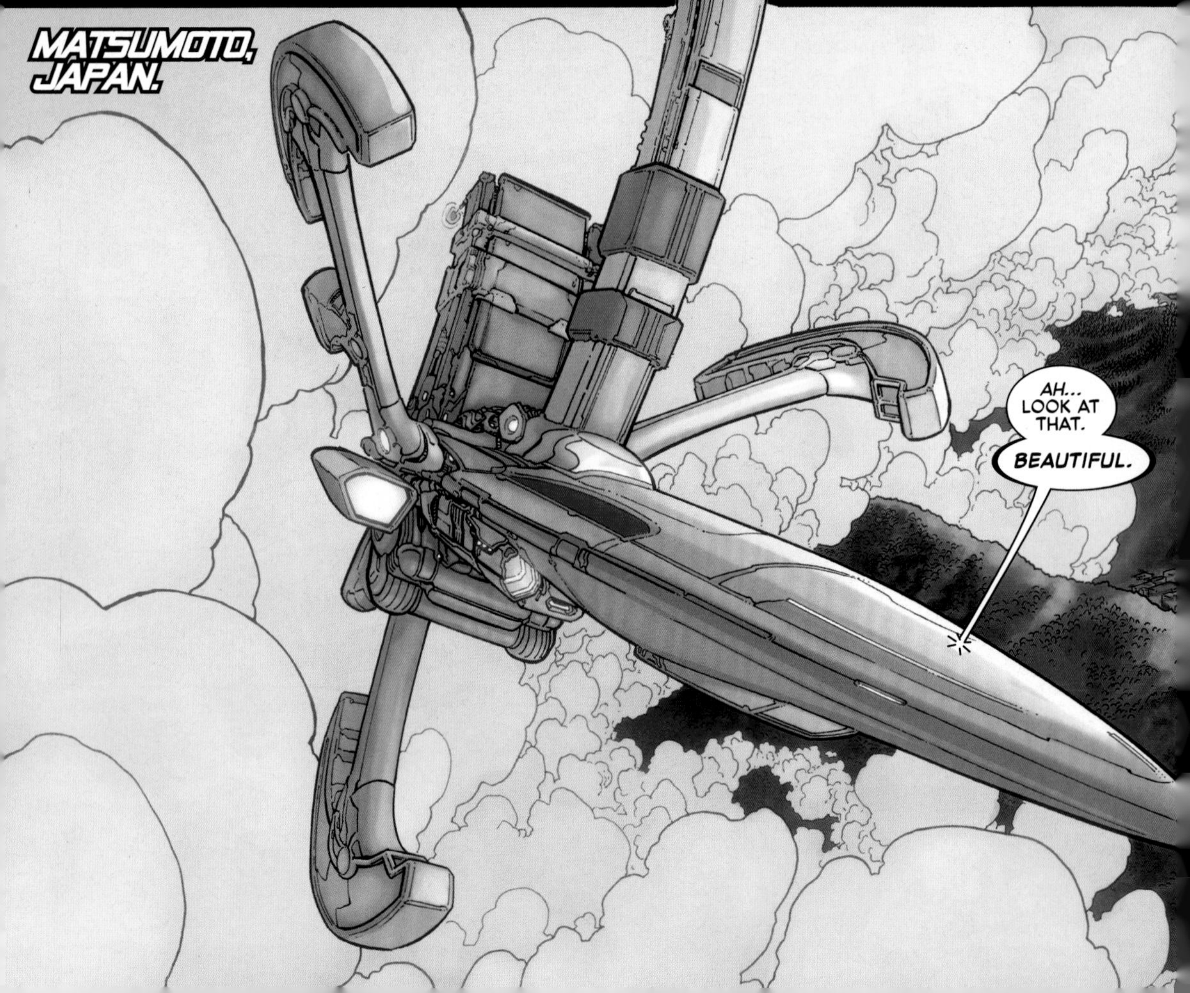
MATSUMOTO, JAPAN.
AH... LOOK AT THAT.
BEAUTIFUL.

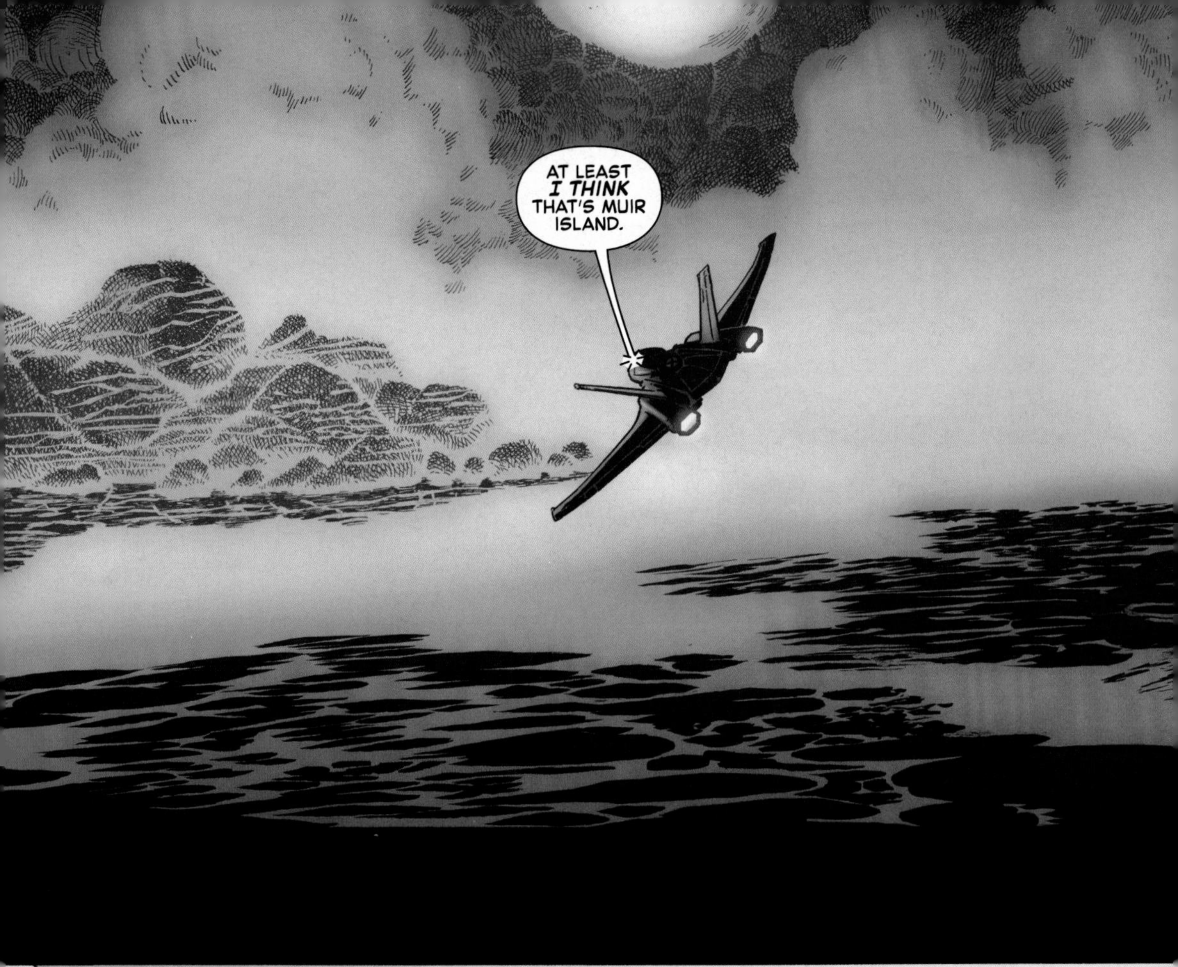
AT LEAST *I THINK* THAT'S MUIR ISLAND.
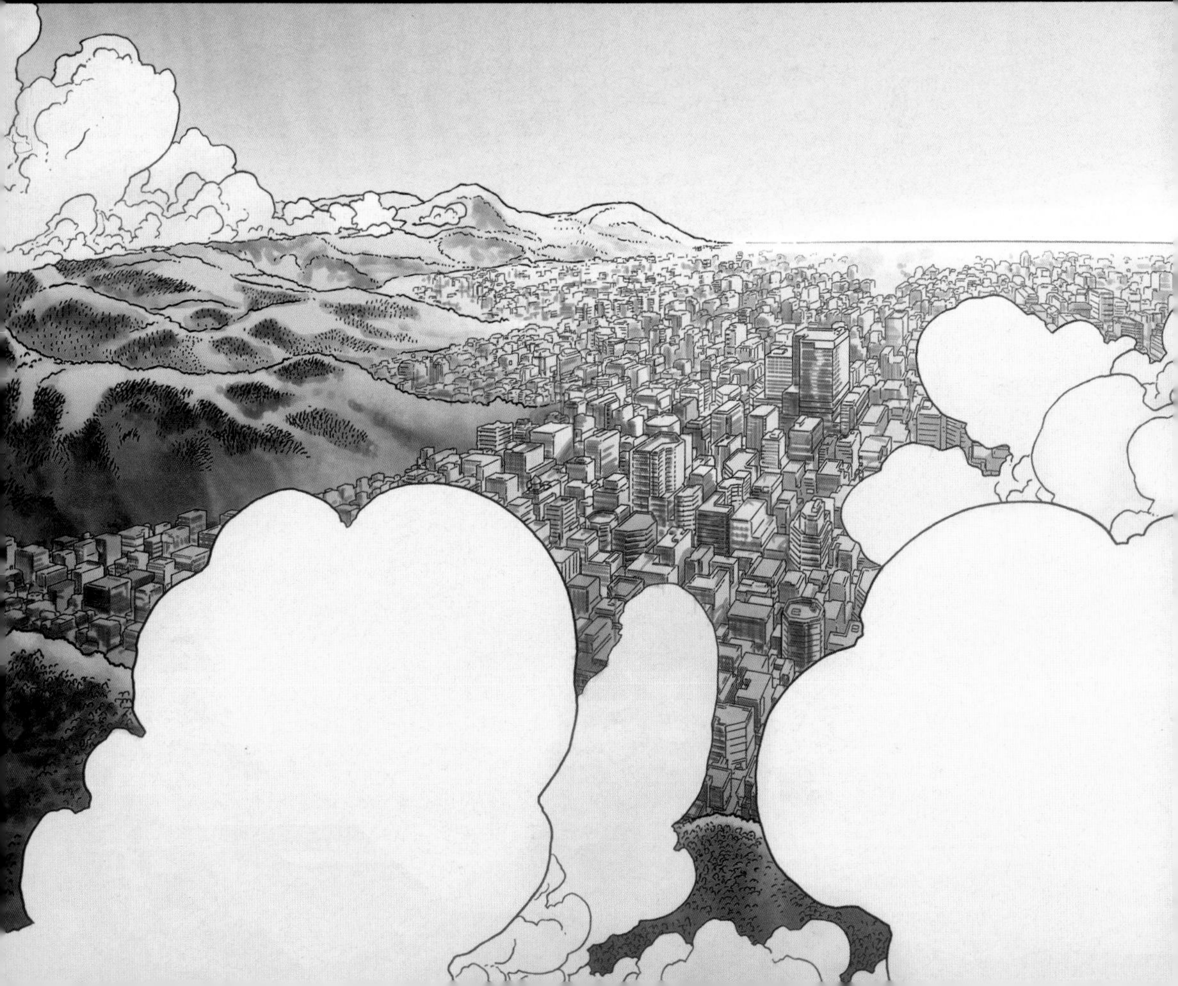

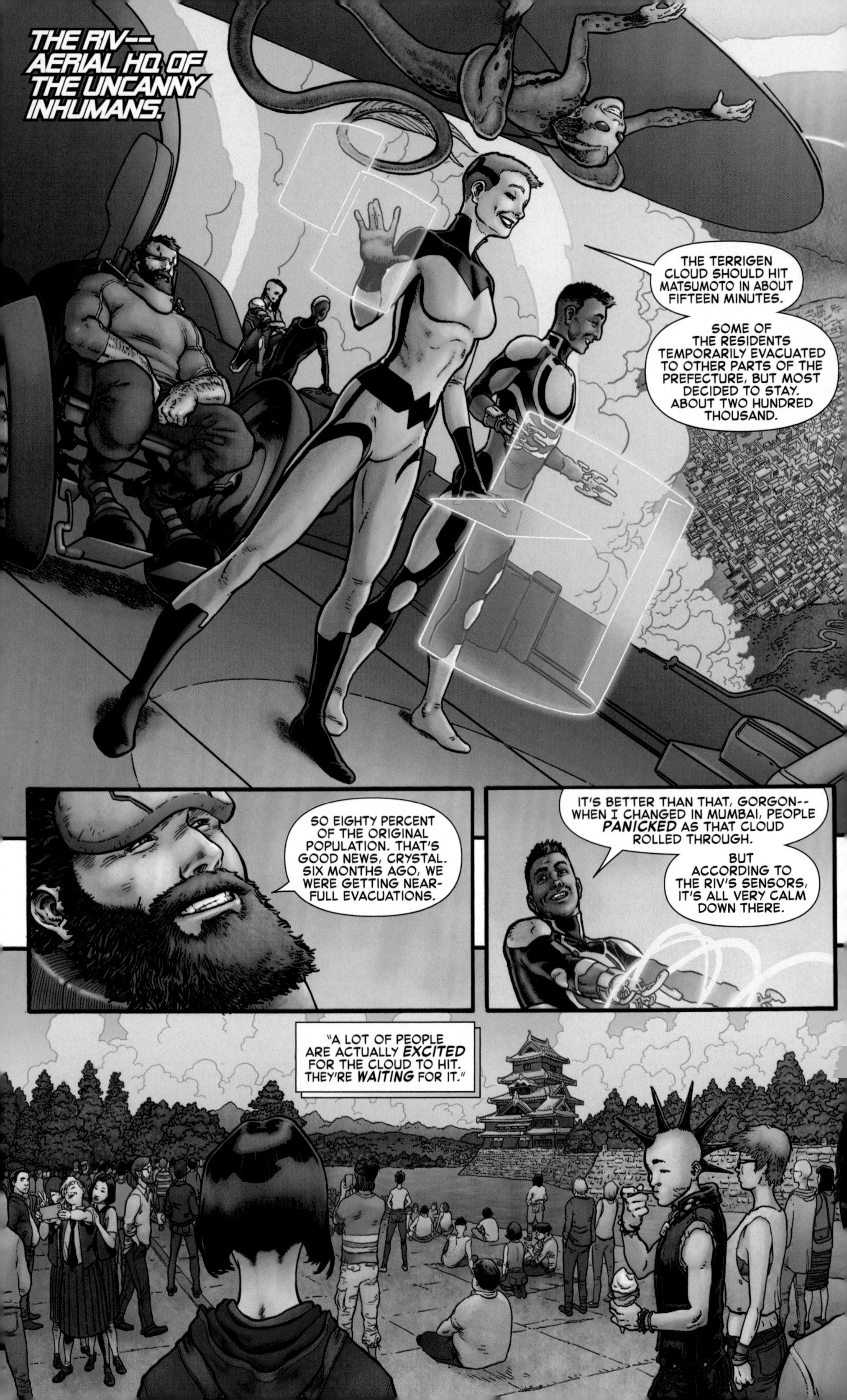
THE RIV-- AERIAL HQ OF THE UNCANNY INHUMANS.
THE TERRIGEN CLOUD SHOULD HIT MATSUMOTO IN ABOUT FIFTEEN MINUTES.
SOME OF THE RESIDENTS TEMPORARILY EVACUATED TO OTHER PARTS OF THE PREFECTURE, BUT MOST DECIDED TO STAY. ABOUT TWO HUNDRED THOUSAND.
SO EIGHTY PERCENT OF THE ORIGINAL POPULATION. THAT'S GOOD NEWS, CRYSTAL. SIX MONTHS AGO, WE WERE GETTING NEAR-FULL EVACUATIONS.
IT'S BETTER THAN THAT, GORGON-- WHEN I CHANGED IN MUMBAI, PEOPLE PANICKED AS THAT CLOUD ROLLED THROUGH.
BUT ACCORDING TO THE RIV'S SENSORS, IT'S ALL VERY CALM DOWN THERE.
"A LOT OF PEOPLE ARE ACTUALLY EXCITED FOR THE CLOUD TO HIT. THEY'RE WAITING FOR IT."

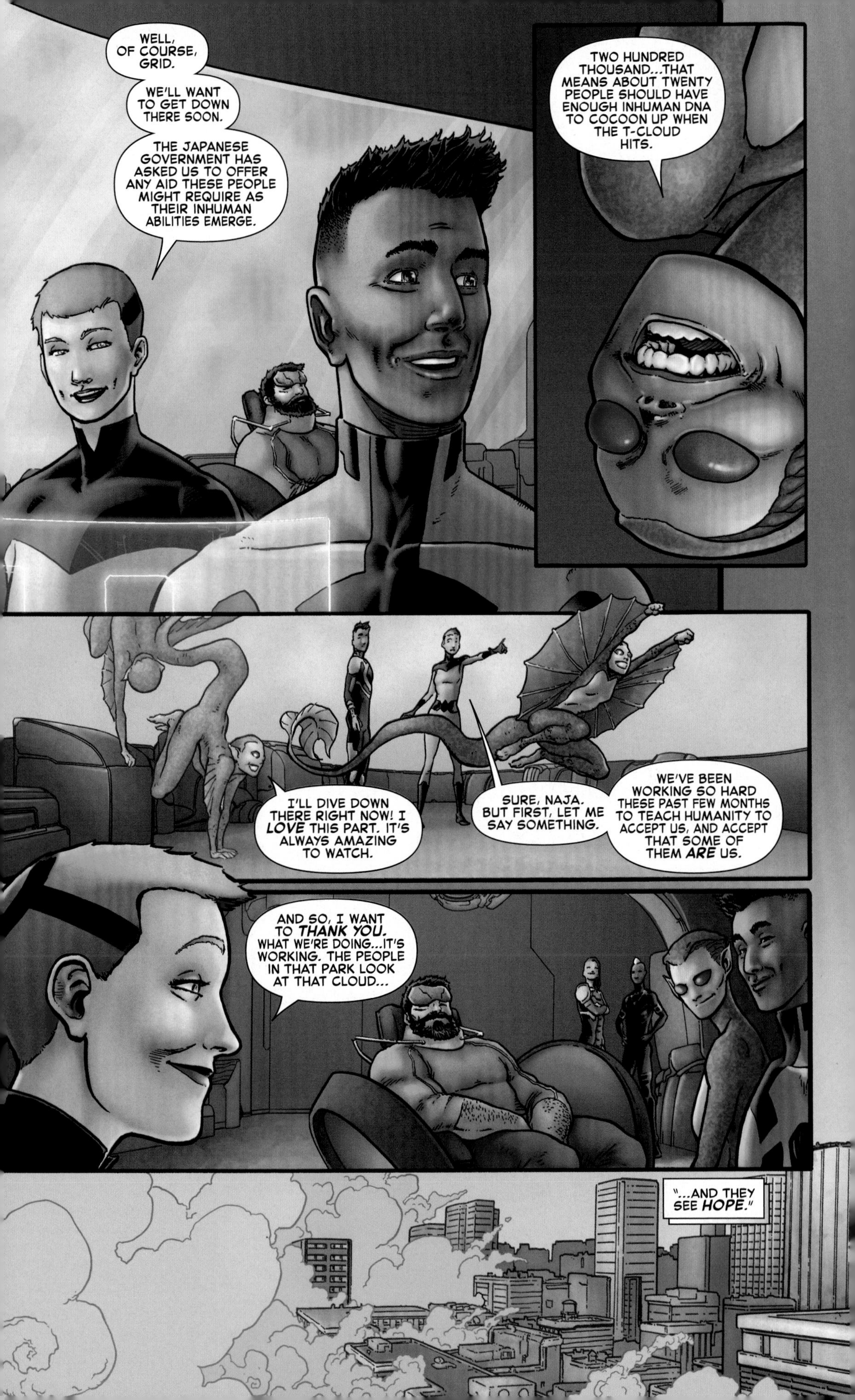
WELL, OF COURSE, GRID.
WE'LL WANT TO GET DOWN THERE SOON.
THE JAPANESE GOVERNMENT HAS ASKED US TO OFFER ANY AID THESE PEOPLE MIGHT REQUIRE AS THEIR INHUMAN ABILITIES EMERGE.
TWO HUNDRED THOUSAND...THAT MEANS ABOUT TWENTY PEOPLE SHOULD HAVE ENOUGH INHUMAN DNA TO COCOON UP WHEN THE T-CLOUD HITS.
I'LL DIVE DOWN THERE RIGHT NOW! I LOVE THIS PART. IT'S ALWAYS AMAZING TO WATCH.
SURE, NAJA. BUT FIRST, LET ME SAY SOMETHING.
WE'VE BEEN WORKING SO HARD THESE PAST FEW MONTHS TO TEACH HUMANITY TO ACCEPT US, AND ACCEPT THAT SOME OF THEM ARE US.
AND SO, I WANT TO THANK YOU. WHAT WE'RE DOING...IT'S WORKING. THE PEOPLE IN THAT PARK LOOK AT THAT CLOUD...
"...AND THEY SEE HOPE."

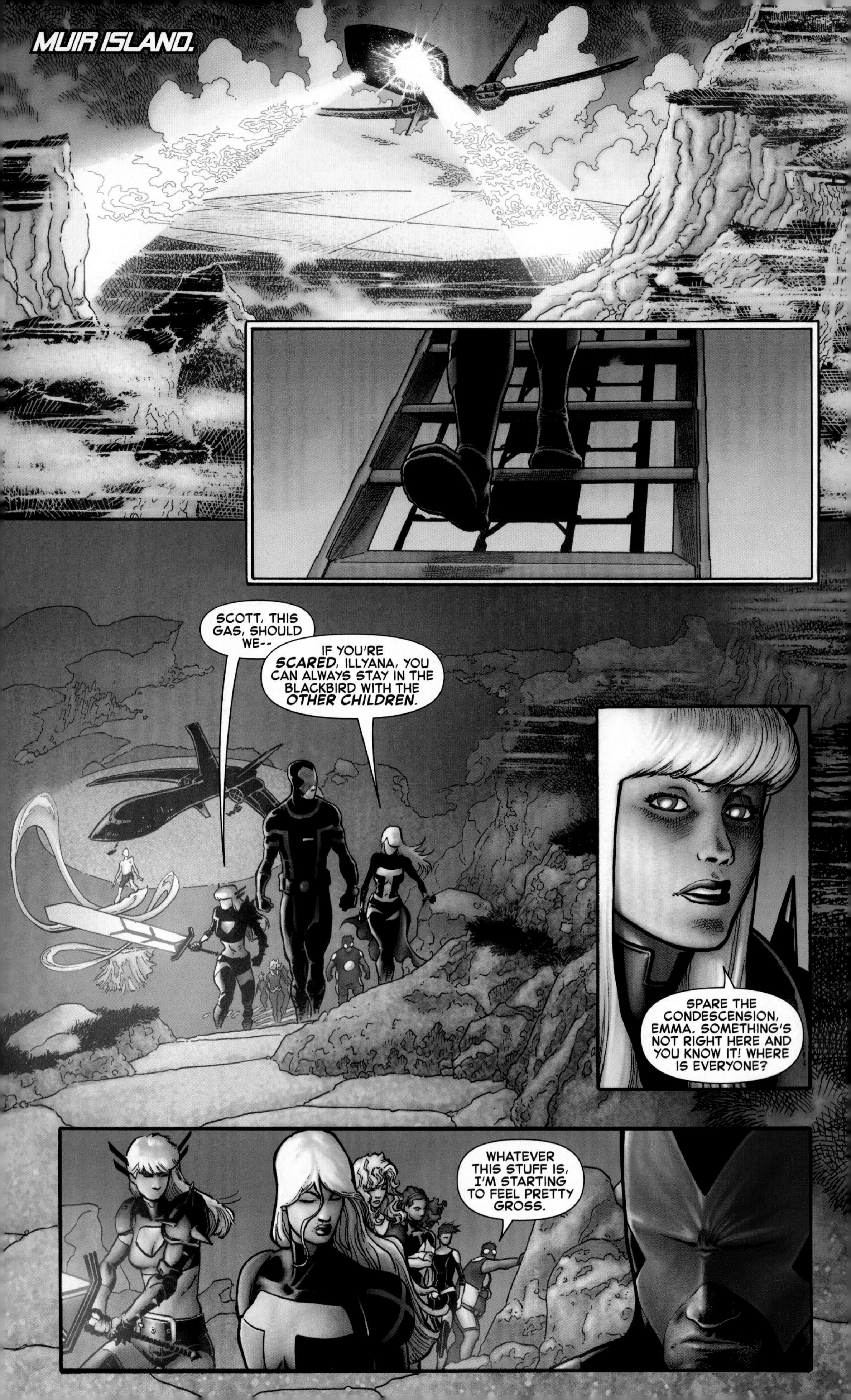
MUIR ISLAND.
SCOTT, THIS GAS, SHOULD WE--
IF YOU'RE SCARED, ILLYANA, YOU CAN ALWAYS STAY IN THE BLACKBIRD WITH THE OTHER CHILDREN.
SPARE THE CONDESCENSION, EMMA. SOMETHING'S NOT RIGHT HERE AND YOU KNOW IT! WHERE IS EVERYONE?
WHATEVER THIS STUFF IS, I'M STARTING TO FEEL PRETTY GROSS.

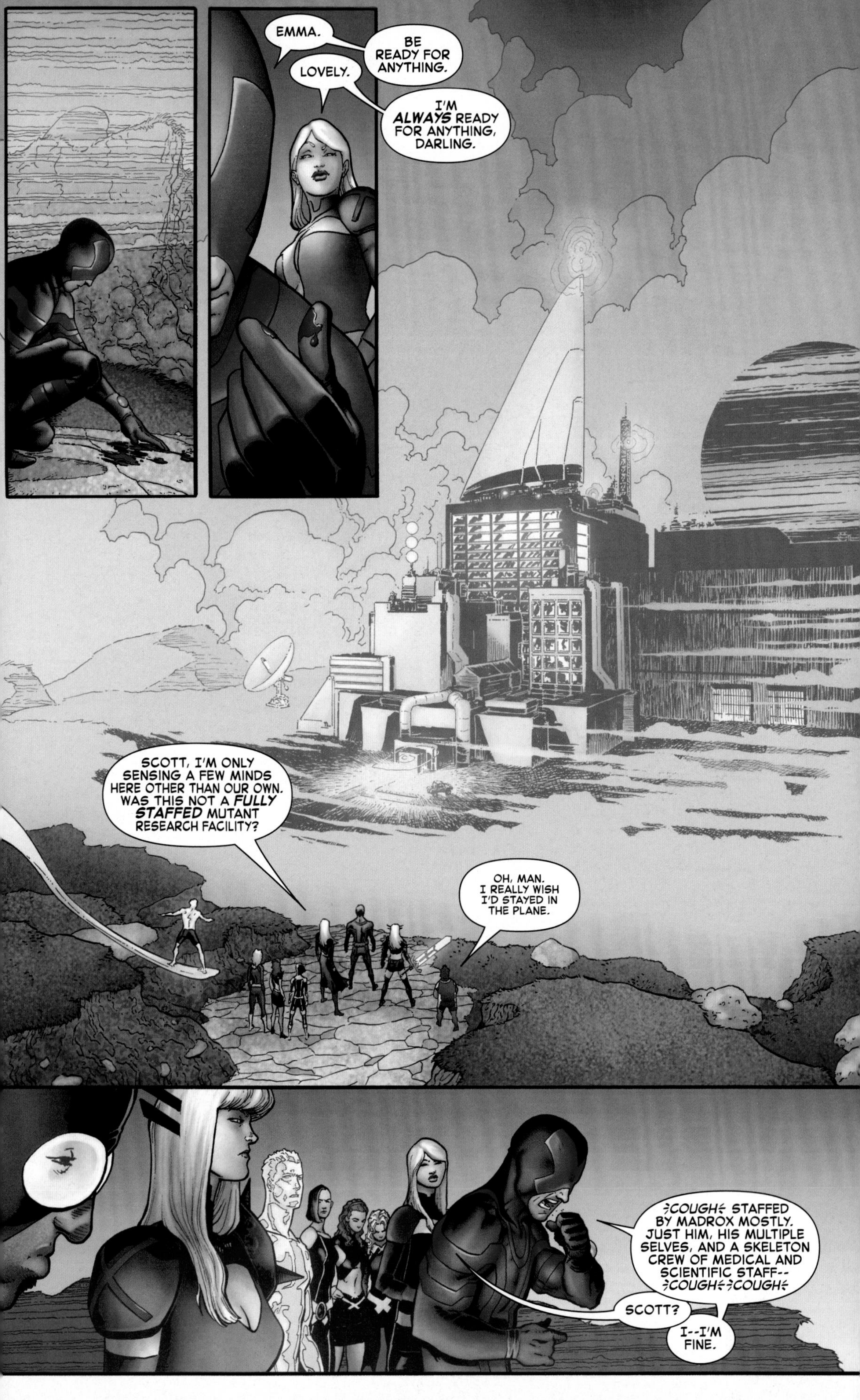
EMMA.
BE READY FOR ANYTHING.
LOVELY.
I'M *ALWAYS* READY FOR ANYTHING, DARLING.
SCOTT, I'M ONLY SENSING A FEW MINDS HERE OTHER THAN OUR OWN. WAS THIS NOT A *FULLY STAFFED* MUTANT RESEARCH FACILITY?
OH, MAN. I REALLY WISH I'D STAYED IN THE PLANE.
COUGH STAFFED BY MADROX MOSTLY. JUST HIM, HIS MULTIPLE SELVES, AND A SKELETON CREW OF MEDICAL AND SCIENTIFIC STAFF-- *COUGH* *COUGH*
SCOTT?
I--I'M FINE.

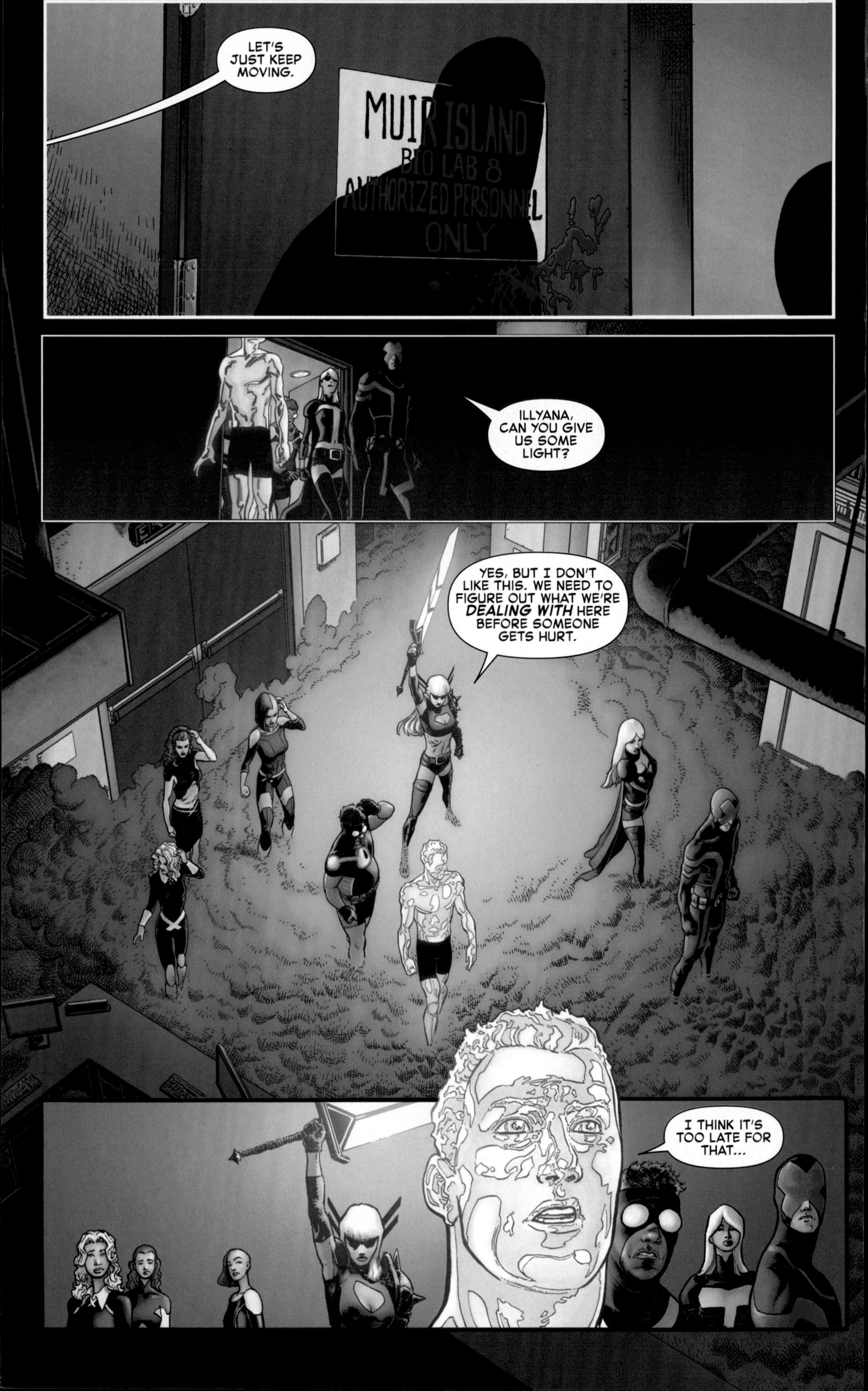
LET'S JUST KEEP MOVING.
MUIR ISLAND
BIO LAB 8
AUTHORIZED PERSONNEL
ONLY
ILLYANA, CAN YOU GIVE US SOME LIGHT?
YES, BUT I DON'T LIKE THIS. WE NEED TO FIGURE OUT WHAT WE'RE *DEALING WITH* HERE BEFORE SOMEONE GETS HURT.
I THINK IT'S TOO LATE FOR THAT...

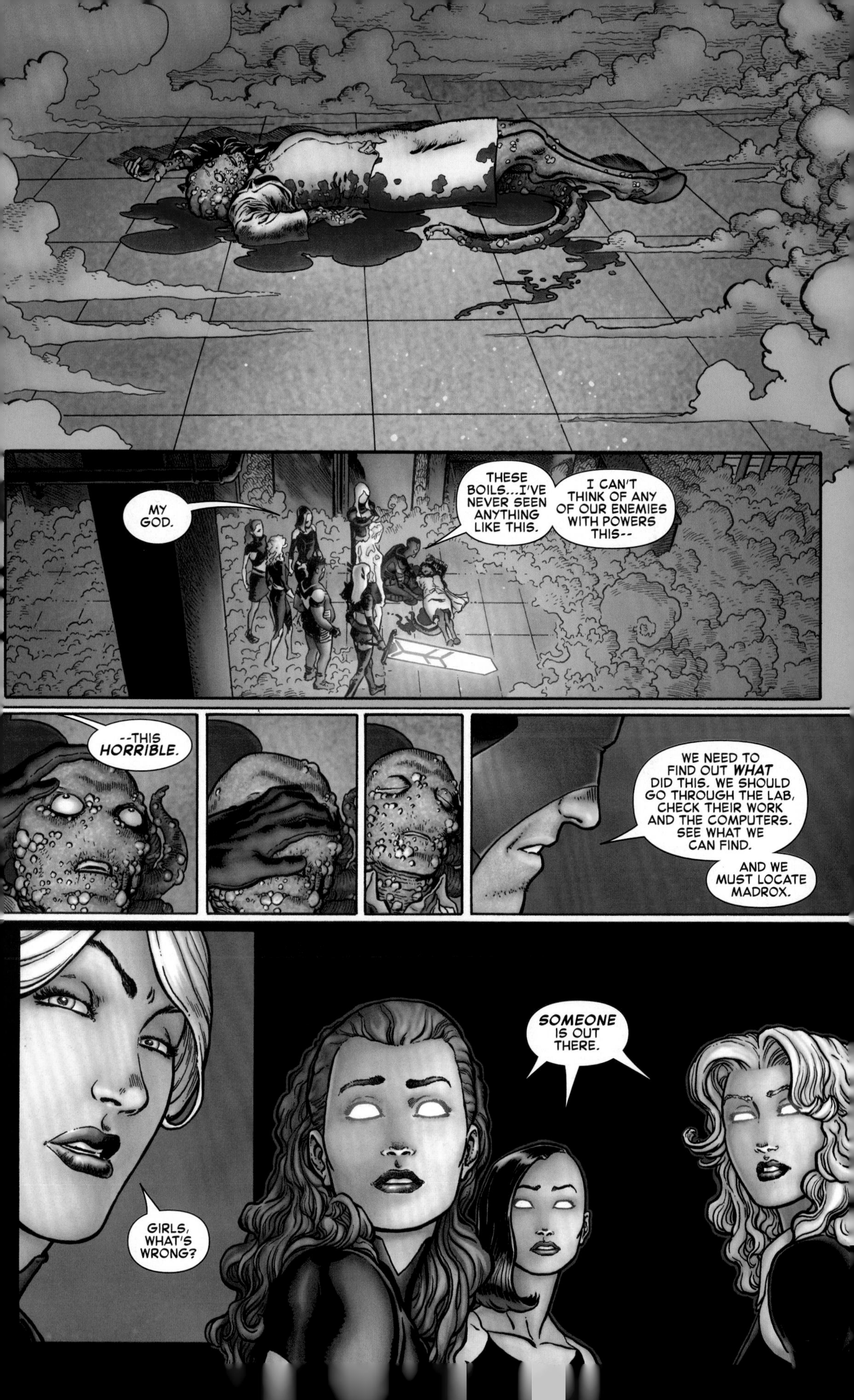
MY GOD.
THESE BOILS...I'VE NEVER SEEN ANYTHING LIKE THIS.
I CAN'T THINK OF ANY OF OUR ENEMIES WITH POWERS THIS--
--THIS HORRIBLE.
WE NEED TO FIND OUT WHAT DID THIS. WE SHOULD GO THROUGH THE LAB, CHECK THEIR WORK AND THE COMPUTERS. SEE WHAT WE CAN FIND.
AND WE MUST LOCATE MADROX.
GIRLS, WHAT'S WRONG?
SOMEONE IS OUT THERE.

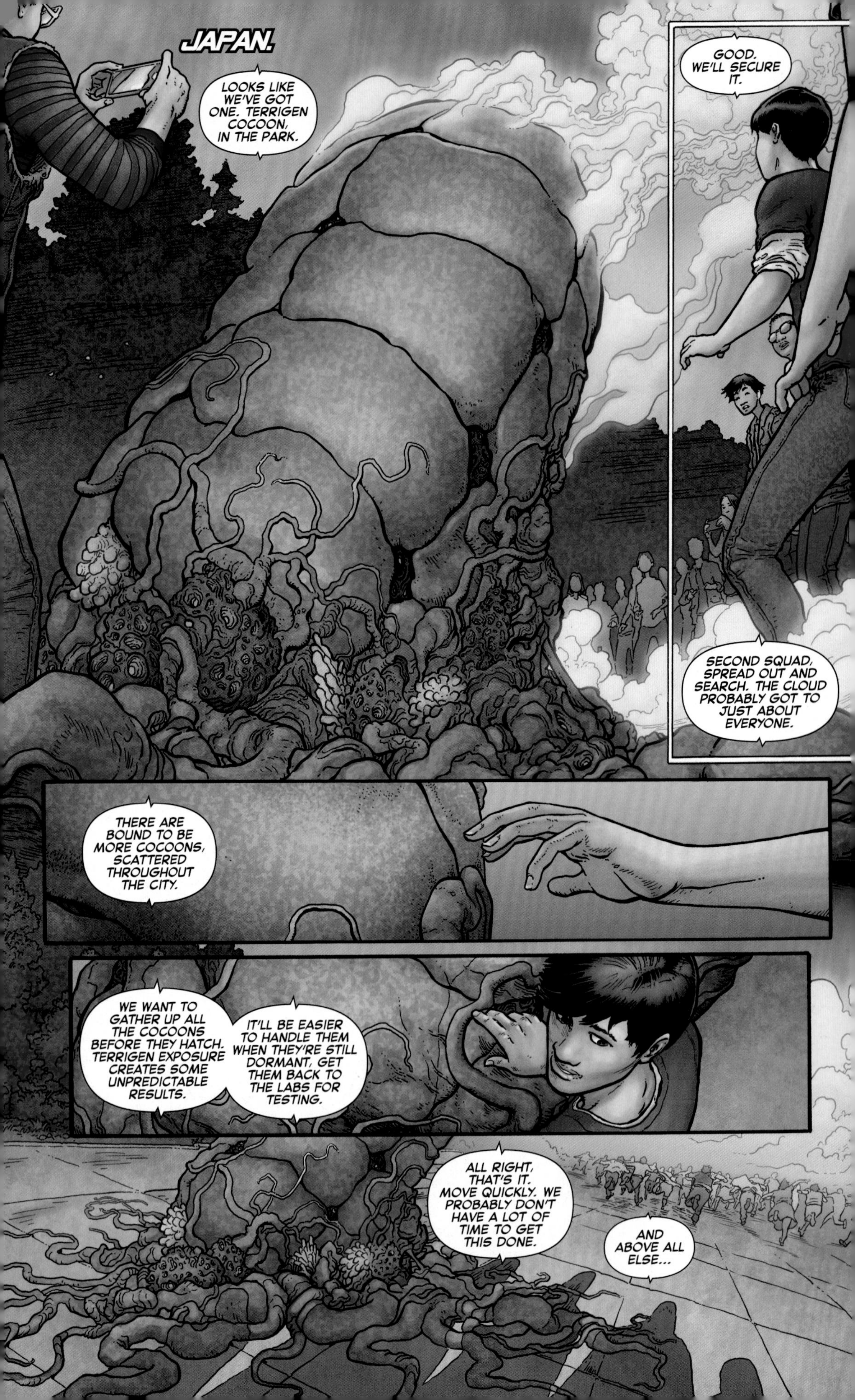
JAPAN.
LOOKS LIKE WE'VE GOT ONE. TERRIGEN COCOON, IN THE PARK.
GOOD. WE'LL SECURE IT.
SECOND SQUAD, SPREAD OUT AND SEARCH. THE CLOUD PROBABLY GOT TO JUST ABOUT EVERYONE.
THERE ARE BOUND TO BE MORE COCOONS, SCATTERED THROUGHOUT THE CITY.
WE WANT TO GATHER UP ALL THE COCOONS BEFORE THEY HATCH. TERRIGEN EXPOSURE CREATES SOME UNPREDICTABLE RESULTS.
IT'LL BE EASIER TO HANDLE THEM WHEN THEY'RE STILL DORMANT, GET THEM BACK TO THE LABS FOR TESTING.
ALL RIGHT, THAT'S IT. MOVE QUICKLY. WE PROBABLY DON'T HAVE A LOT OF TIME TO GET THIS DONE.
AND ABOVE ALL ELSE...

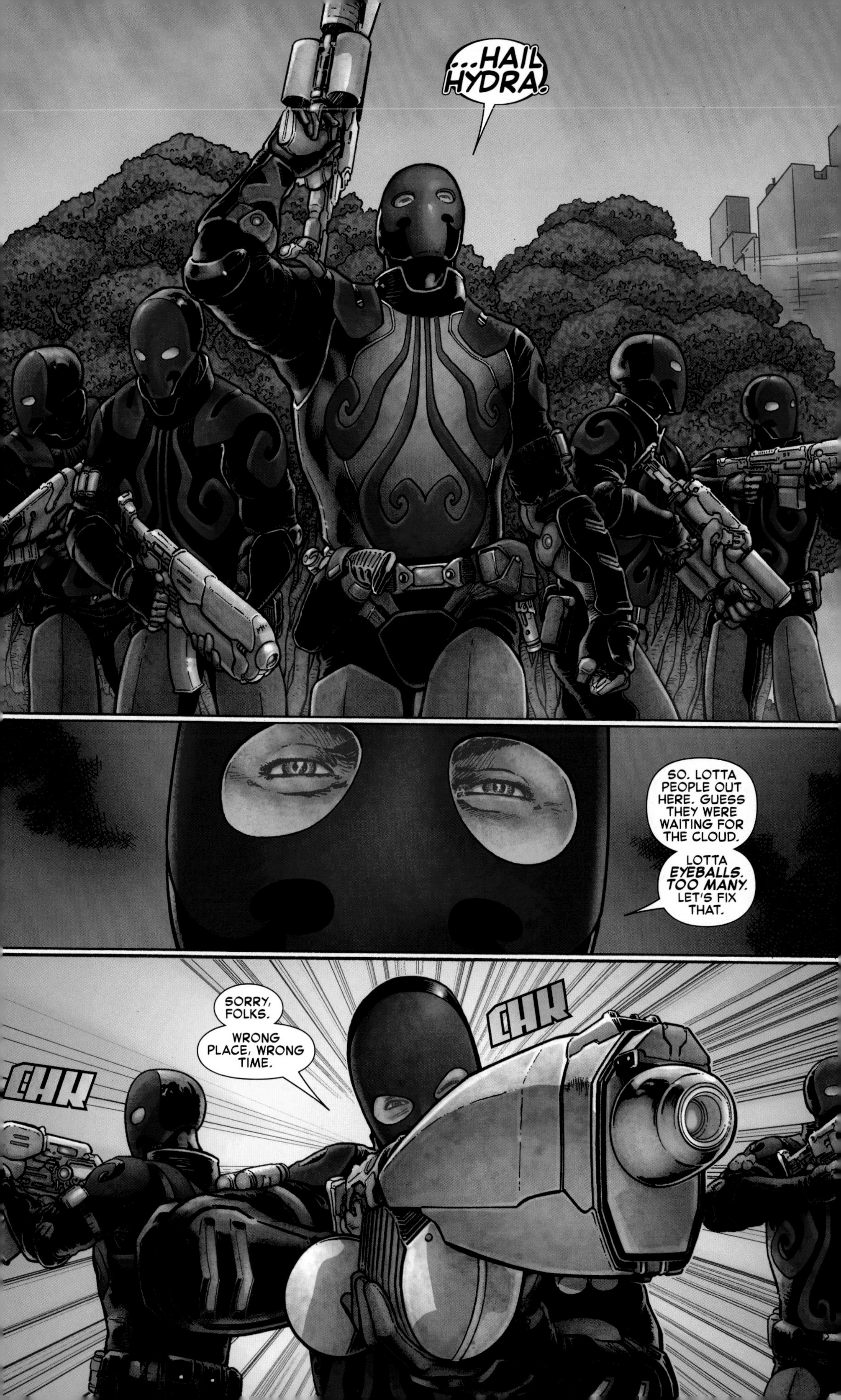
...HAIL HYDRA.
SO. LOTTA PEOPLE OUT HERE. GUESS THEY WERE WAITING FOR THE CLOUD.
LOTTA EYEBALLS. TOO MANY. LET'S FIX THAT.
SORRY, FOLKS.
WRONG PLACE, WRONG TIME.
CHK
CHK

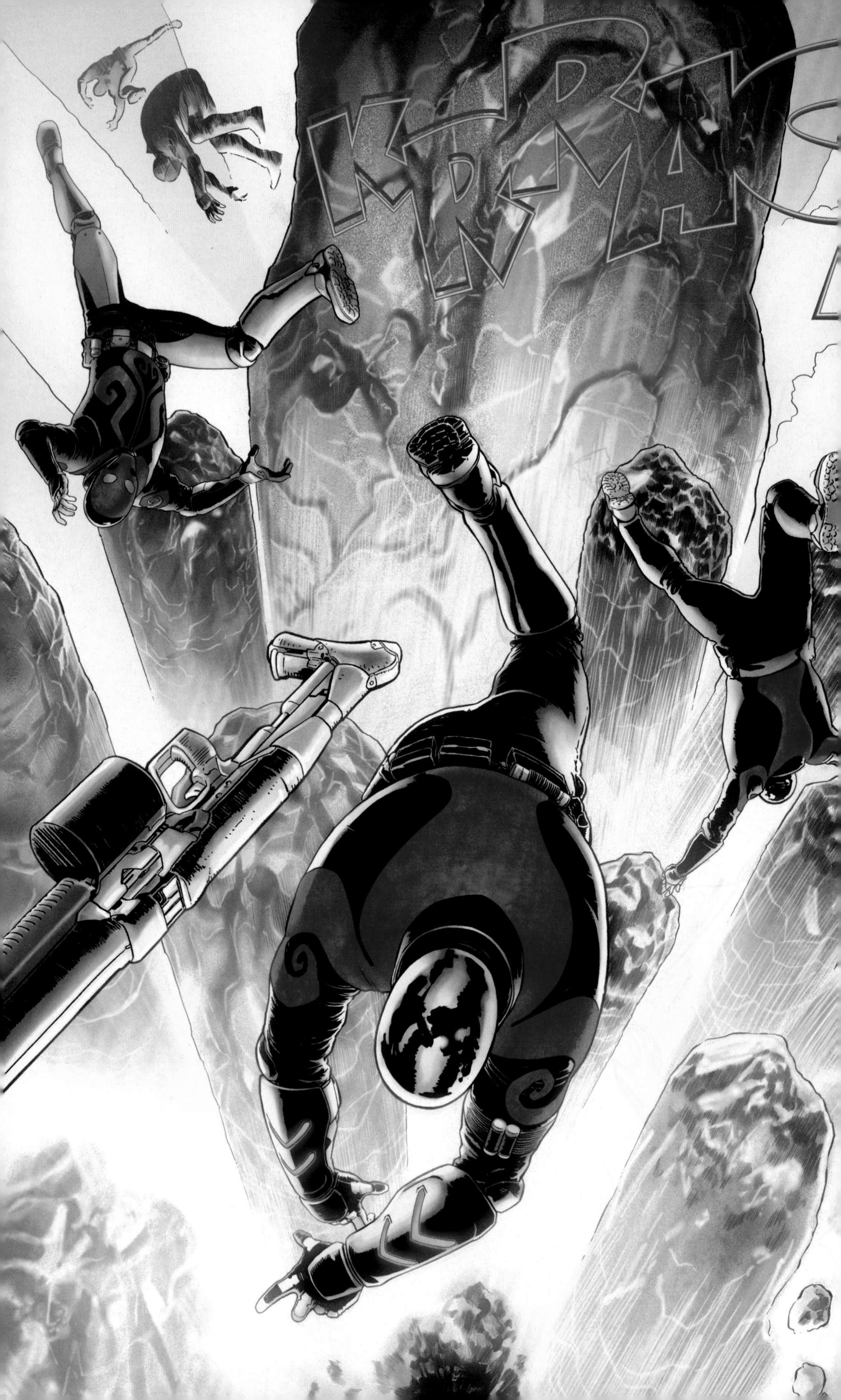

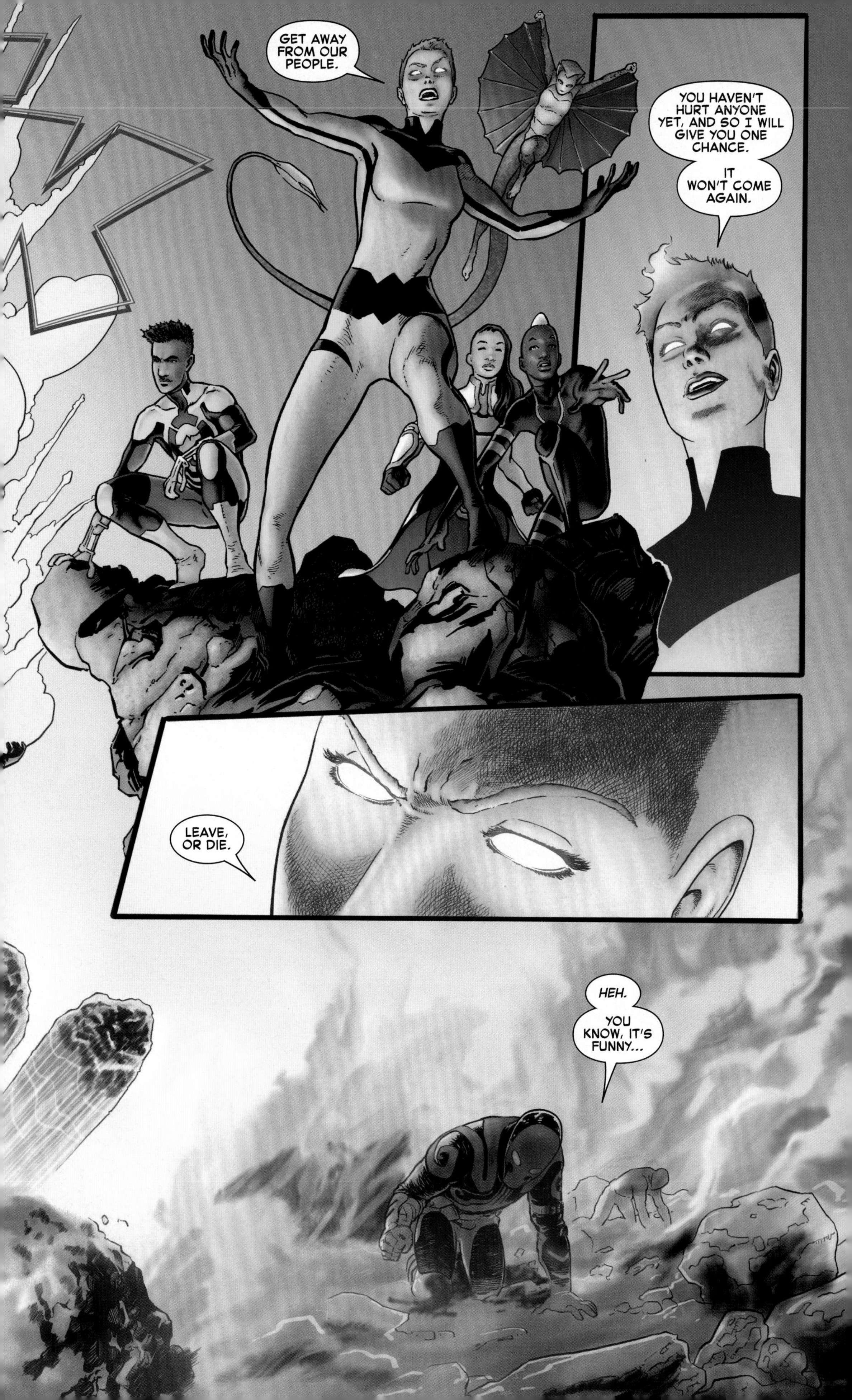
GET AWAY FROM OUR PEOPLE.
YOU HAVEN'T HURT ANYONE YET, AND SO I WILL GIVE YOU ONE CHANCE.
IT WON'T COME AGAIN.
LEAVE, OR DIE.
HEH.
YOU KNOW, IT'S FUNNY...

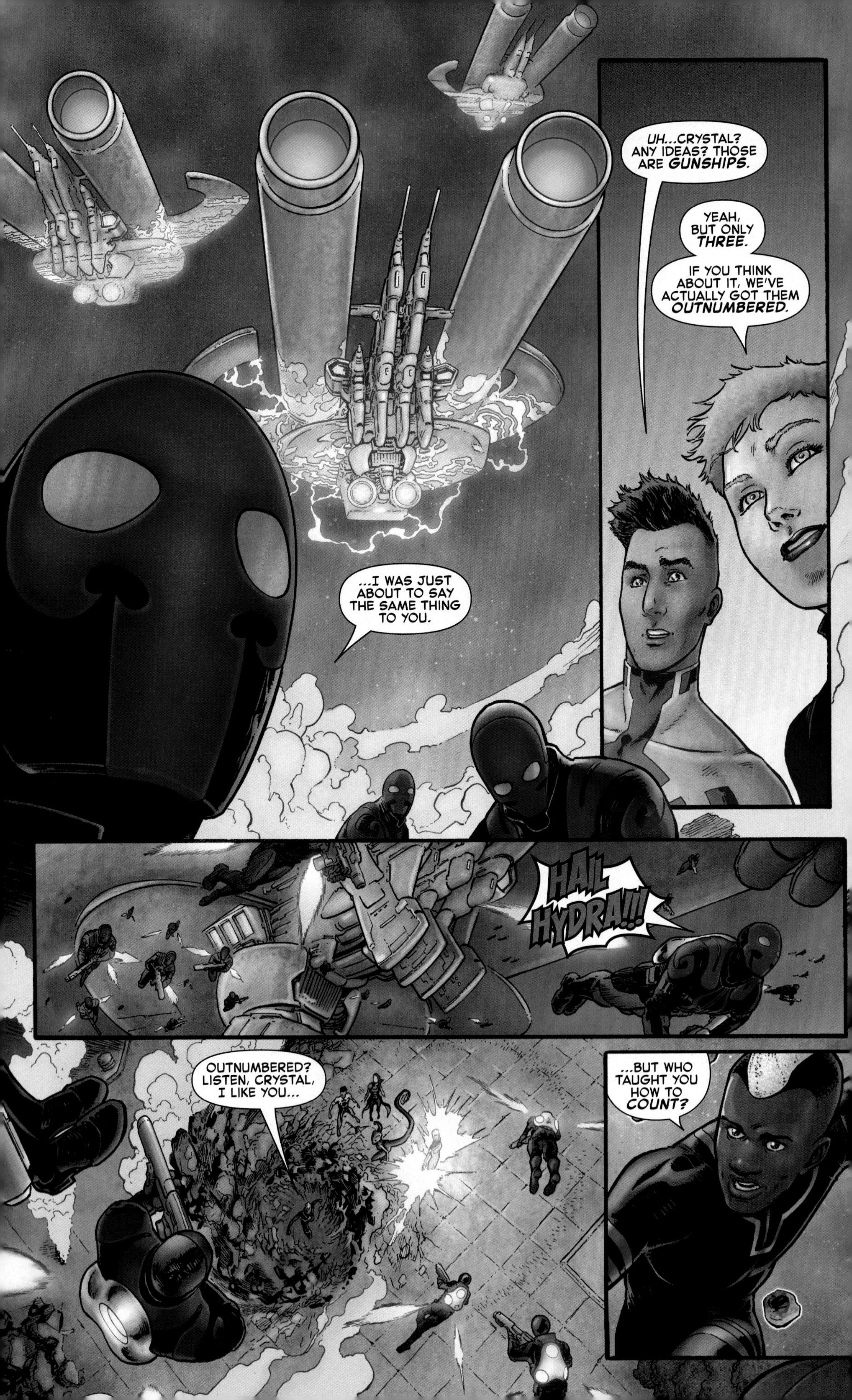
UH...CRYSTAL? ANY IDEAS? THOSE ARE GUNSHIPS.
YEAH, BUT ONLY THREE.
IF YOU THINK ABOUT IT, WE'VE ACTUALLY GOT THEM OUTNUMBERED.
...I WAS JUST ABOUT TO SAY THE SAME THING TO YOU.
HAIL HYDRA!!!
OUTNUMBERED? LISTEN, CRYSTAL, I LIKE YOU...
...BUT WHO TAUGHT YOU HOW TO COUNT?

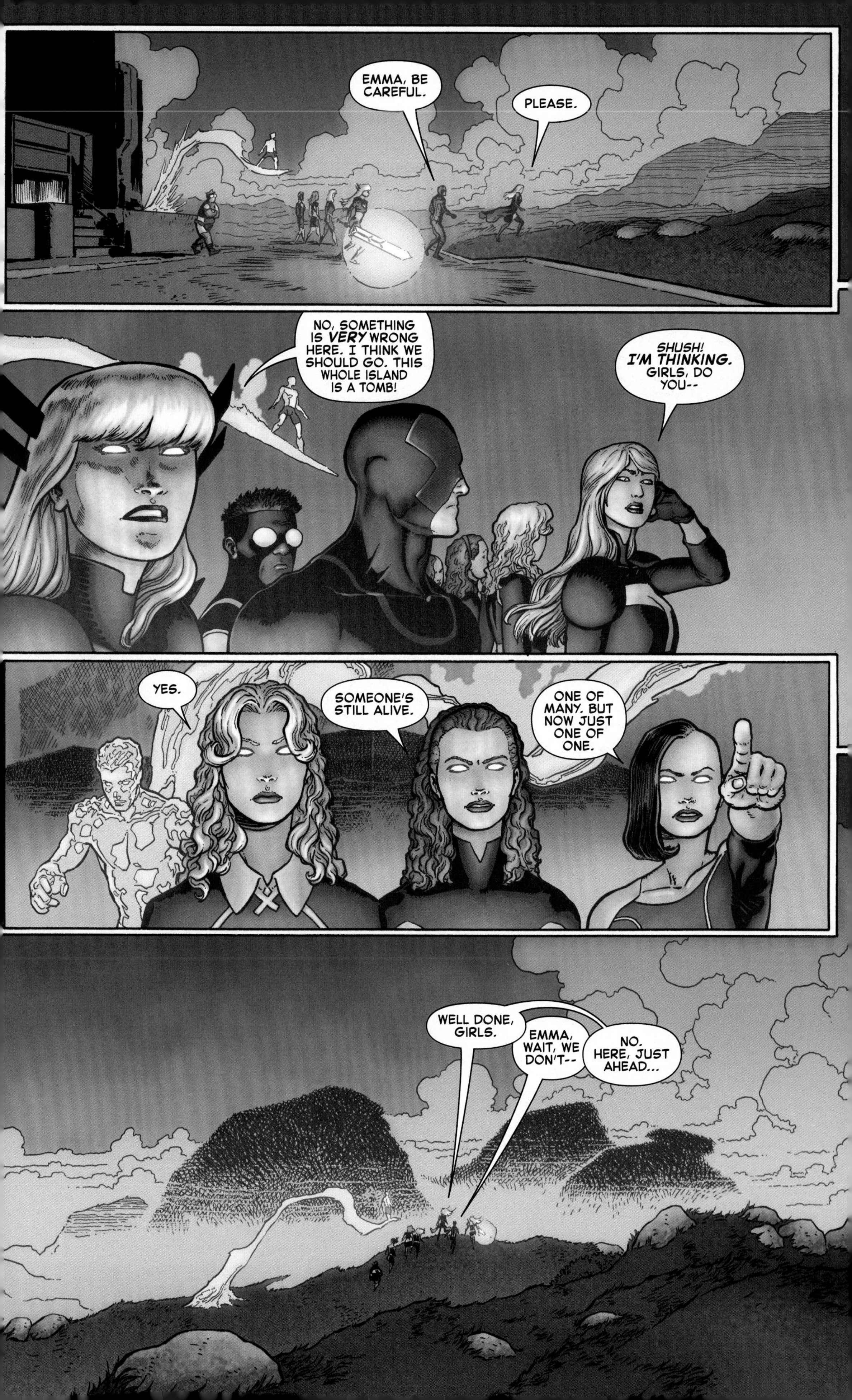

EMMA, BE CAREFUL.
PLEASE.
NO, SOMETHING IS VERY WRONG HERE. I THINK WE SHOULD GO. THIS WHOLE ISLAND IS A TOMB!
SHUSH! I'M THINKING. GIRLS, DO YOU--
YES.
SOMEONE'S STILL ALIVE.
ONE OF MANY. BUT NOW JUST ONE OF ONE.
WELL DONE, GIRLS.
EMMA, WAIT, WE DON'T--
NO. HERE, JUST AHEAD...

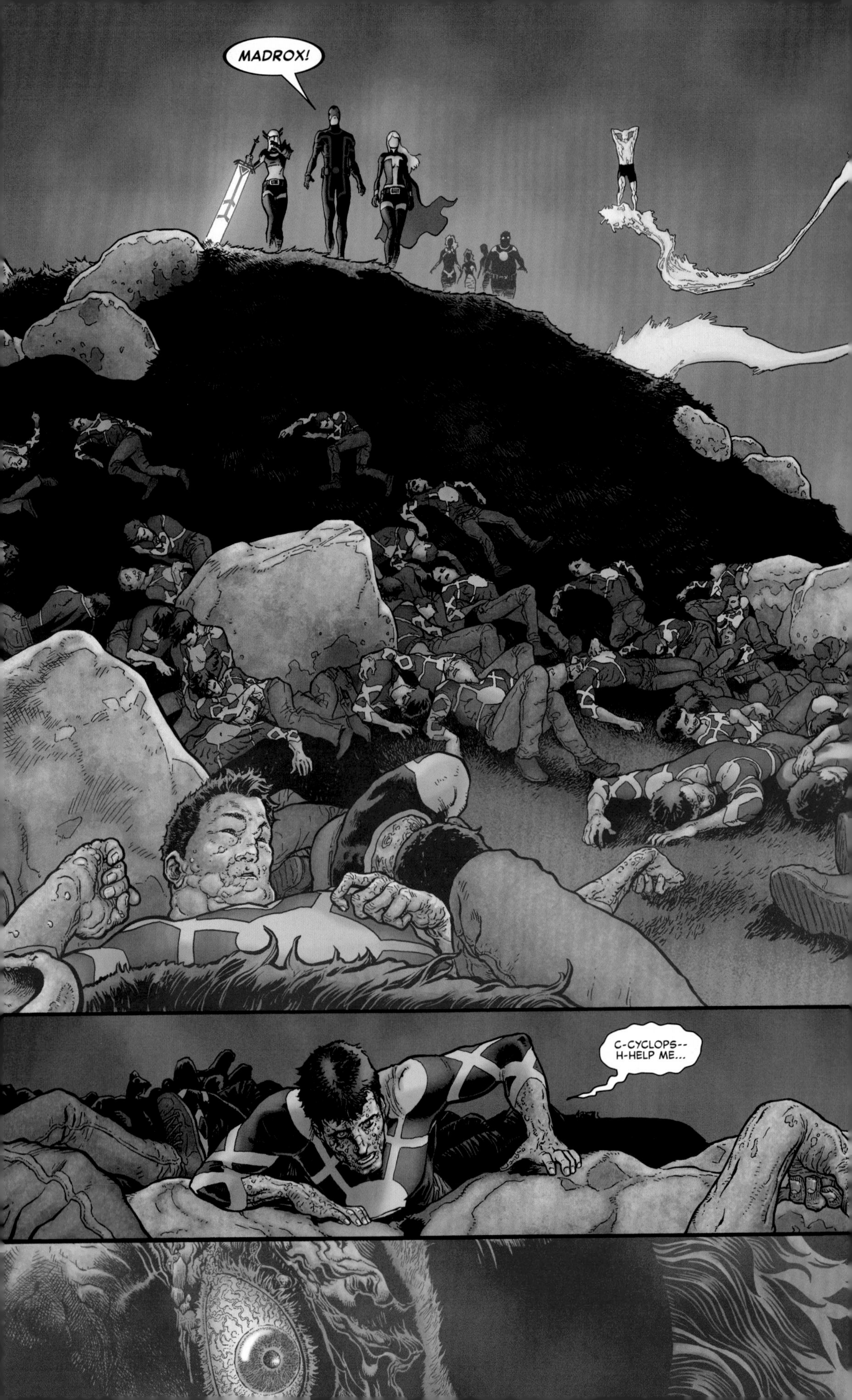
MADROX!
C-CYCLOPS--
H-HELP ME...

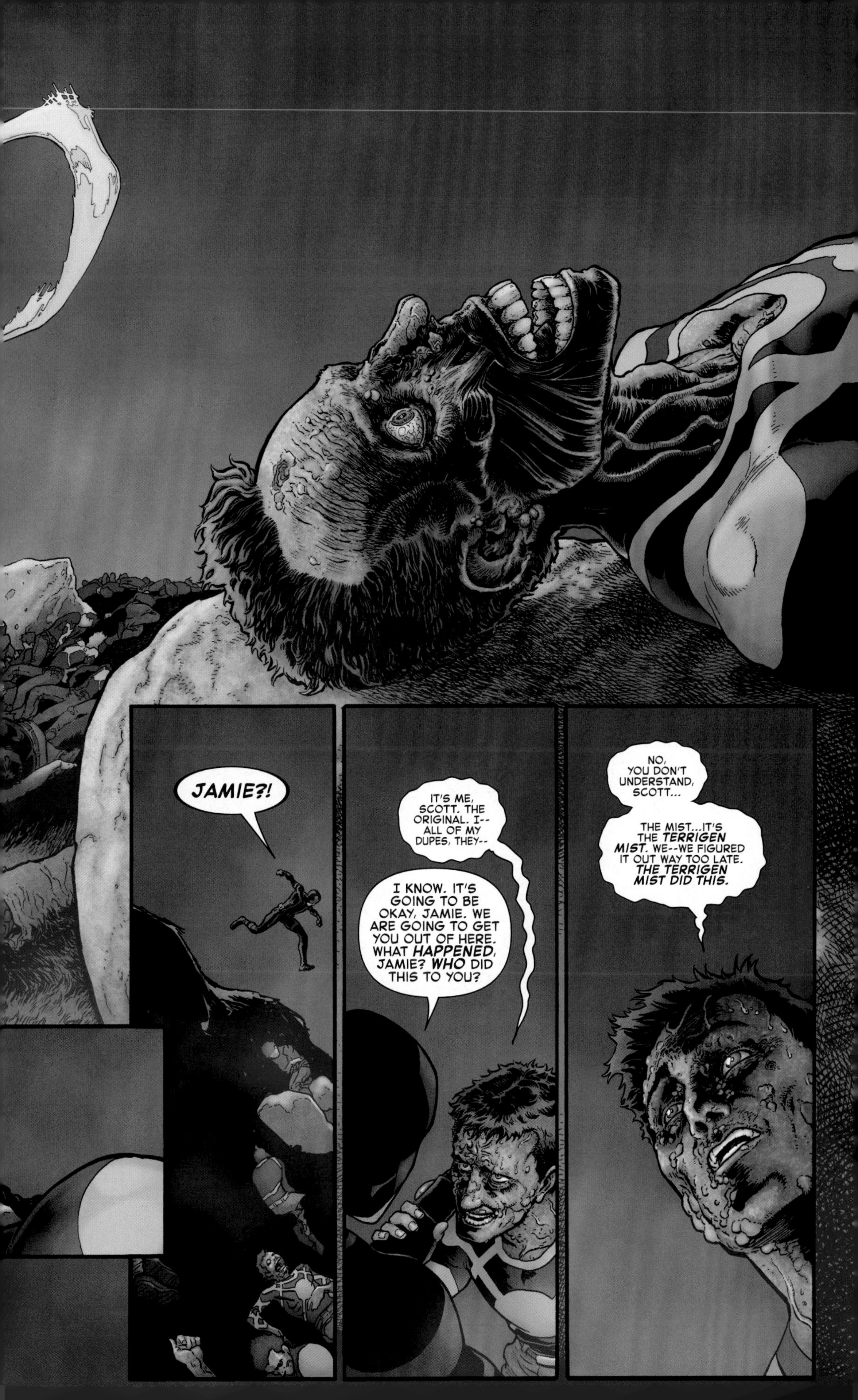
JAMIE?!
IT'S ME, SCOTT. THE ORIGINAL. I-- ALL OF MY DUPES, THEY--
I KNOW. IT'S GOING TO BE OKAY, JAMIE. WE ARE GOING TO GET YOU OUT OF HERE. WHAT HAPPENED, JAMIE? WHO DID THIS TO YOU?
NO, YOU DON'T UNDERSTAND, SCOTT...
THE MIST...IT'S THE TERRIGEN MIST. WE--WE FIGURED IT OUT WAY TOO LATE. THE TERRIGEN MIST DID THIS.

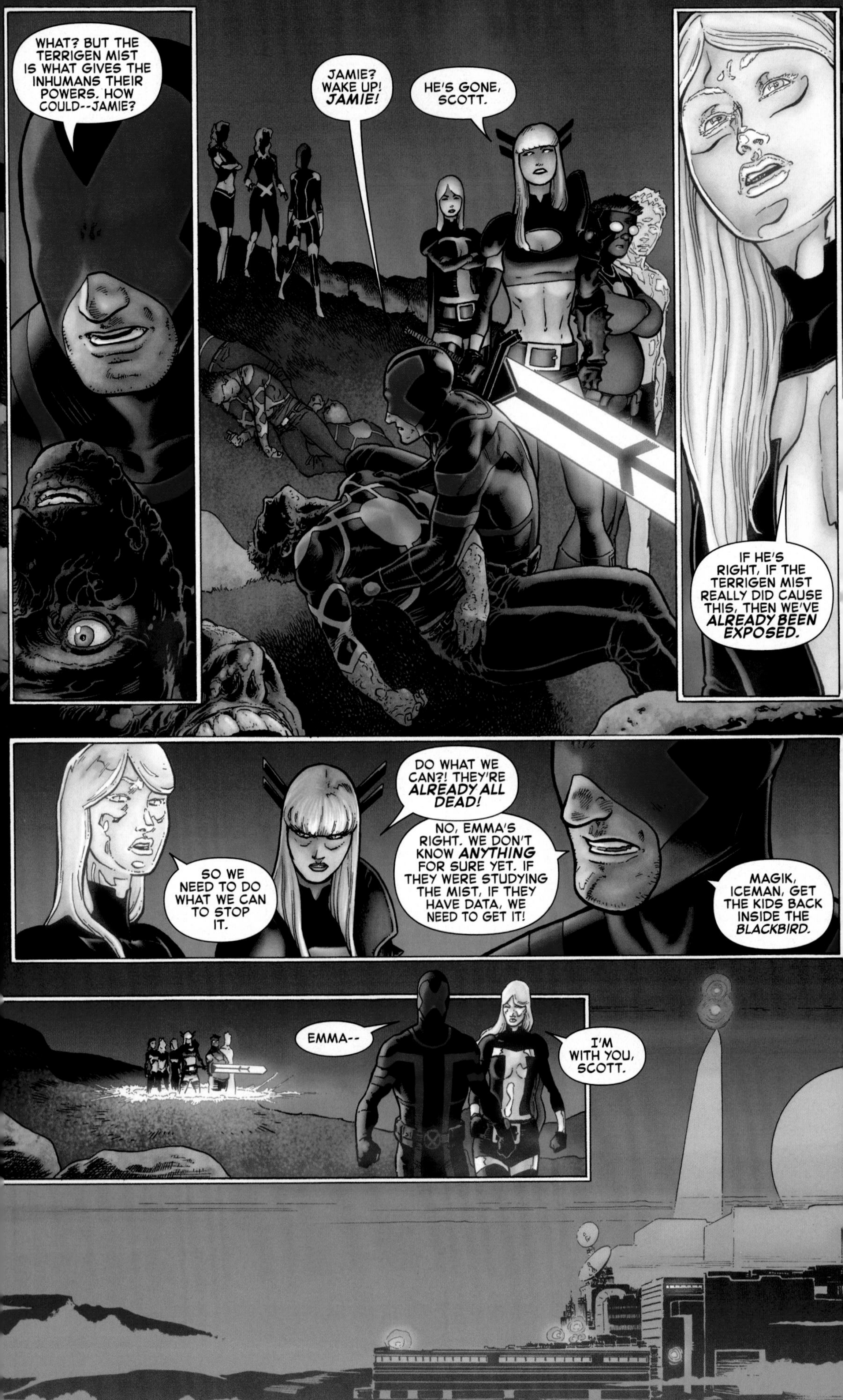
WHAT? BUT THE TERRIGEN MIST IS WHAT GIVES THE INHUMANS THEIR POWERS. HOW COULD--JAMIE?
JAMIE? WAKE UP! *JAMIE!*
HE'S GONE, SCOTT.
IF HE'S RIGHT, IF THE TERRIGEN MIST REALLY DID CAUSE THIS, THEN WE'VE *ALREADY BEEN EXPOSED.*
SO WE NEED TO DO WHAT WE CAN TO STOP IT.
DO WHAT WE CAN?! THEY'RE *ALREADY ALL DEAD!*
NO, EMMA'S RIGHT. WE DON'T KNOW *ANYTHING* FOR SURE YET. IF THEY WERE STUDYING THE MIST, IF THEY HAVE DATA, WE NEED TO GET IT!
MAGIK, ICEMAN, GET THE KIDS BACK INSIDE THE *BLACKBIRD.*
EMMA--
I'M WITH YOU, SCOTT.

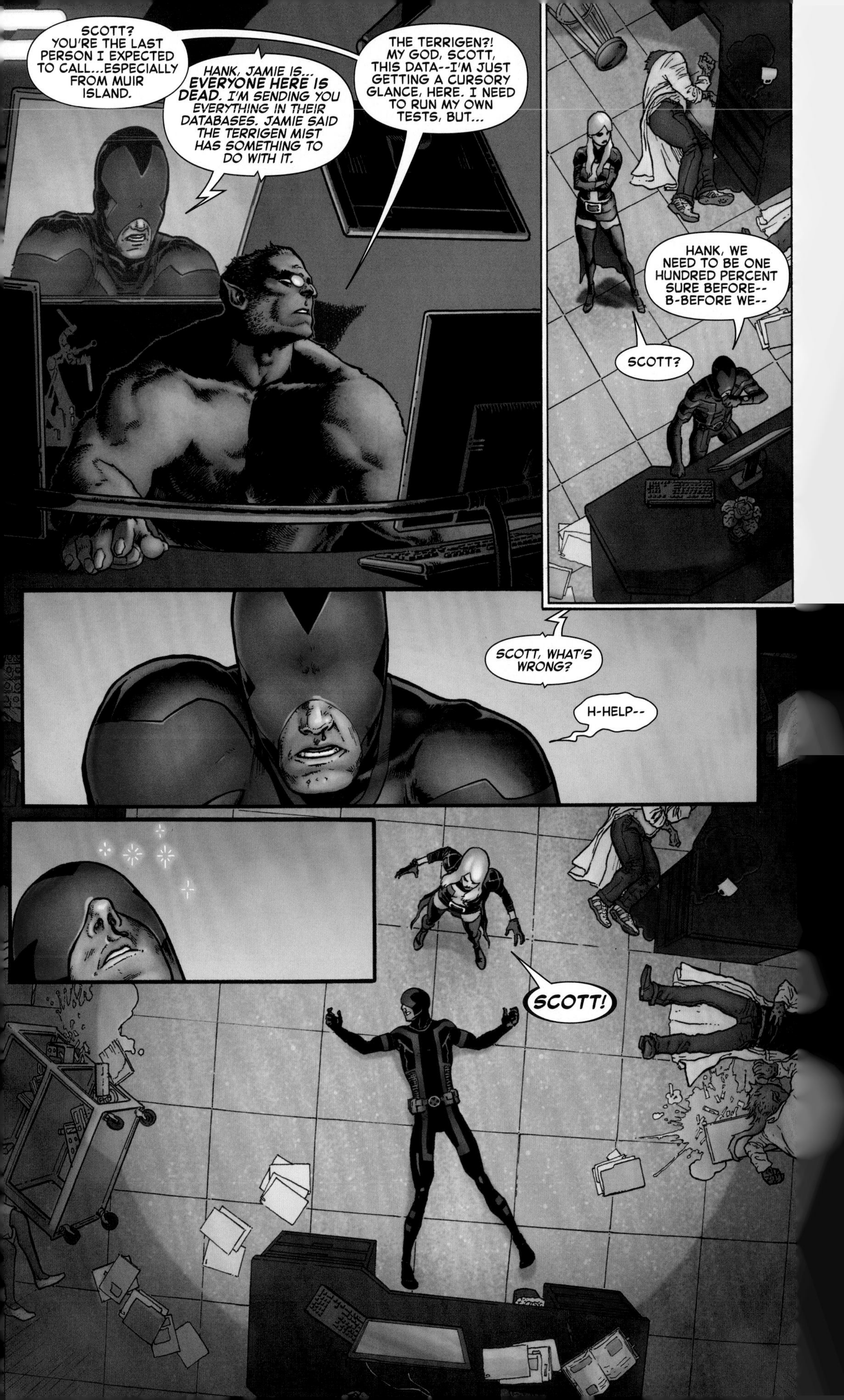

SCOTT? YOU'RE THE LAST PERSON I EXPECTED TO CALL...ESPECIALLY FROM MUIR ISLAND.
HANK, JAMIE IS... EVERYONE HERE IS DEAD. I'M SENDING YOU EVERYTHING IN THEIR DATABASES. JAMIE SAID THE TERRIGEN MIST HAS SOMETHING TO DO WITH IT.
THE TERRIGEN?! MY GOD, SCOTT, THIS DATA--I'M JUST GETTING A CURSORY GLANCE, HERE. I NEED TO RUN MY OWN TESTS, BUT...
HANK, WE NEED TO BE ONE HUNDRED PERCENT SURE BEFORE-- B-BEFORE WE--
SCOTT?
SCOTT, WHAT'S WRONG?
H-HELP--
SCOTT!

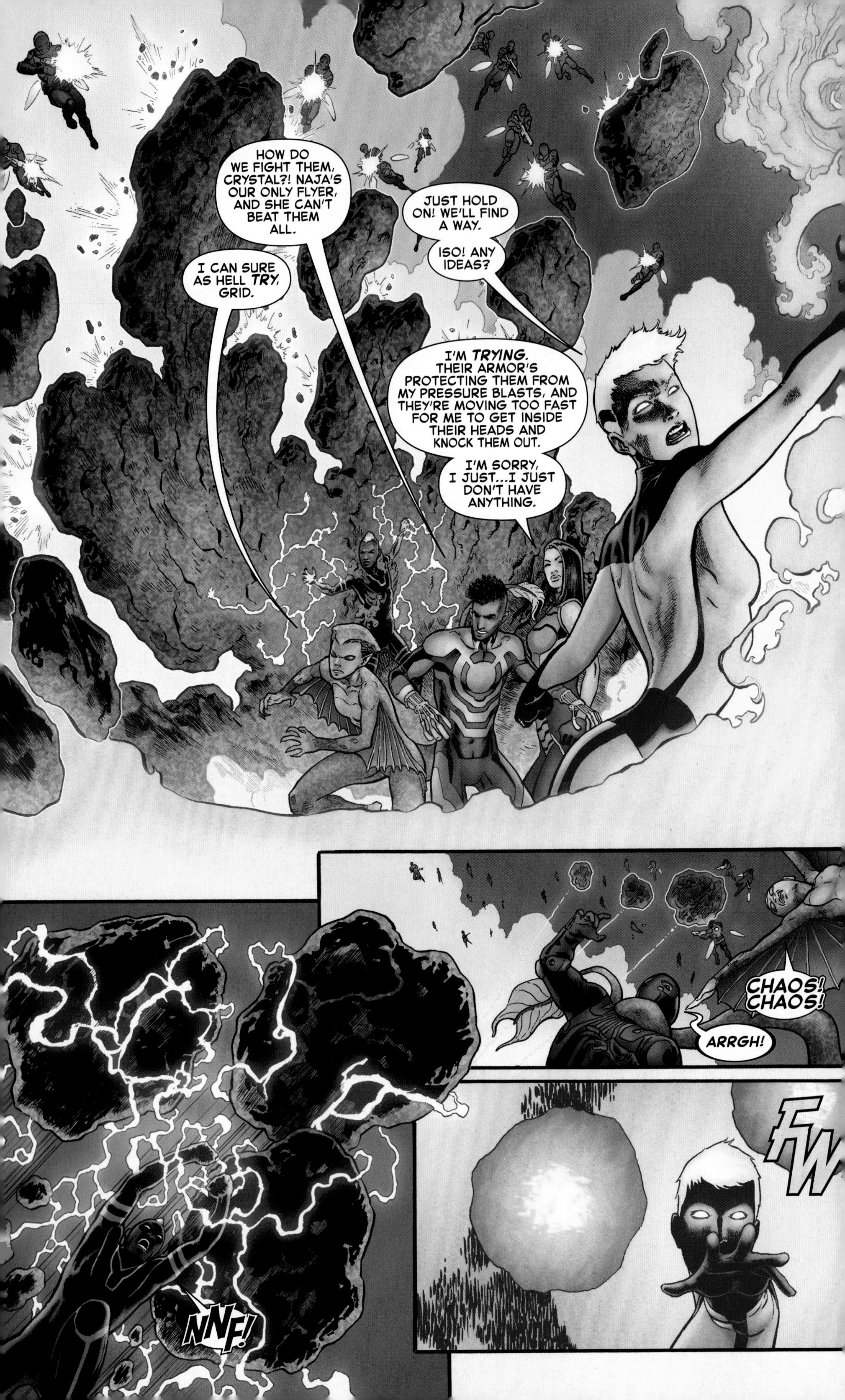
HOW DO WE FIGHT THEM, CRYSTAL?! NAJA'S OUR ONLY FLYER, AND SHE CAN'T BEAT THEM ALL.
I CAN SURE AS HELL TRY, GRID.
JUST HOLD ON! WE'LL FIND A WAY.
ISO! ANY IDEAS?
I'M TRYING. THEIR ARMOR'S PROTECTING THEM FROM MY PRESSURE BLASTS, AND THEY'RE MOVING TOO FAST FOR ME TO GET INSIDE THEIR HEADS AND KNOCK THEM OUT.
I'M SORRY, I JUST...I JUST DON'T HAVE ANYTHING.
NNF!
CHAOS! CHAOS!
ARRGH!
FW

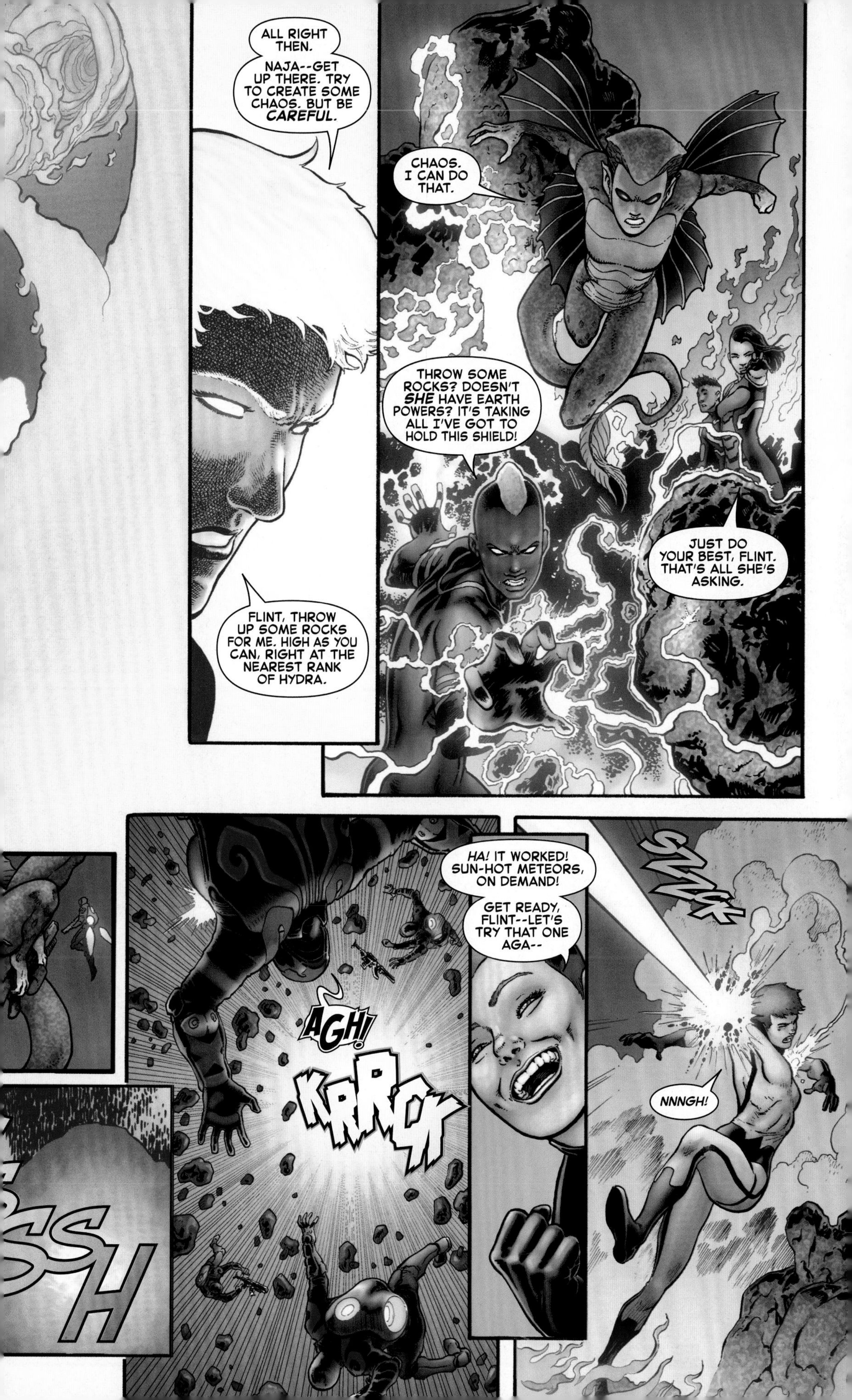
ALL RIGHT THEN.
NAJA--GET UP THERE. TRY TO CREATE SOME CHAOS. BUT BE *CAREFUL*.
CHAOS. I CAN DO THAT.
FLINT, THROW UP SOME ROCKS FOR ME. HIGH AS YOU CAN, RIGHT AT THE NEAREST RANK OF HYDRA.
THROW SOME ROCKS? DOESN'T *SHE* HAVE EARTH POWERS? IT'S TAKING ALL I'VE GOT TO HOLD THIS SHIELD!
JUST DO YOUR BEST, FLINT. THAT'S ALL SHE'S ASKING.
AGH!
KRRRK
HA! IT WORKED! SUN-HOT METEORS, ON DEMAND!
GET READY, FLINT--LET'S TRY THAT ONE AGA--
SZZZK
NNNGH!

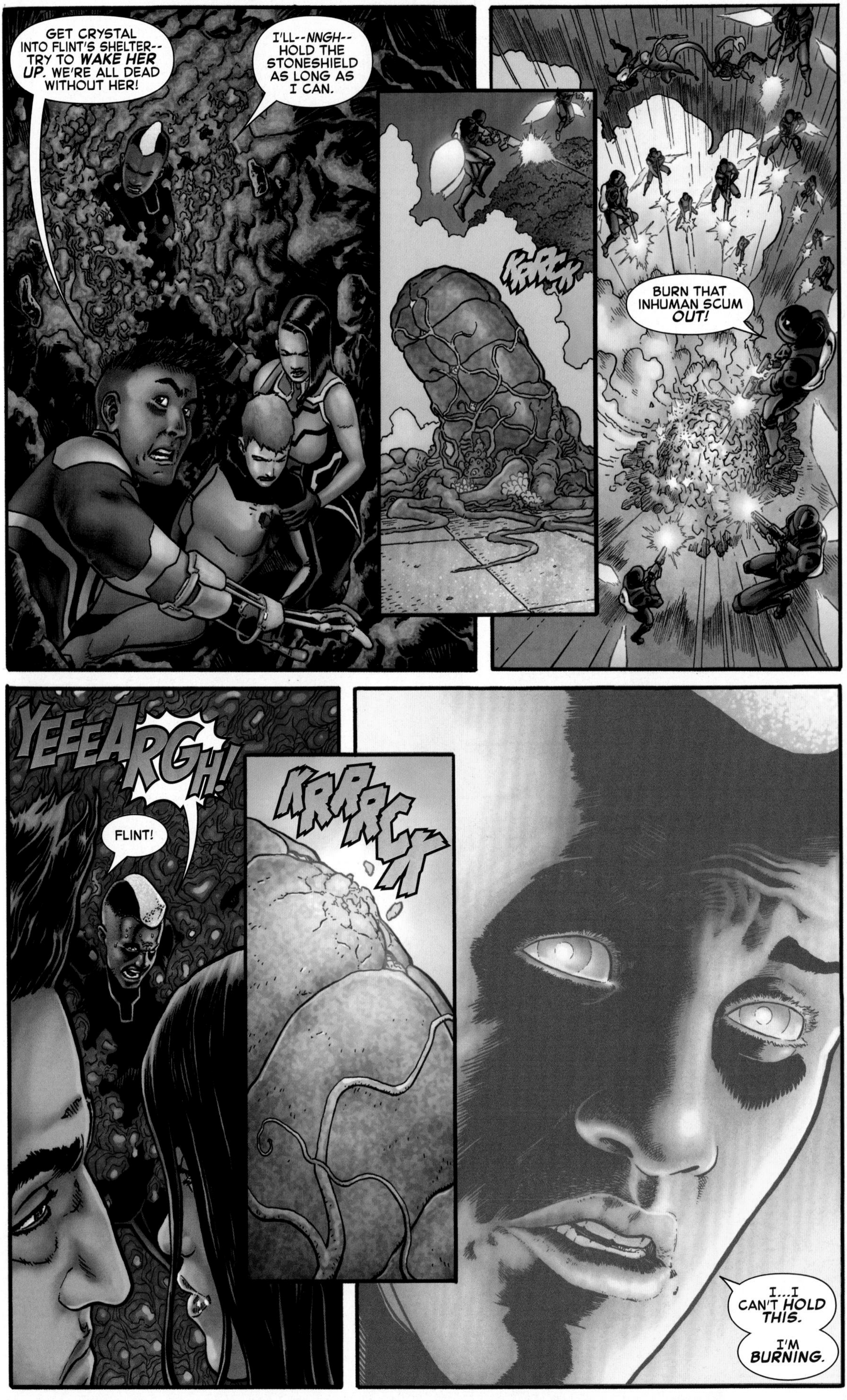
GET CRYSTAL INTO FLINT'S SHELTER-- TRY TO WAKE HER UP. WE'RE ALL DEAD WITHOUT HER!
I'LL--NNGH-- HOLD THE STONESHIELD AS LONG AS I CAN.
KRRRCK
BURN THAT INHUMAN SCUM OUT!
YEEEARGH!
FLINT!
KRRRCK
I...I CAN'T HOLD THIS.
I'M BURNING.

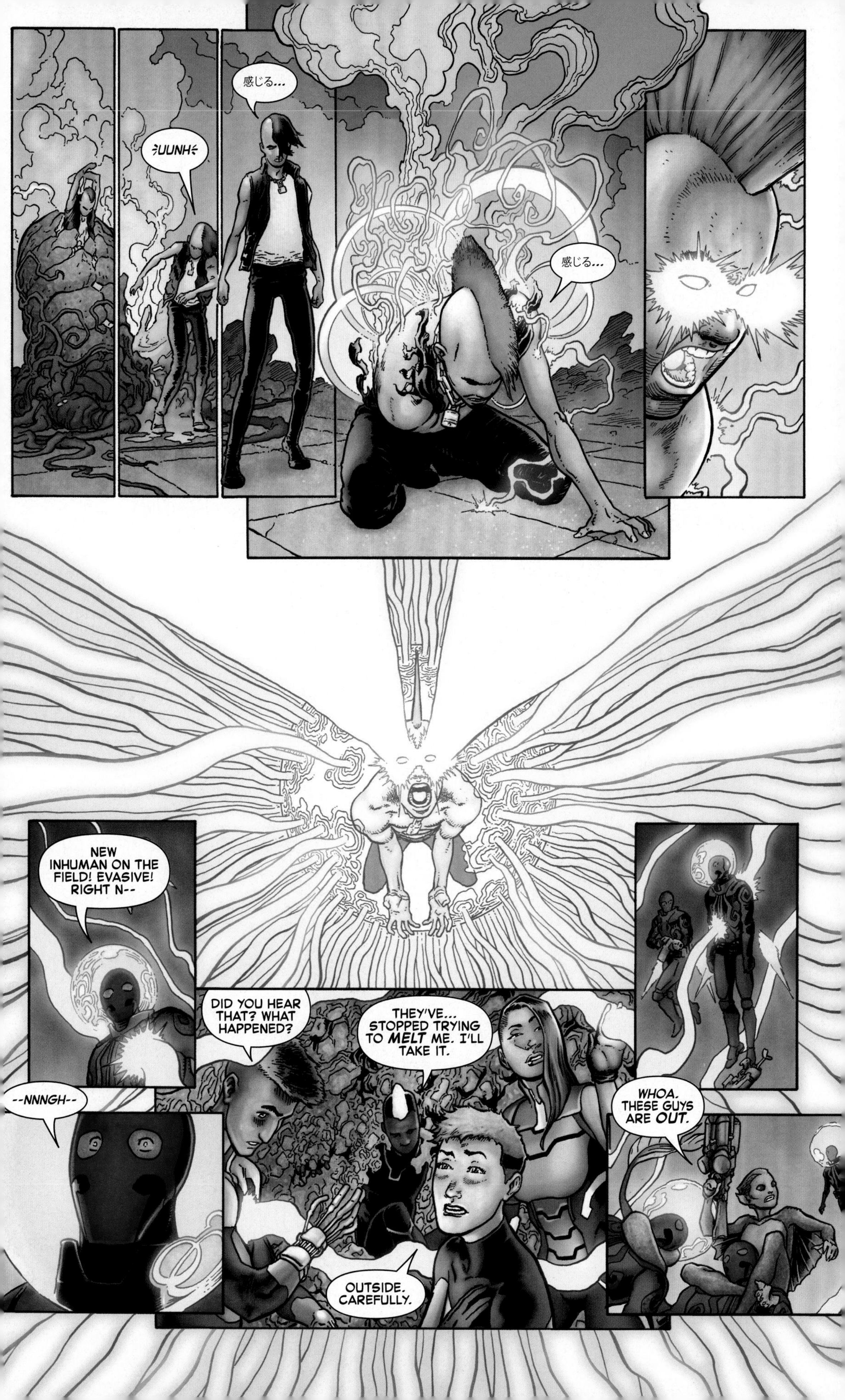

UUNH
感じる...
感じる...
NEW INHUMAN ON THE FIELD! EVASIVE! RIGHT N--
--NNNGH--
DID YOU HEAR THAT? WHAT HAPPENED?
THEY'VE... STOPPED TRYING TO MELT ME. I'LL TAKE IT.
OUTSIDE. CAREFULLY.
WHOA. THESE GUYS ARE OUT.

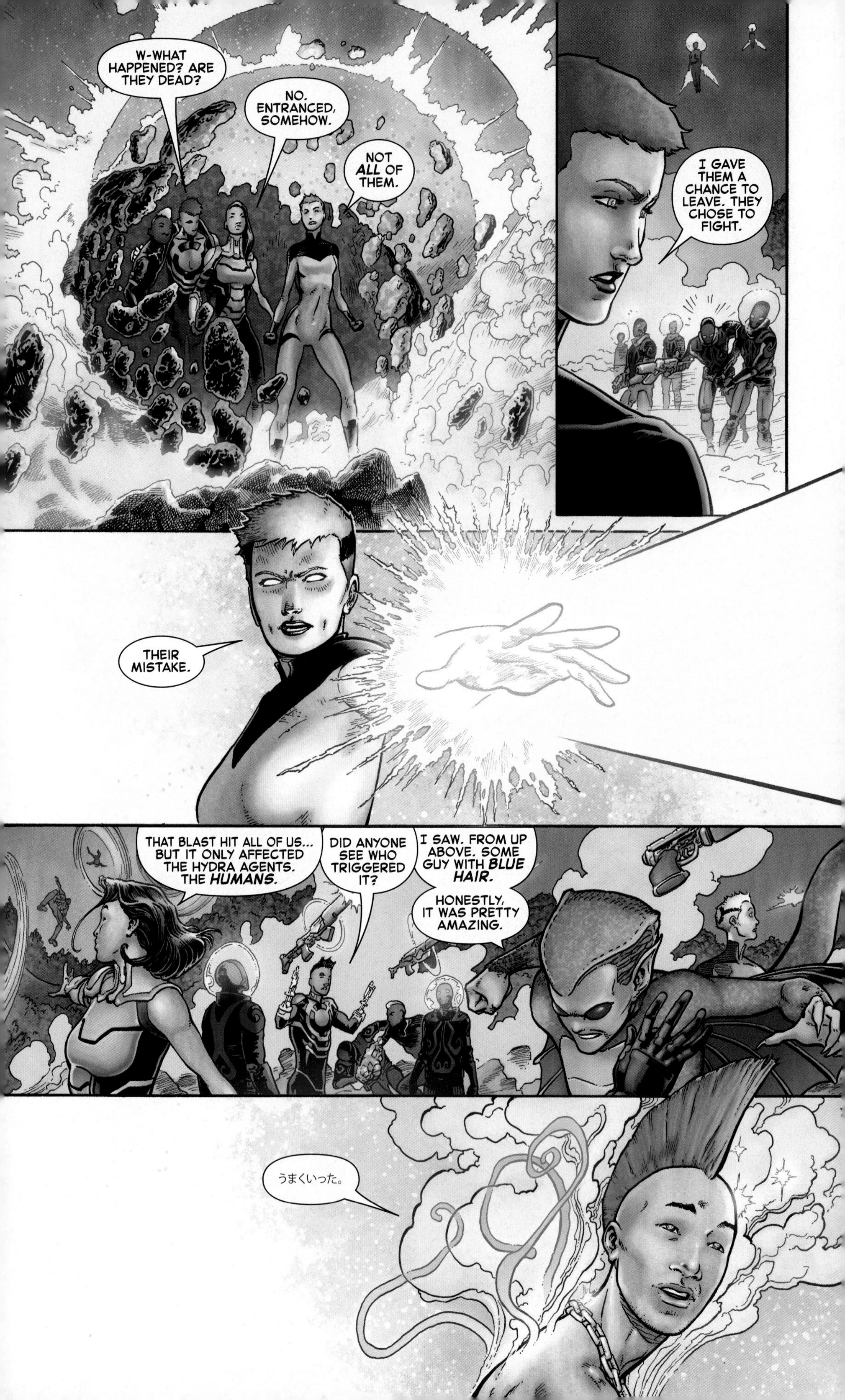
W-WHAT HAPPENED? ARE THEY DEAD?
NO. ENTRANCED, SOMEHOW.
NOT ALL OF THEM.
I GAVE THEM A CHANCE TO LEAVE. THEY CHOSE TO FIGHT.
THEIR MISTAKE.
THAT BLAST HIT ALL OF US... BUT IT ONLY AFFECTED THE HYDRA AGENTS. THE HUMANS.
DID ANYONE SEE WHO TRIGGERED IT?
I SAW. FROM UP ABOVE. SOME GUY WITH BLUE HAIR.
HONESTLY, IT WAS PRETTY AMAZING.
うまくいった。

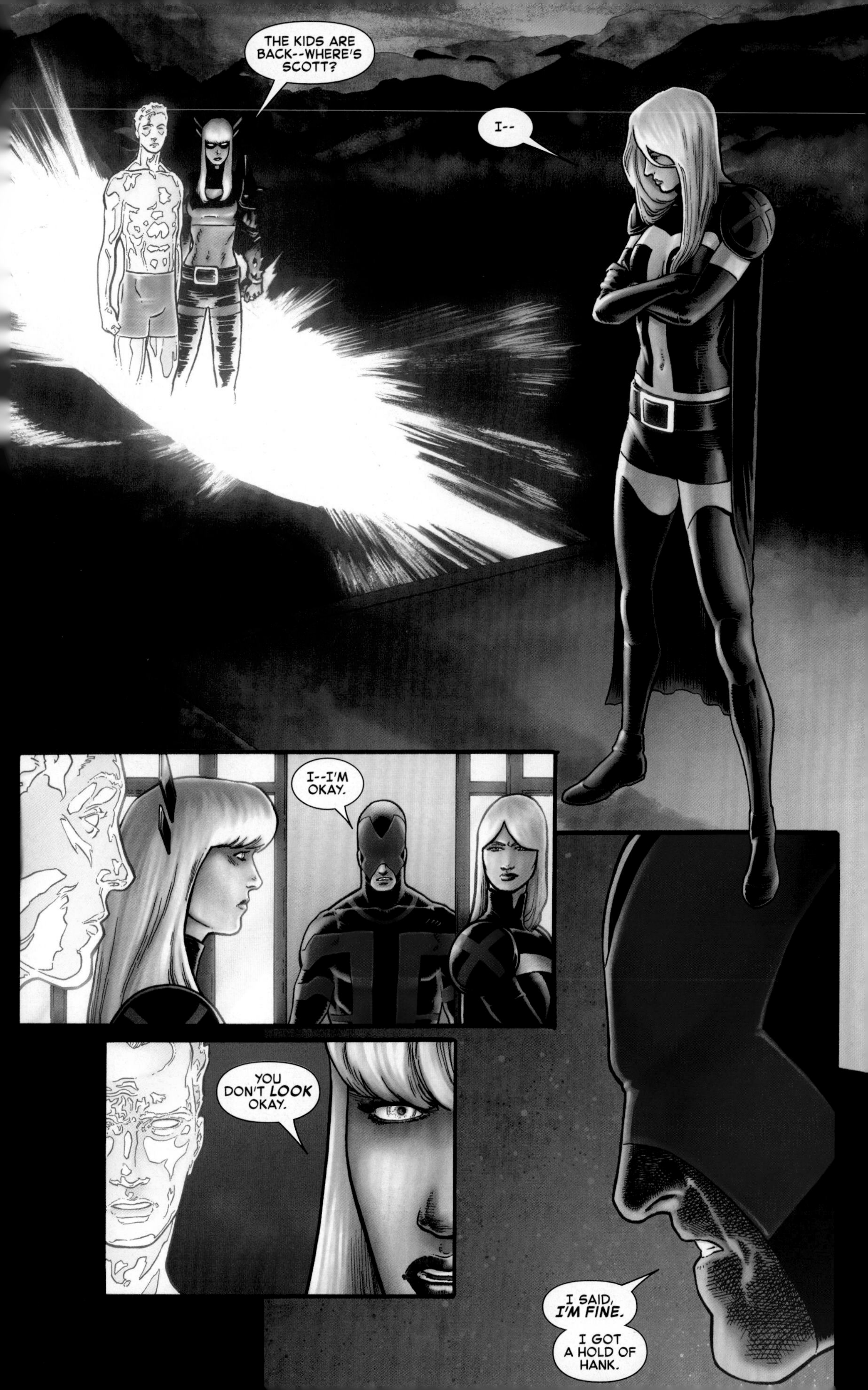
THE KIDS ARE BACK--WHERE'S SCOTT?
I--
I--I'M OKAY.
YOU DON'T LOOK OKAY.
I SAID, I'M FINE.
I GOT A HOLD OF HANK.

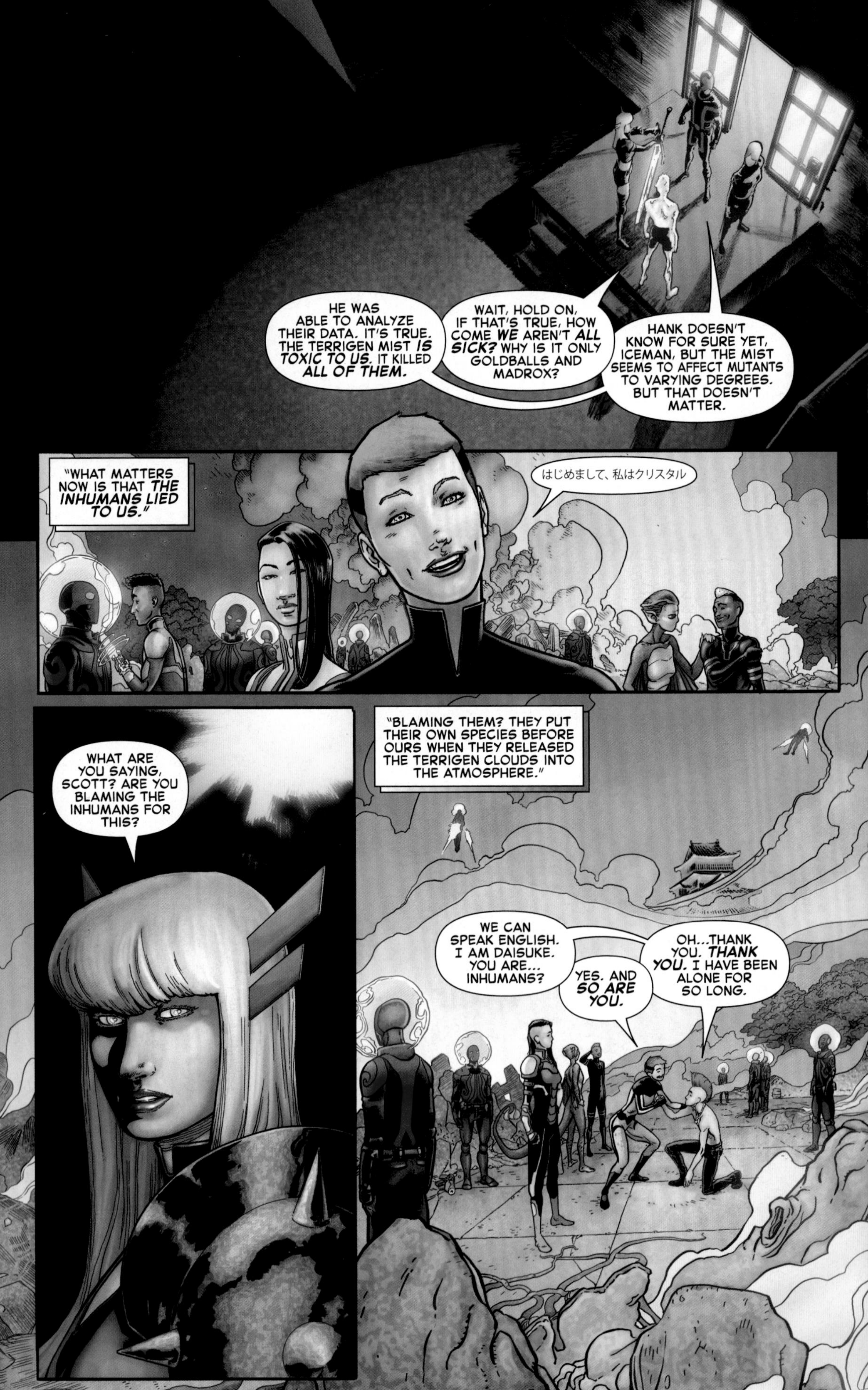
HE WAS ABLE TO ANALYZE THEIR DATA. IT'S TRUE. THE TERRIGEN MIST IS TOXIC TO US. IT KILLED ALL OF THEM.
WAIT, HOLD ON, IF THAT'S TRUE, HOW COME WE AREN'T ALL SICK? WHY IS IT ONLY GOLDBALLS AND MADROX?
HANK DOESN'T KNOW FOR SURE YET, ICEMAN, BUT THE MIST SEEMS TO AFFECT MUTANTS TO VARYING DEGREES. BUT THAT DOESN'T MATTER.
"WHAT MATTERS NOW IS THAT THE INHUMANS LIED TO US."
はじめまして、私はクリスタル
WHAT ARE YOU SAYING, SCOTT? ARE YOU BLAMING THE INHUMANS FOR THIS?
"BLAMING THEM? THEY PUT THEIR OWN SPECIES BEFORE OURS WHEN THEY RELEASED THE TERRIGEN CLOUDS INTO THE ATMOSPHERE."
WE CAN SPEAK ENGLISH. I AM DAISUKE. YOU ARE... INHUMANS?
YES. AND SO ARE YOU.
OH...THANK YOU. THANK YOU. I HAVE BEEN ALONE FOR SO LONG.

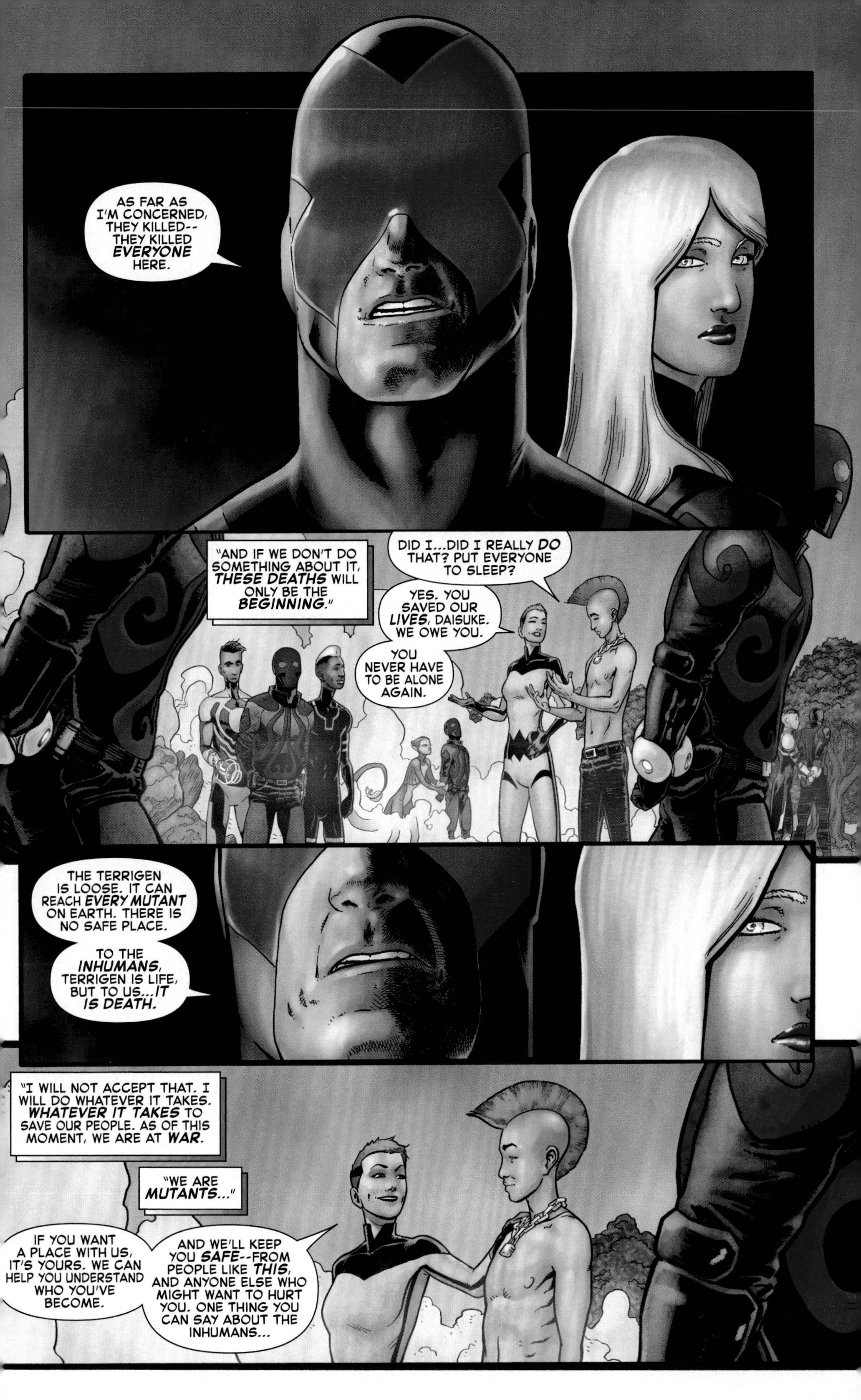
AS FAR AS I'M CONCERNED, THEY KILLED-- THEY KILLED EVERYONE HERE.
"AND IF WE DON'T DO SOMETHING ABOUT IT, THESE DEATHS WILL ONLY BE THE BEGINNING."
DID I...DID I REALLY DO THAT? PUT EVERYONE TO SLEEP?
YES. YOU SAVED OUR LIVES, DAISUKE. WE OWE YOU.
YOU NEVER HAVE TO BE ALONE AGAIN.
THE TERRIGEN IS LOOSE. IT CAN REACH EVERY MUTANT ON EARTH. THERE IS NO SAFE PLACE.
TO THE INHUMANS, TERRIGEN IS LIFE, BUT TO US...IT IS DEATH.
"I WILL NOT ACCEPT THAT. I WILL DO WHATEVER IT TAKES. WHATEVER IT TAKES TO SAVE OUR PEOPLE. AS OF THIS MOMENT, WE ARE AT WAR.
"WE ARE MUTANTS..."
IF YOU WANT A PLACE WITH US, IT'S YOURS. WE CAN HELP YOU UNDERSTAND WHO YOU'VE BECOME.
AND WE'LL KEEP YOU SAFE--FROM PEOPLE LIKE THIS, AND ANYONE ELSE WHO MIGHT WANT TO HURT YOU. ONE THING YOU CAN SAY ABOUT THE INHUMANS...

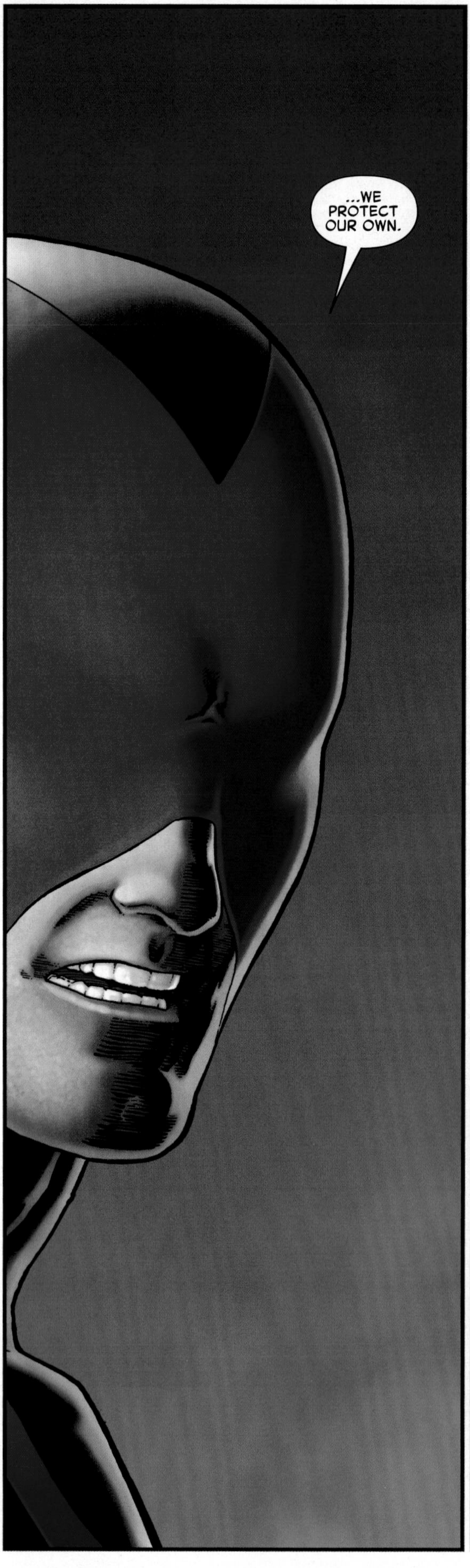
...WE PROTECT OUR OWN.

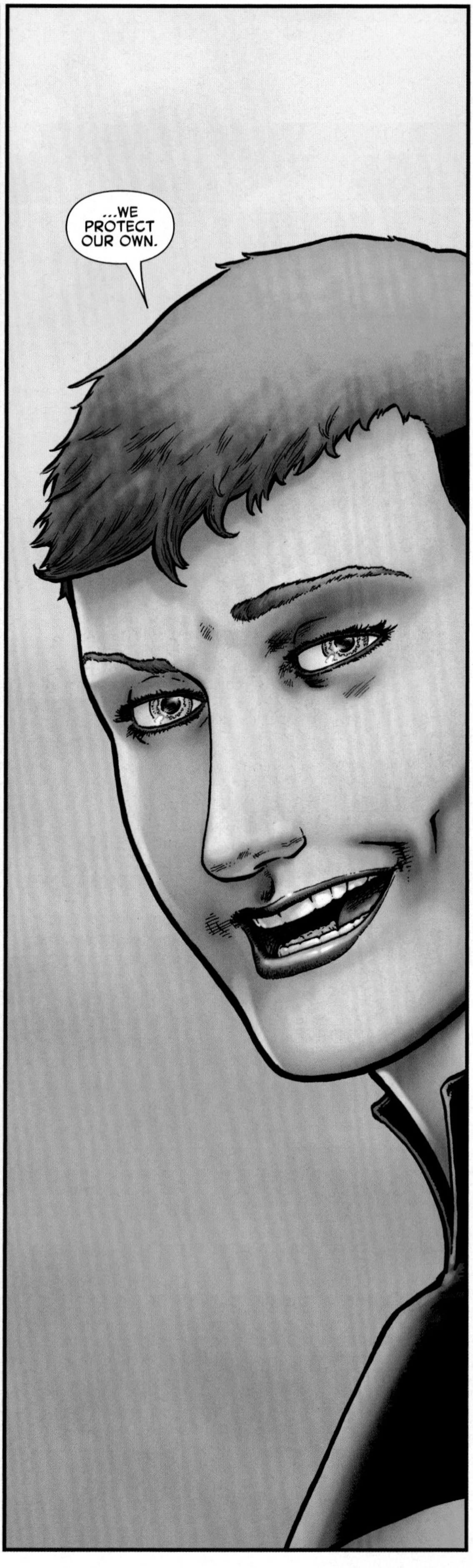
...WE PROTECT OUR OWN.

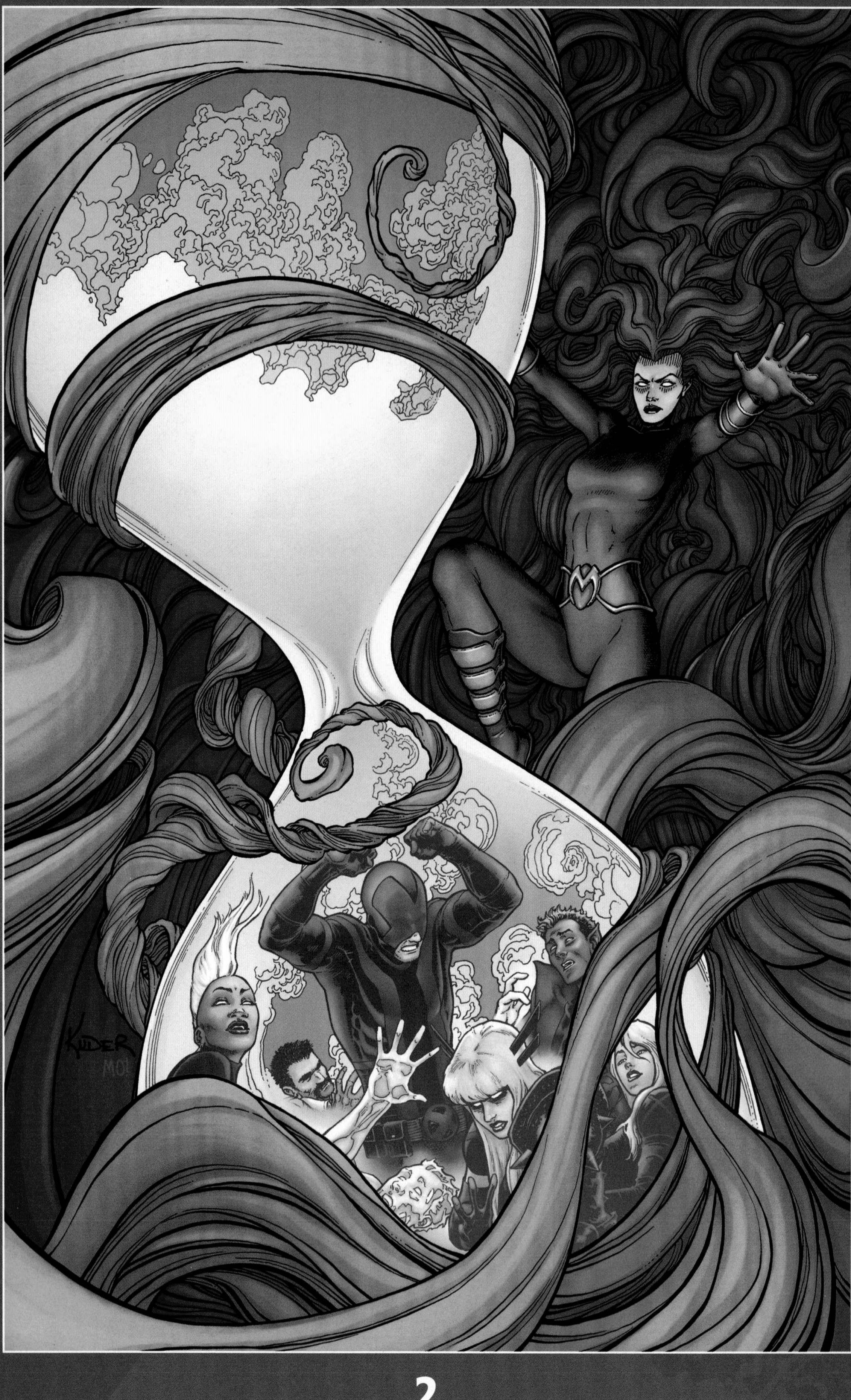

2

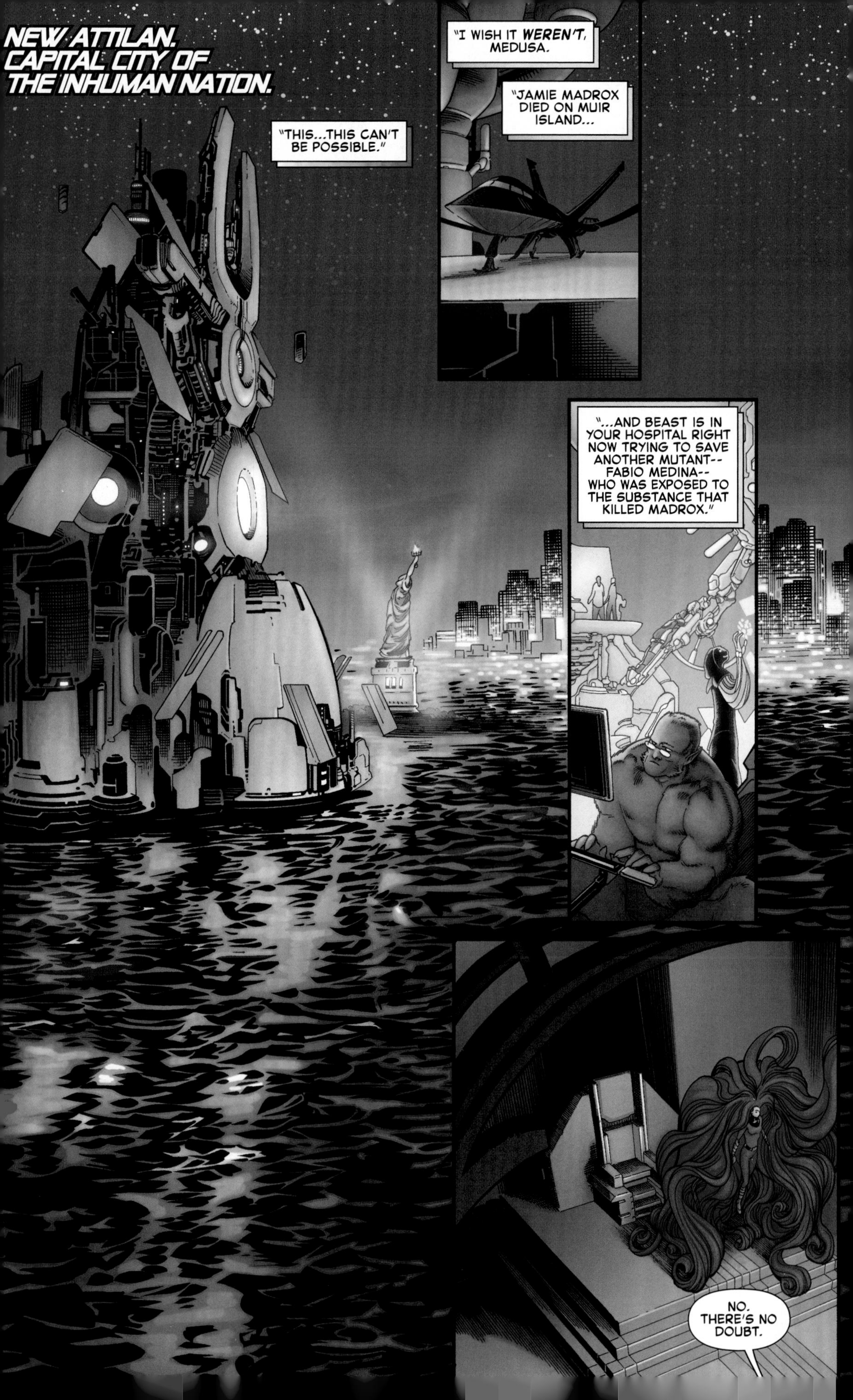
NEW ATTILAN. CAPITAL CITY OF THE INHUMAN NATION.
"THIS...THIS CAN'T BE POSSIBLE."
"I WISH IT WEREN'T, MEDUSA.
"JAMIE MADROX DIED ON MUIR ISLAND...
"...AND BEAST IS IN YOUR HOSPITAL RIGHT NOW TRYING TO SAVE ANOTHER MUTANT--FABIO MEDINA--WHO WAS EXPOSED TO THE SUBSTANCE THAT KILLED MADROX."
NO. THERE'S NO DOUBT.

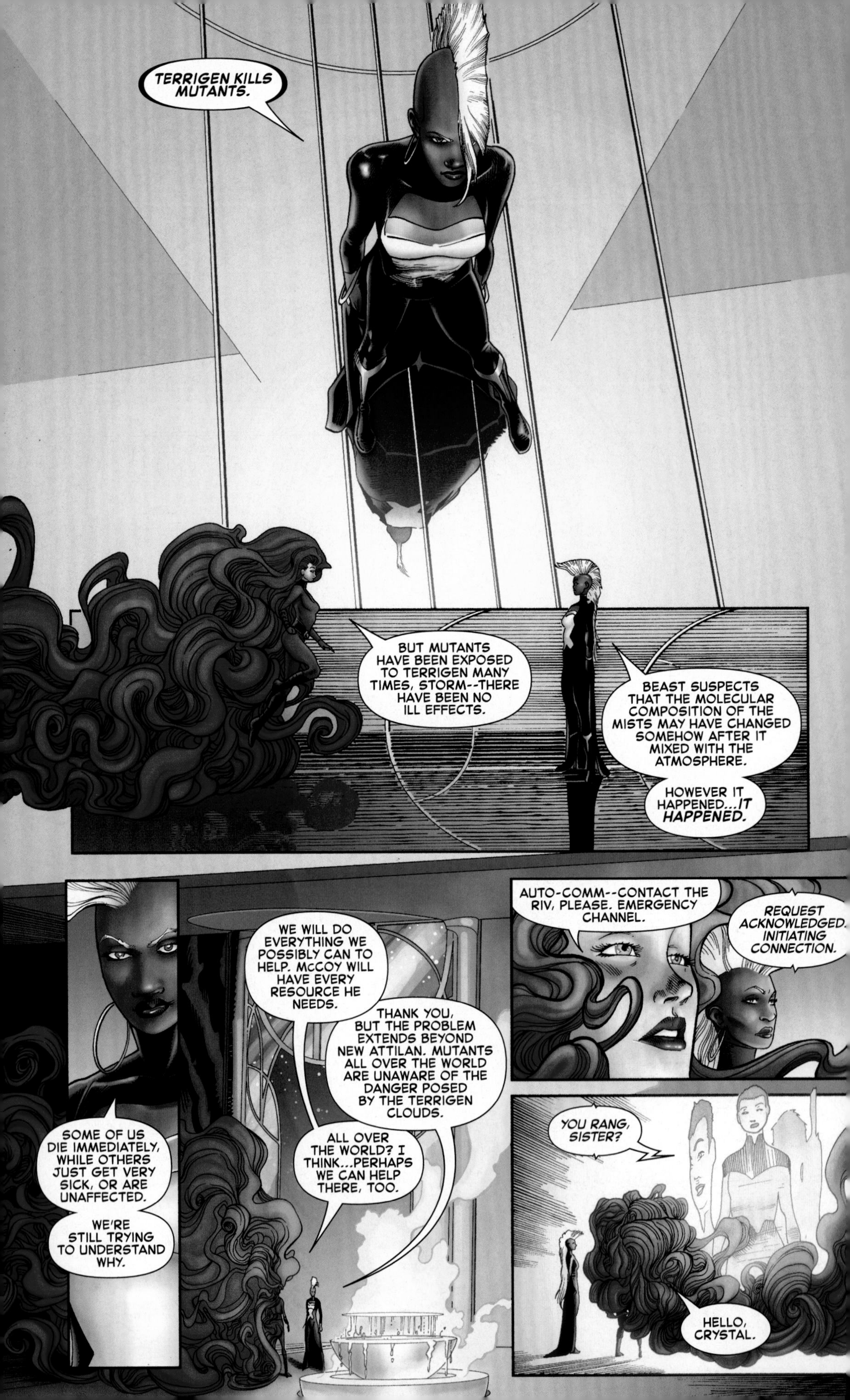
TERRIGEN KILLS MUTANTS.
BUT MUTANTS HAVE BEEN EXPOSED TO TERRIGEN MANY TIMES, STORM--THERE HAVE BEEN NO ILL EFFECTS.
BEAST SUSPECTS THAT THE MOLECULAR COMPOSITION OF THE MISTS MAY HAVE CHANGED SOMEHOW AFTER IT MIXED WITH THE ATMOSPHERE.
HOWEVER IT HAPPENED...*IT HAPPENED.*
SOME OF US DIE IMMEDIATELY, WHILE OTHERS JUST GET VERY SICK, OR ARE UNAFFECTED.
WE'RE STILL TRYING TO UNDERSTAND WHY.
WE WILL DO EVERYTHING WE POSSIBLY CAN TO HELP. McCOY WILL HAVE EVERY RESOURCE HE NEEDS.
THANK YOU, BUT THE PROBLEM EXTENDS BEYOND NEW ATTILAN. MUTANTS ALL OVER THE WORLD ARE UNAWARE OF THE DANGER POSED BY THE TERRIGEN CLOUDS.
ALL OVER THE WORLD? I THINK...PERHAPS WE CAN HELP THERE, TOO.
AUTO-COMM--CONTACT THE RIV, PLEASE. EMERGENCY CHANNEL.
REQUEST ACKNOWLEDGED. INITIATING CONNECTION.
YOU RANG, SISTER?
HELLO, CRYSTAL.

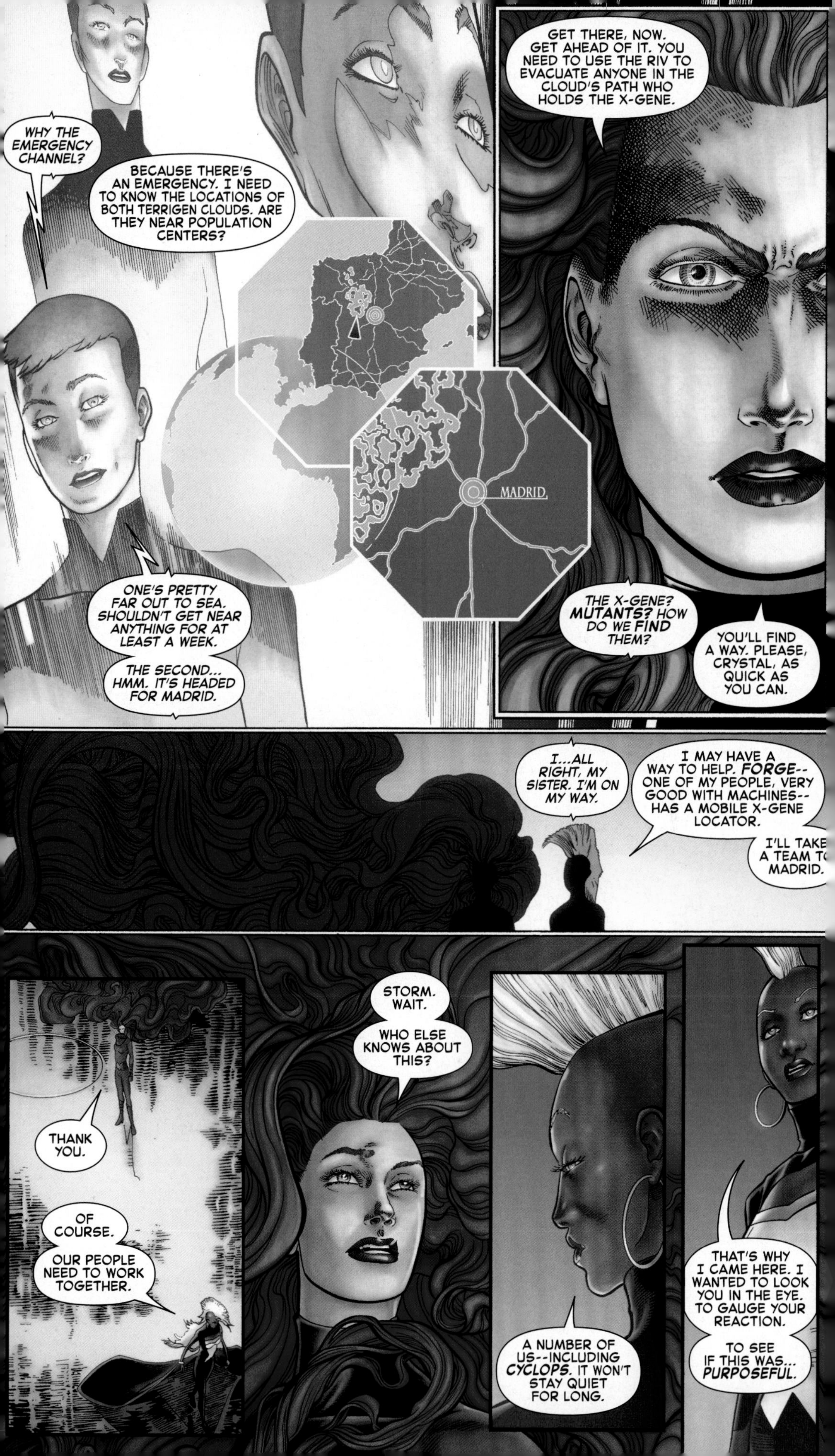
WHY THE EMERGENCY CHANNEL?
BECAUSE THERE'S AN EMERGENCY. I NEED TO KNOW THE LOCATIONS OF BOTH TERRIGEN CLOUDS. ARE THEY NEAR POPULATION CENTERS?
MADRID
ONE'S PRETTY FAR OUT TO SEA. SHOULDN'T GET NEAR ANYTHING FOR AT LEAST A WEEK.
THE SECOND... HMM. IT'S HEADED FOR MADRID.
GET THERE, NOW. GET AHEAD OF IT. YOU NEED TO USE THE RIV TO EVACUATE ANYONE IN THE CLOUD'S PATH WHO HOLDS THE X-GENE.
THE X-GENE? MUTANTS? HOW DO WE FIND THEM?
YOU'LL FIND A WAY. PLEASE, CRYSTAL, AS QUICK AS YOU CAN.
I...ALL RIGHT, MY SISTER. I'M ON MY WAY.
I MAY HAVE A WAY TO HELP. FORGE-- ONE OF MY PEOPLE, VERY GOOD WITH MACHINES-- HAS A MOBILE X-GENE LOCATOR.
I'LL TAKE A TEAM TO MADRID.
THANK YOU.
OF COURSE.
OUR PEOPLE NEED TO WORK TOGETHER.
STORM. WAIT.
WHO ELSE KNOWS ABOUT THIS?
A NUMBER OF US--INCLUDING CYCLOPS. IT WON'T STAY QUIET FOR LONG.
THAT'S WHY I CAME HERE. I WANTED TO LOOK YOU IN THE EYE. TO GAUGE YOUR REACTION.
TO SEE IF THIS WAS... PURPOSEFUL.

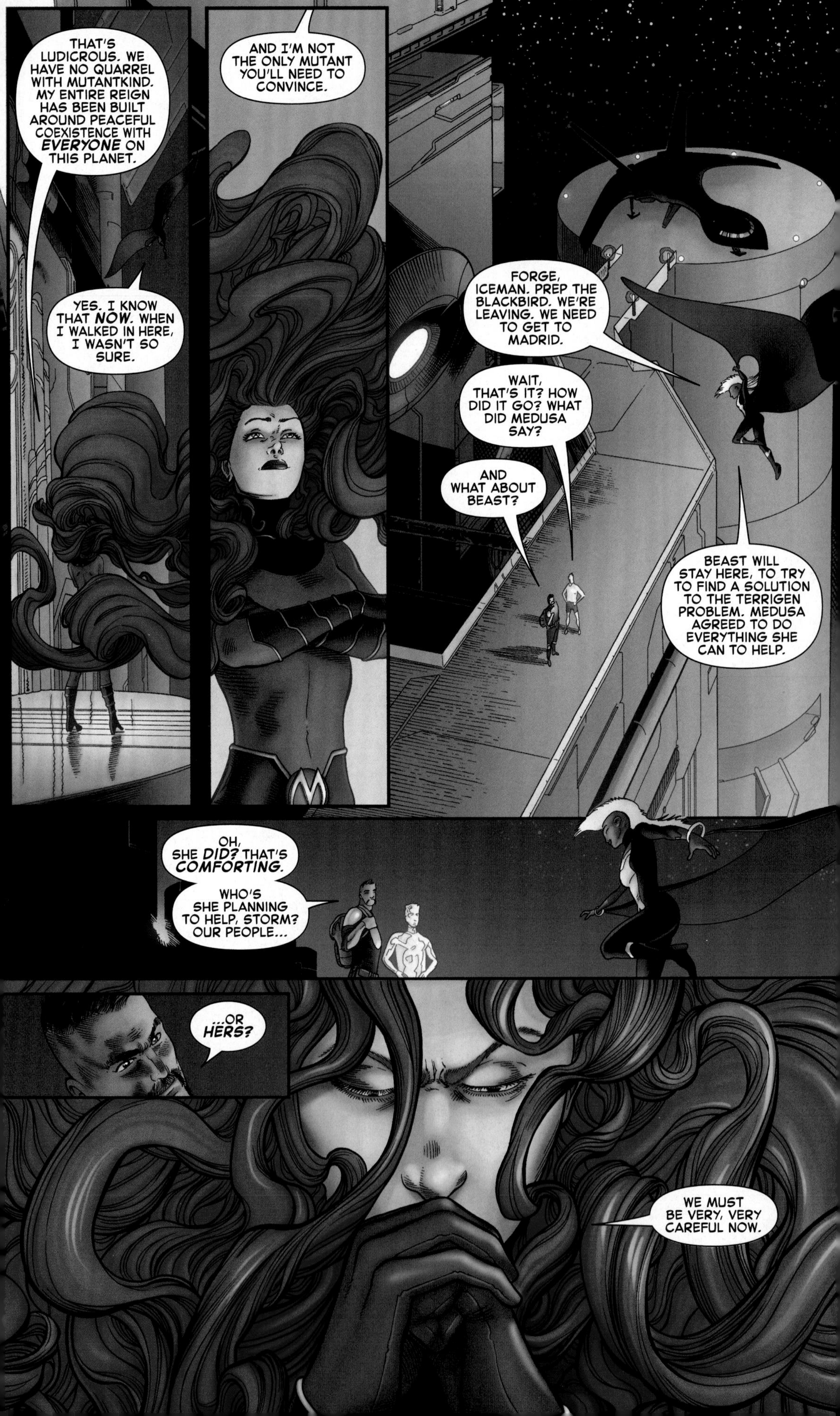
THAT'S LUDICROUS. WE HAVE NO QUARREL WITH MUTANTKIND. MY ENTIRE REIGN HAS BEEN BUILT AROUND PEACEFUL COEXISTENCE WITH *EVERYONE* ON THIS PLANET.
YES. I KNOW THAT *NOW*. WHEN I WALKED IN HERE, I WASN'T SO SURE.
AND I'M NOT THE ONLY MUTANT YOU'LL NEED TO CONVINCE.
FORGE, ICEMAN. PREP THE BLACKBIRD. WE'RE LEAVING. WE NEED TO GET TO MADRID.
WAIT, THAT'S IT? HOW DID IT GO? WHAT DID MEDUSA SAY?
AND WHAT ABOUT BEAST?
BEAST WILL STAY HERE, TO TRY TO FIND A SOLUTION TO THE TERRIGEN PROBLEM. MEDUSA AGREED TO DO EVERYTHING SHE CAN TO HELP.
OH, SHE *DID?* THAT'S *COMFORTING*.
WHO'S SHE PLANNING TO HELP, STORM? OUR PEOPLE...
...OR *HERS?*
WE MUST BE VERY, VERY CAREFUL NOW.

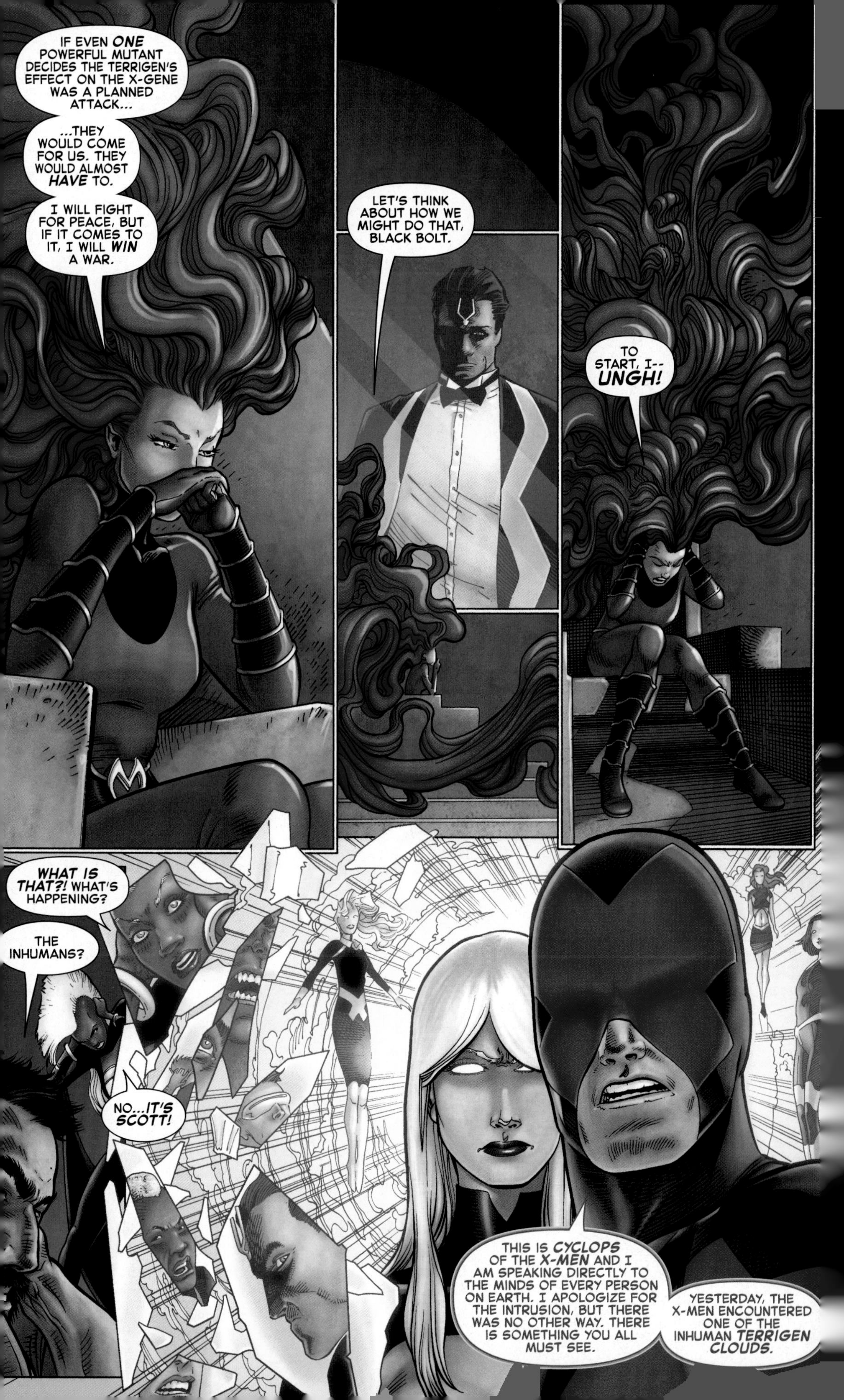

IF EVEN ONE POWERFUL MUTANT DECIDES THE TERRIGEN'S EFFECT ON THE X-GENE WAS A PLANNED ATTACK...
...THEY WOULD COME FOR US. THEY WOULD ALMOST HAVE TO.
I WILL FIGHT FOR PEACE, BUT IF IT COMES TO IT, I WILL WIN A WAR.
LET'S THINK ABOUT HOW WE MIGHT DO THAT, BLACK BOLT.
TO START, I-- UNGH!
WHAT IS THAT?! WHAT'S HAPPENING?
THE INHUMANS?
NO...IT'S SCOTT!
THIS IS CYCLOPS OF THE X-MEN AND I AM SPEAKING DIRECTLY TO THE MINDS OF EVERY PERSON ON EARTH. I APOLOGIZE FOR THE INTRUSION, BUT THERE WAS NO OTHER WAY. THERE IS SOMETHING YOU ALL MUST SEE.
YESTERDAY, THE X-MEN ENCOUNTERED ONE OF THE INHUMAN TERRIGEN CLOUDS.

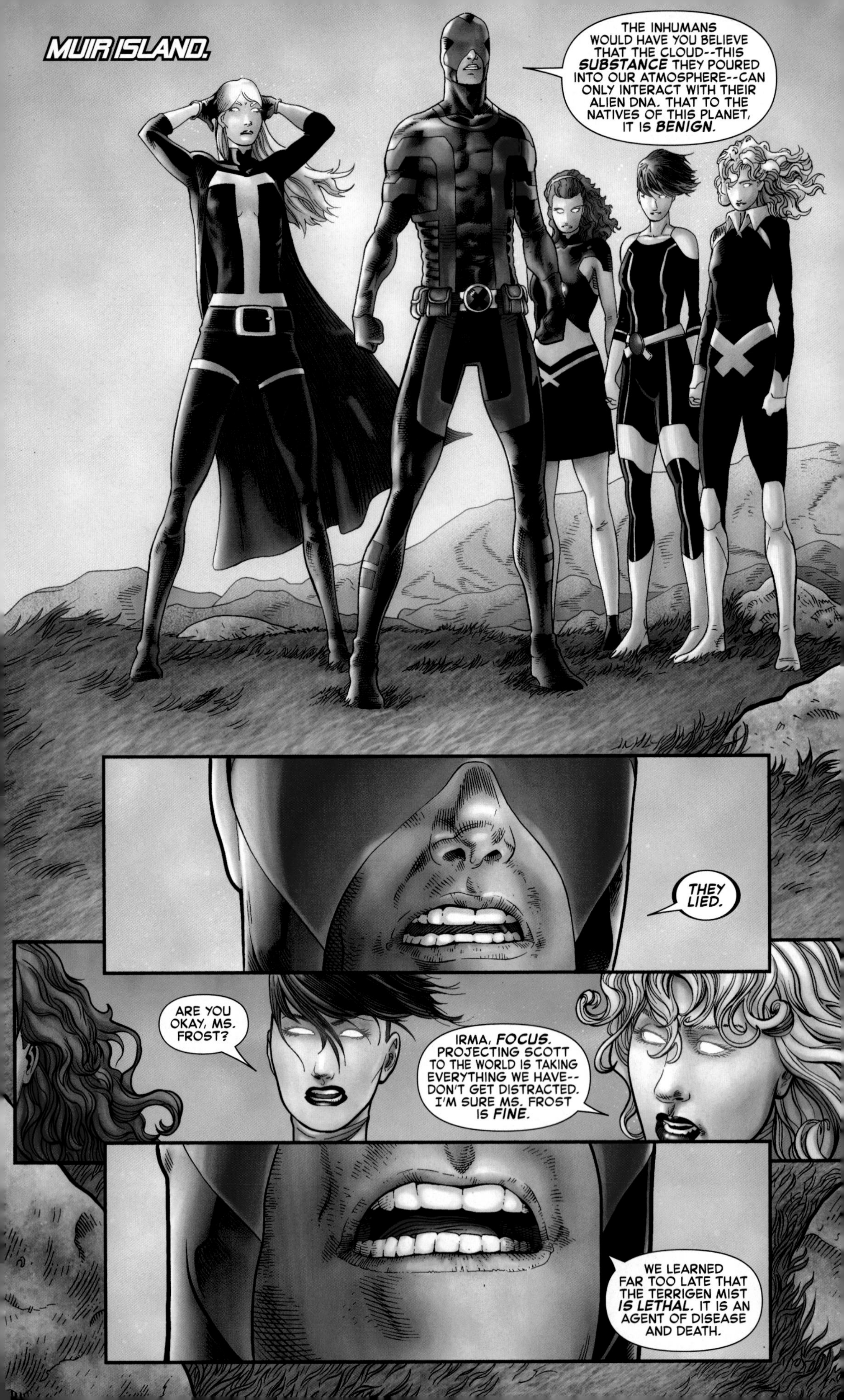
MUIR ISLAND.
THE INHUMANS WOULD HAVE YOU BELIEVE THAT THE CLOUD--THIS SUBSTANCE THEY POURED INTO OUR ATMOSPHERE--CAN ONLY INTERACT WITH THEIR ALIEN DNA. THAT TO THE NATIVES OF THIS PLANET, IT IS BENIGN.
THEY LIED.
ARE YOU OKAY, MS. FROST?
IRMA, FOCUS. PROJECTING SCOTT TO THE WORLD IS TAKING EVERYTHING WE HAVE--DON'T GET DISTRACTED. I'M SURE MS. FROST IS FINE.
WE LEARNED FAR TOO LATE THAT THE TERRIGEN MIST IS LETHAL. IT IS AN AGENT OF DISEASE AND DEATH.

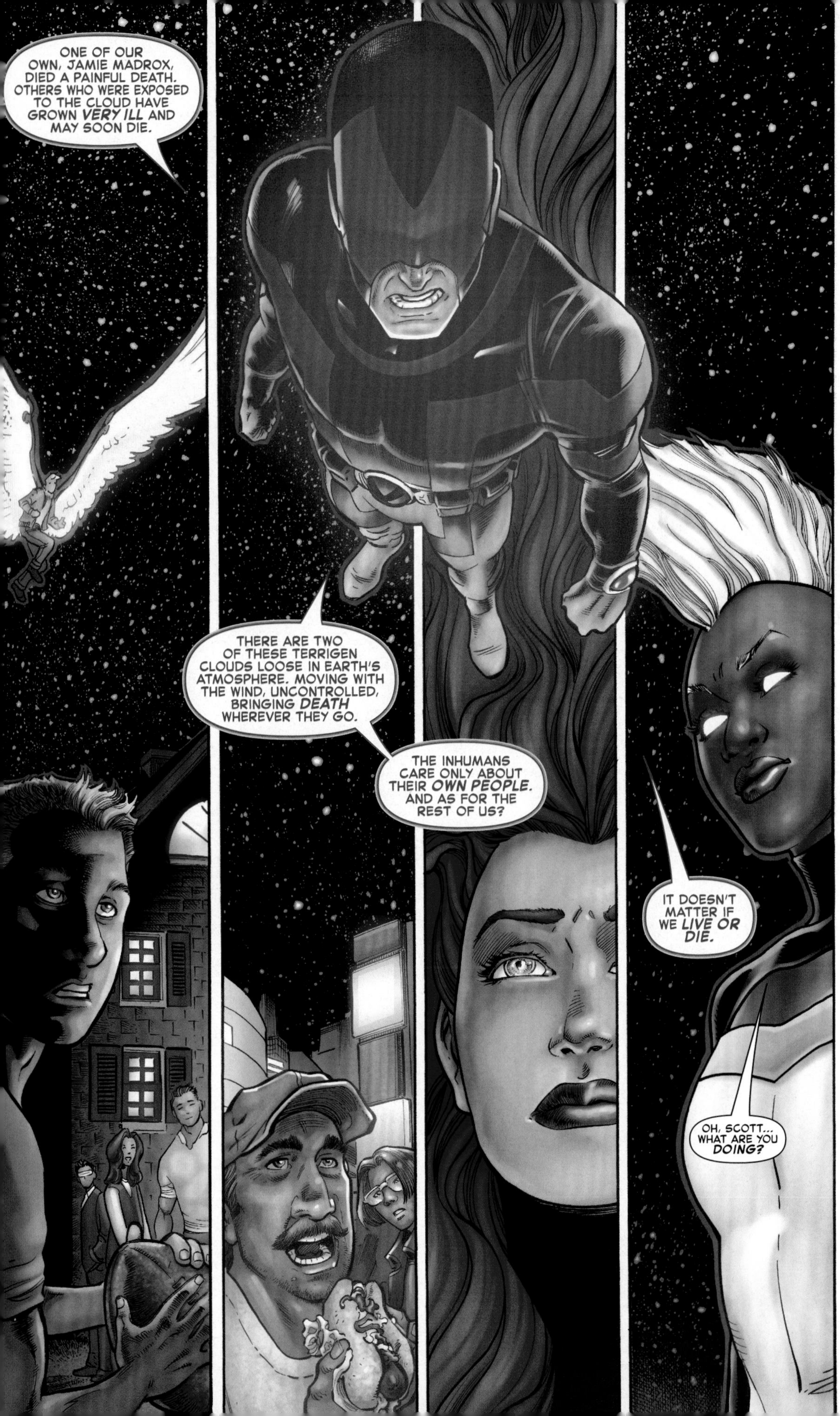

ONE OF OUR OWN, JAMIE MADROX, DIED A PAINFUL DEATH. OTHERS WHO WERE EXPOSED TO THE CLOUD HAVE GROWN VERY ILL AND MAY SOON DIE.
THERE ARE TWO OF THESE TERRIGEN CLOUDS LOOSE IN EARTH'S ATMOSPHERE. MOVING WITH THE WIND, UNCONTROLLED, BRINGING DEATH WHEREVER THEY GO.
THE INHUMANS CARE ONLY ABOUT THEIR OWN PEOPLE. AND AS FOR THE REST OF US?
IT DOESN'T MATTER IF WE LIVE OR DIE.
OH, SCOTT... WHAT ARE YOU DOING?

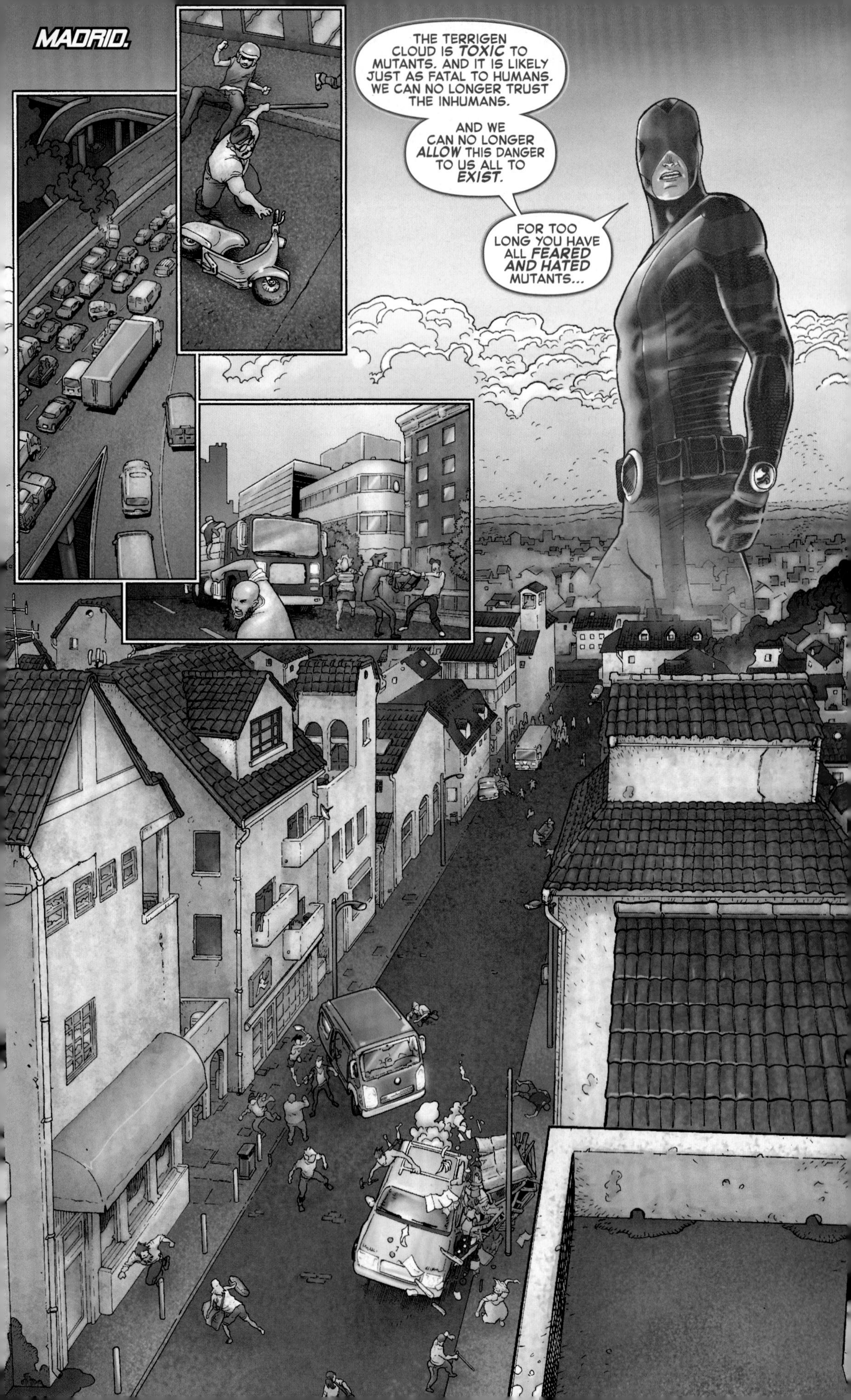
MADRID.
THE TERRIGEN CLOUD IS TOXIC TO MUTANTS. AND IT IS LIKELY JUST AS FATAL TO HUMANS. WE CAN NO LONGER TRUST THE INHUMANS.
AND WE CAN NO LONGER ALLOW THIS DANGER TO US ALL TO EXIST.
FOR TOO LONG YOU HAVE ALL FEARED AND HATED MUTANTS...

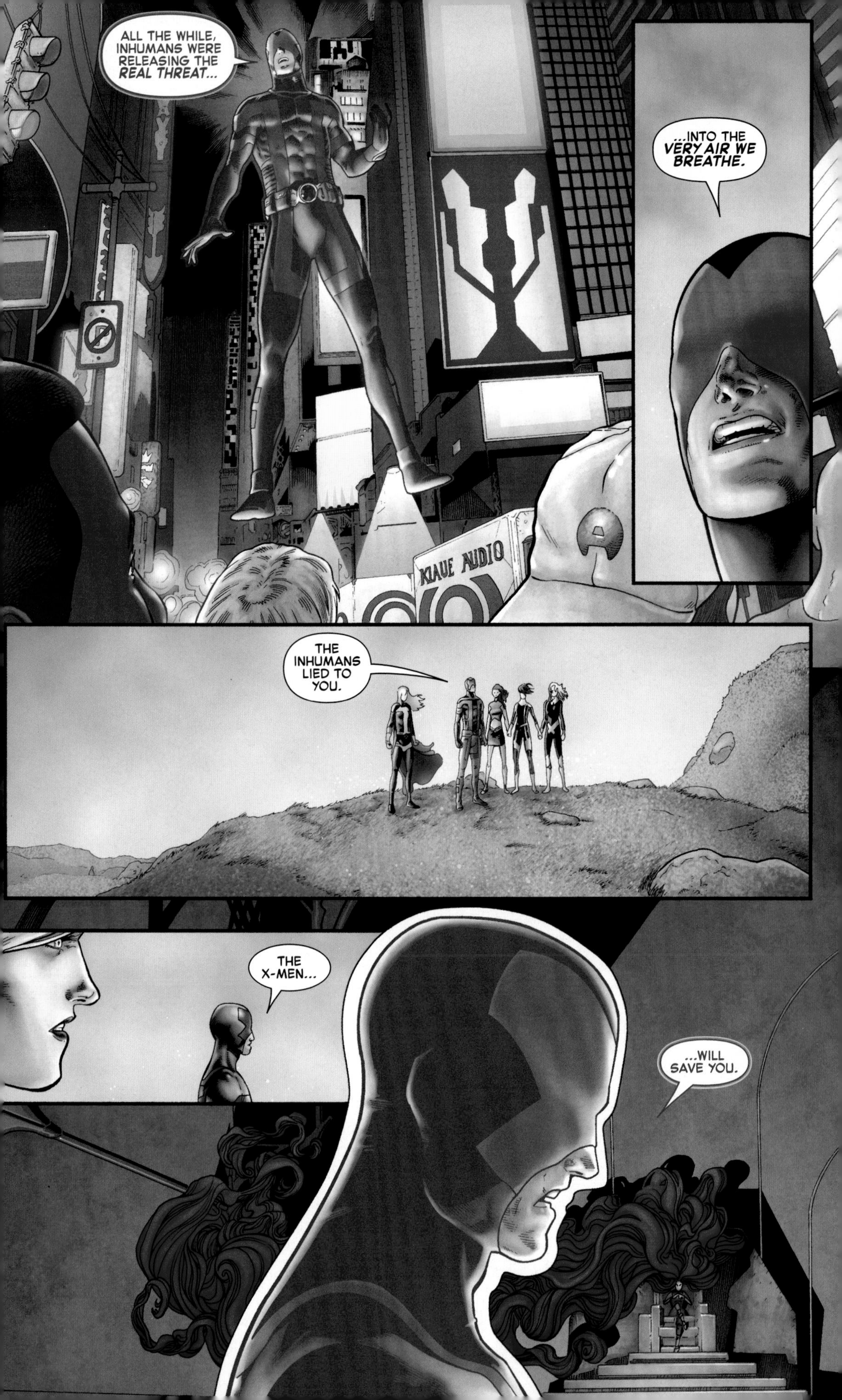

ALL THE WHILE, INHUMANS WERE RELEASING THE REAL THREAT...
...INTO THE VERY AIR WE BREATHE.
KIAUE AUDIO
THE INHUMANS LIED TO YOU.
THE X-MEN...
...WILL SAVE YOU.

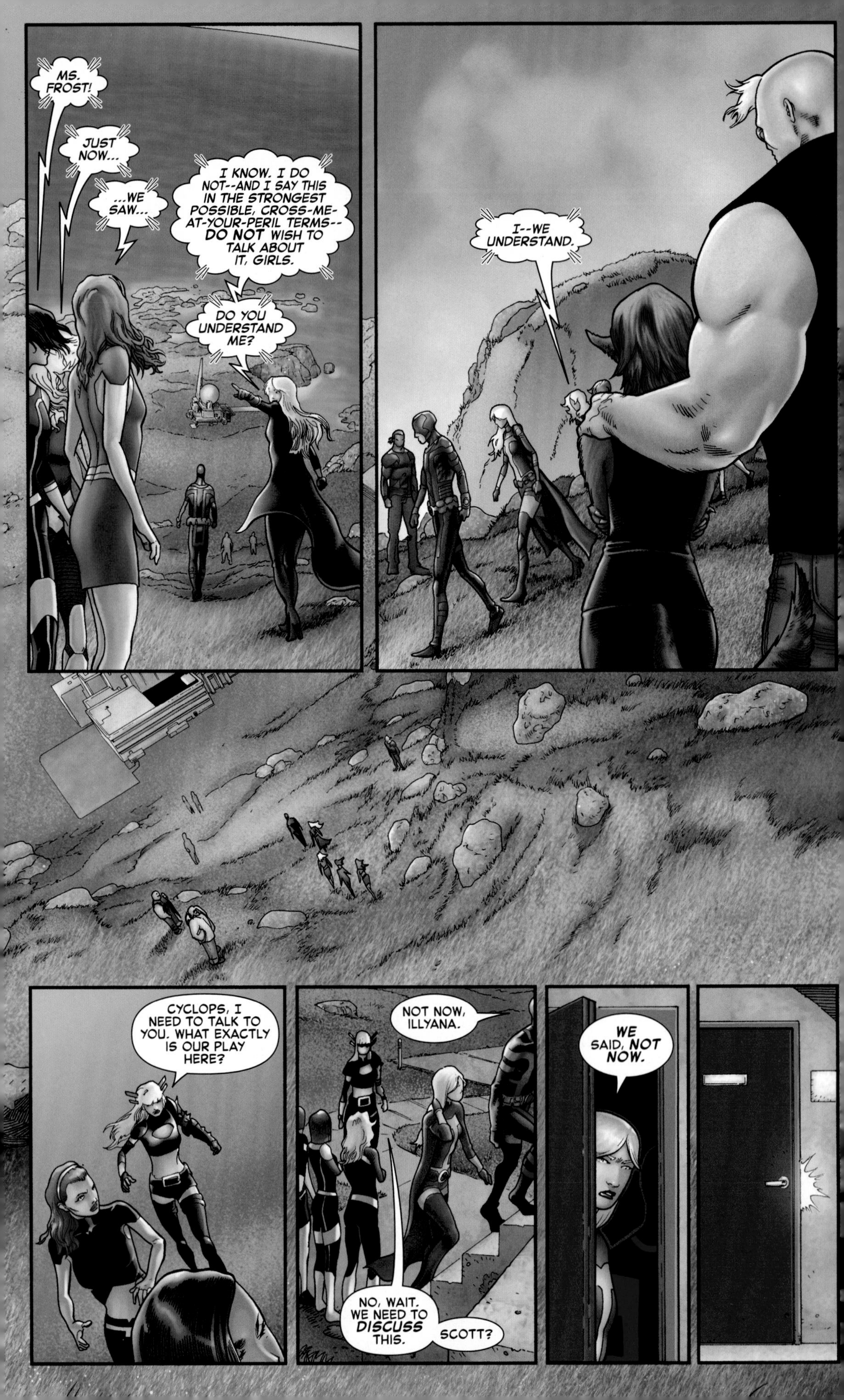
MS. FROST!
JUST NOW...
...WE SAW...
I KNOW. I DO NOT--AND I SAY THIS IN THE STRONGEST POSSIBLE, CROSS-ME-AT-YOUR-PERIL TERMS--DO NOT WISH TO TALK ABOUT IT, GIRLS.
DO YOU UNDERSTAND ME?
I--WE UNDERSTAND.
CYCLOPS, I NEED TO TALK TO YOU. WHAT EXACTLY IS OUR PLAY HERE?
NOT NOW, ILLYANA.
NO, WAIT. WE NEED TO DISCUSS THIS.
SCOTT?
WE SAID, NOT NOW.

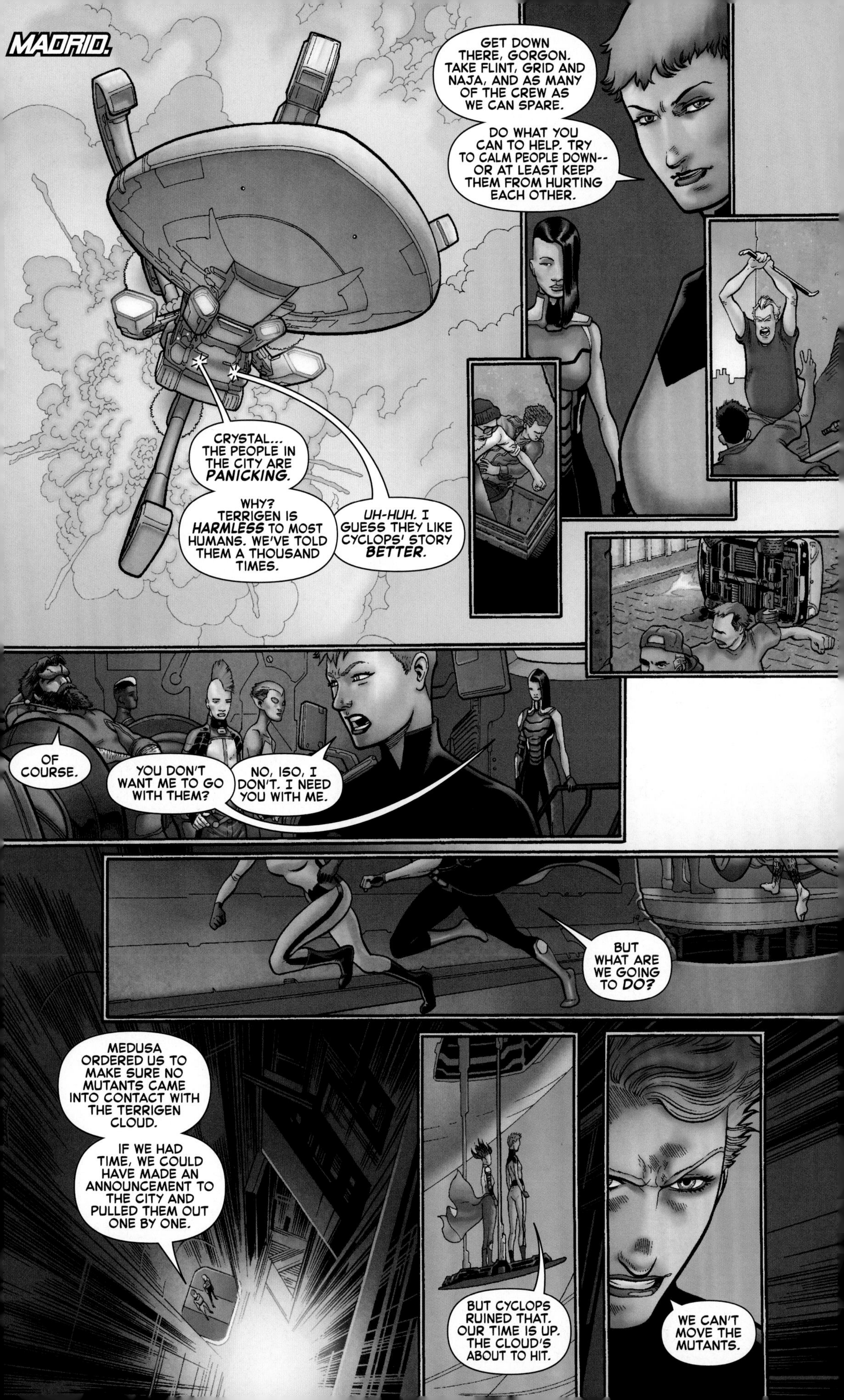
MADRID.
GET DOWN THERE, GORGON. TAKE FLINT, GRID AND NAJA, AND AS MANY OF THE CREW AS WE CAN SPARE.
DO WHAT YOU CAN TO HELP. TRY TO CALM PEOPLE DOWN-- OR AT LEAST KEEP THEM FROM HURTING EACH OTHER.
CRYSTAL... THE PEOPLE IN THE CITY ARE PANICKING.
WHY? TERRIGEN IS HARMLESS TO MOST HUMANS. WE'VE TOLD THEM A THOUSAND TIMES.
UH-HUH. I GUESS THEY LIKE CYCLOPS' STORY BETTER.
OF COURSE.
YOU DON'T WANT ME TO GO WITH THEM?
NO, ISO, I DON'T. I NEED YOU WITH ME.
BUT WHAT ARE WE GOING TO DO?
MEDUSA ORDERED US TO MAKE SURE NO MUTANTS CAME INTO CONTACT WITH THE TERRIGEN CLOUD.
IF WE HAD TIME, WE COULD HAVE MADE AN ANNOUNCEMENT TO THE CITY AND PULLED THEM OUT ONE BY ONE.
BUT CYCLOPS RUINED THAT. OUR TIME IS UP. THE CLOUD'S ABOUT TO HIT.
WE CAN'T MOVE THE MUTANTS.

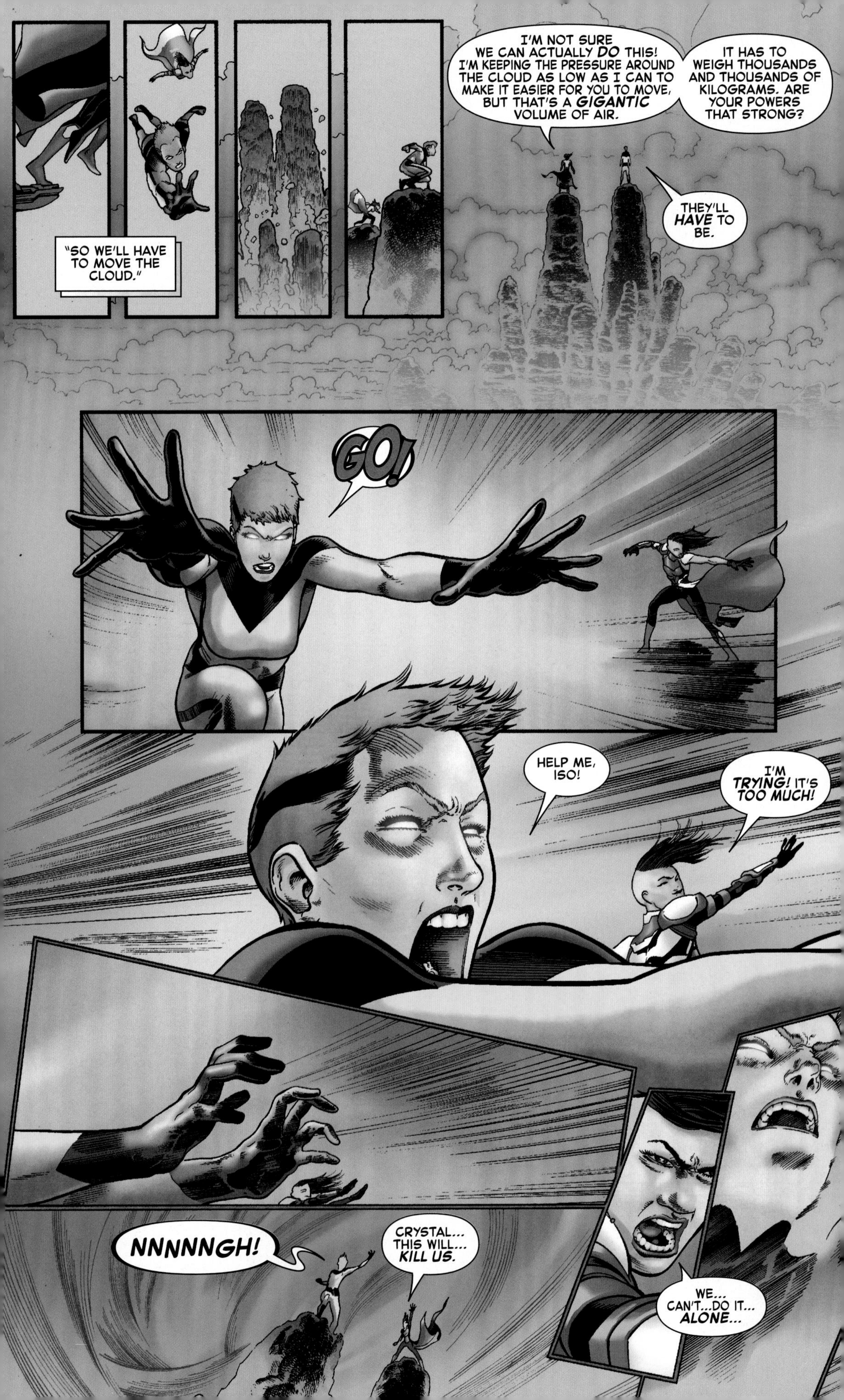
"SO WE'LL HAVE TO MOVE THE CLOUD."
I'M NOT SURE WE CAN ACTUALLY DO THIS! I'M KEEPING THE PRESSURE AROUND THE CLOUD AS LOW AS I CAN TO MAKE IT EASIER FOR YOU TO MOVE, BUT THAT'S A GIGANTIC VOLUME OF AIR.
IT HAS TO WEIGH THOUSANDS AND THOUSANDS OF KILOGRAMS. ARE YOUR POWERS THAT STRONG?
THEY'LL HAVE TO BE.
GO!
HELP ME, ISO!
I'M TRYING! IT'S TOO MUCH!
NNNNNGH!
CRYSTAL... THIS WILL... KILL US.
WE... CAN'T...DO IT... ALONE...

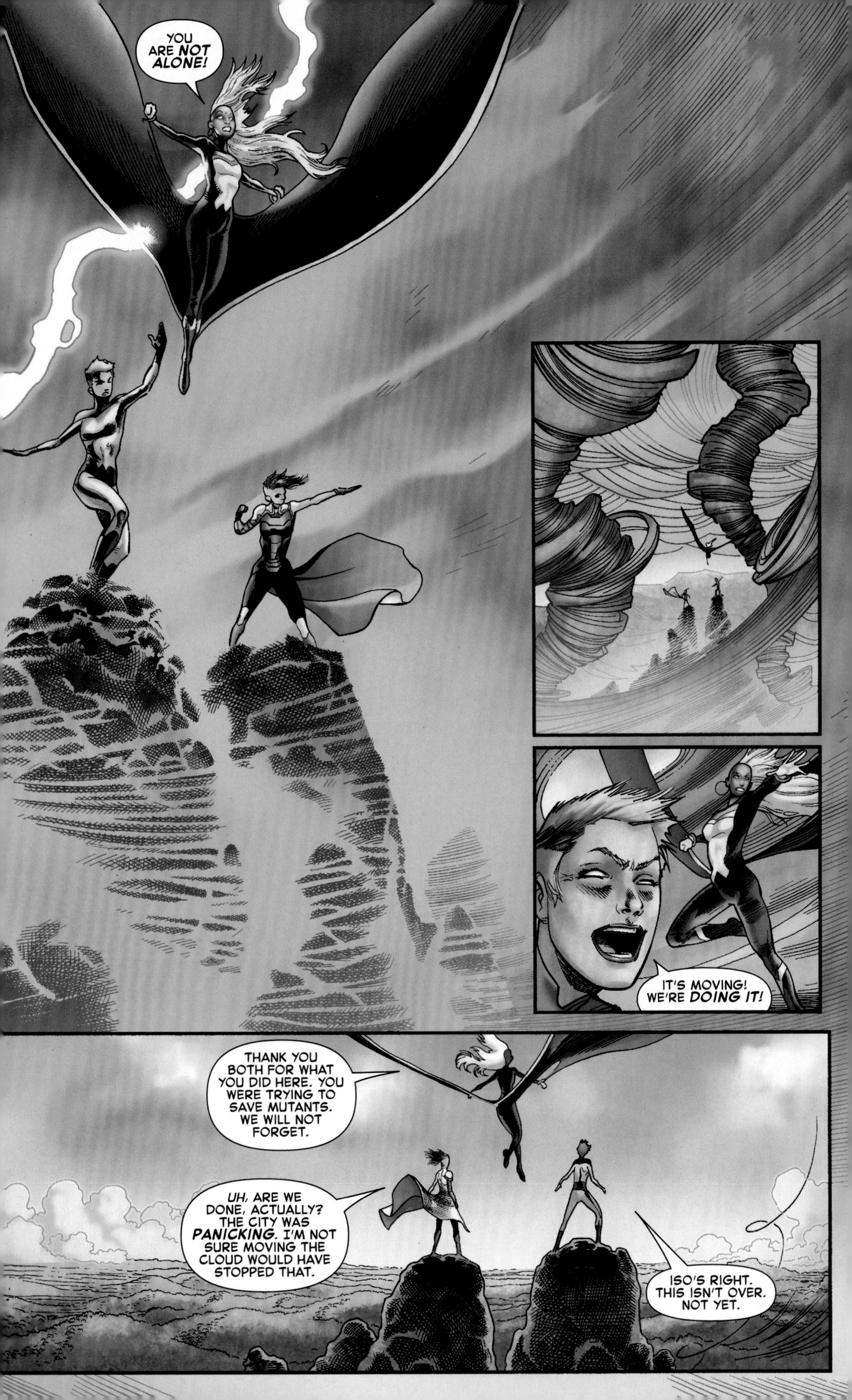
YOU ARE NOT ALONE!
IT'S MOVING! WE'RE DOING IT!
THANK YOU BOTH FOR WHAT YOU DID HERE. YOU WERE TRYING TO SAVE MUTANTS. WE WILL NOT FORGET.
UH, ARE WE DONE, ACTUALLY? THE CITY WAS PANICKING. I'M NOT SURE MOVING THE CLOUD WOULD HAVE STOPPED THAT.
ISO'S RIGHT. THIS ISN'T OVER. NOT YET.

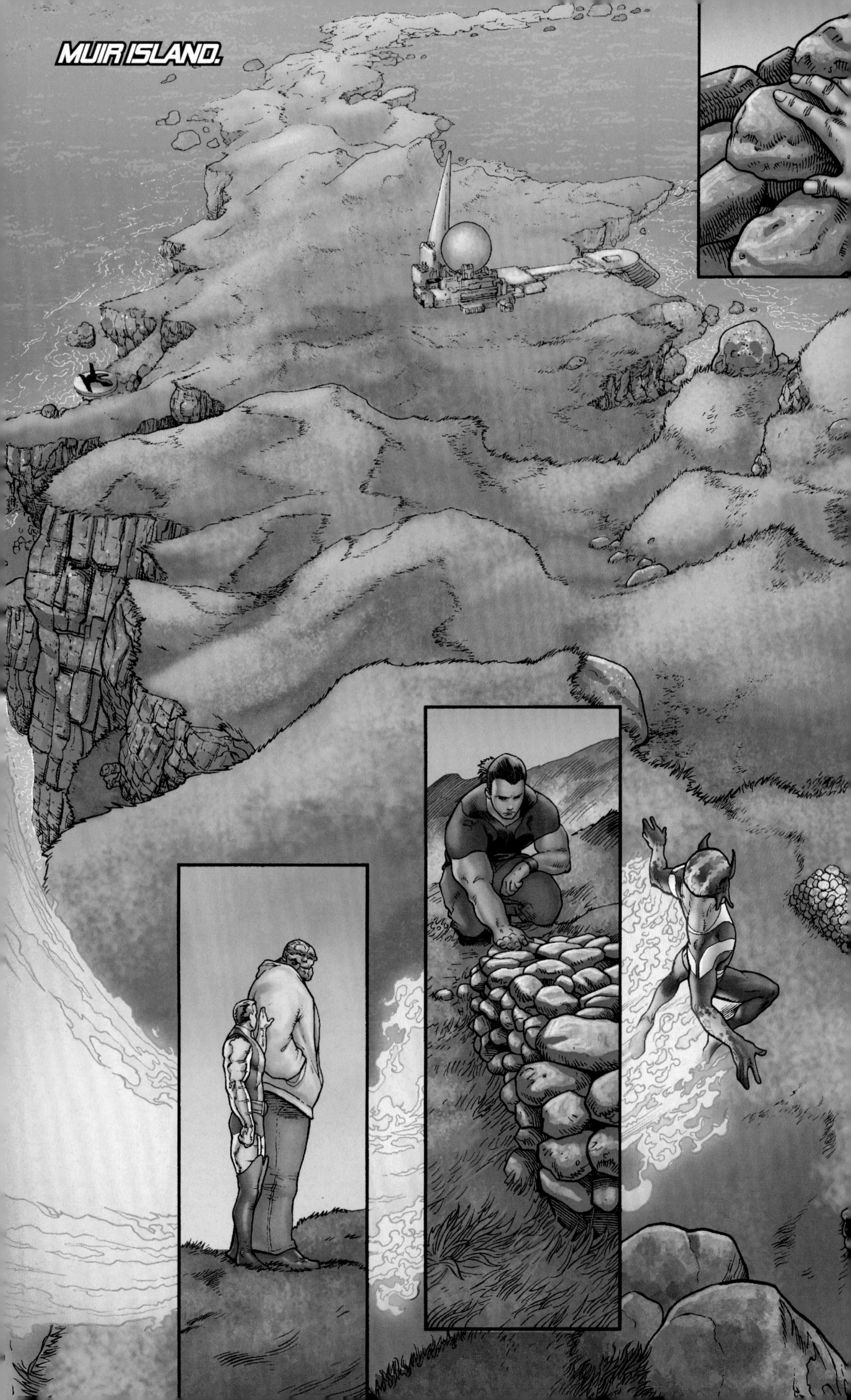
MUIR ISLAND.

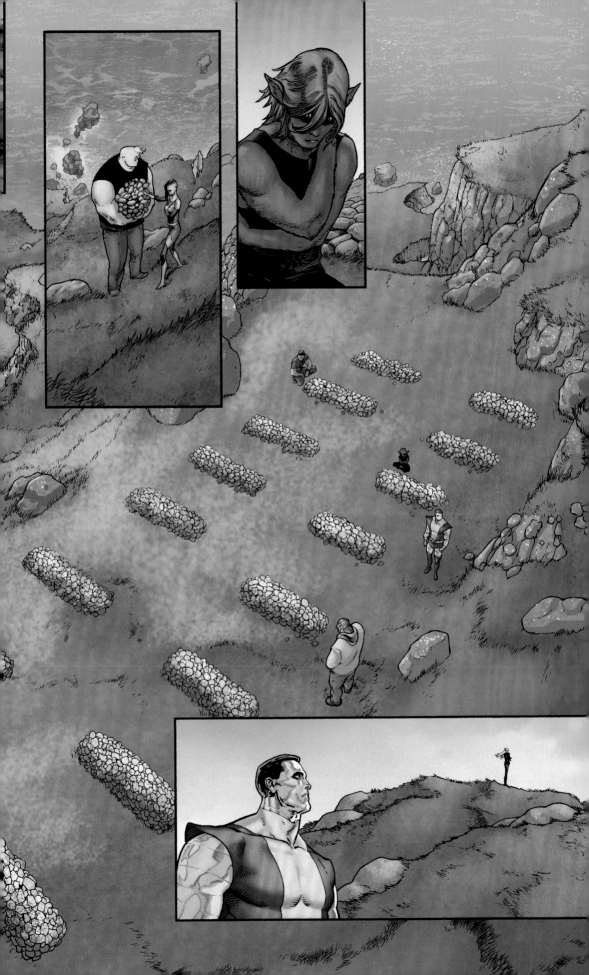

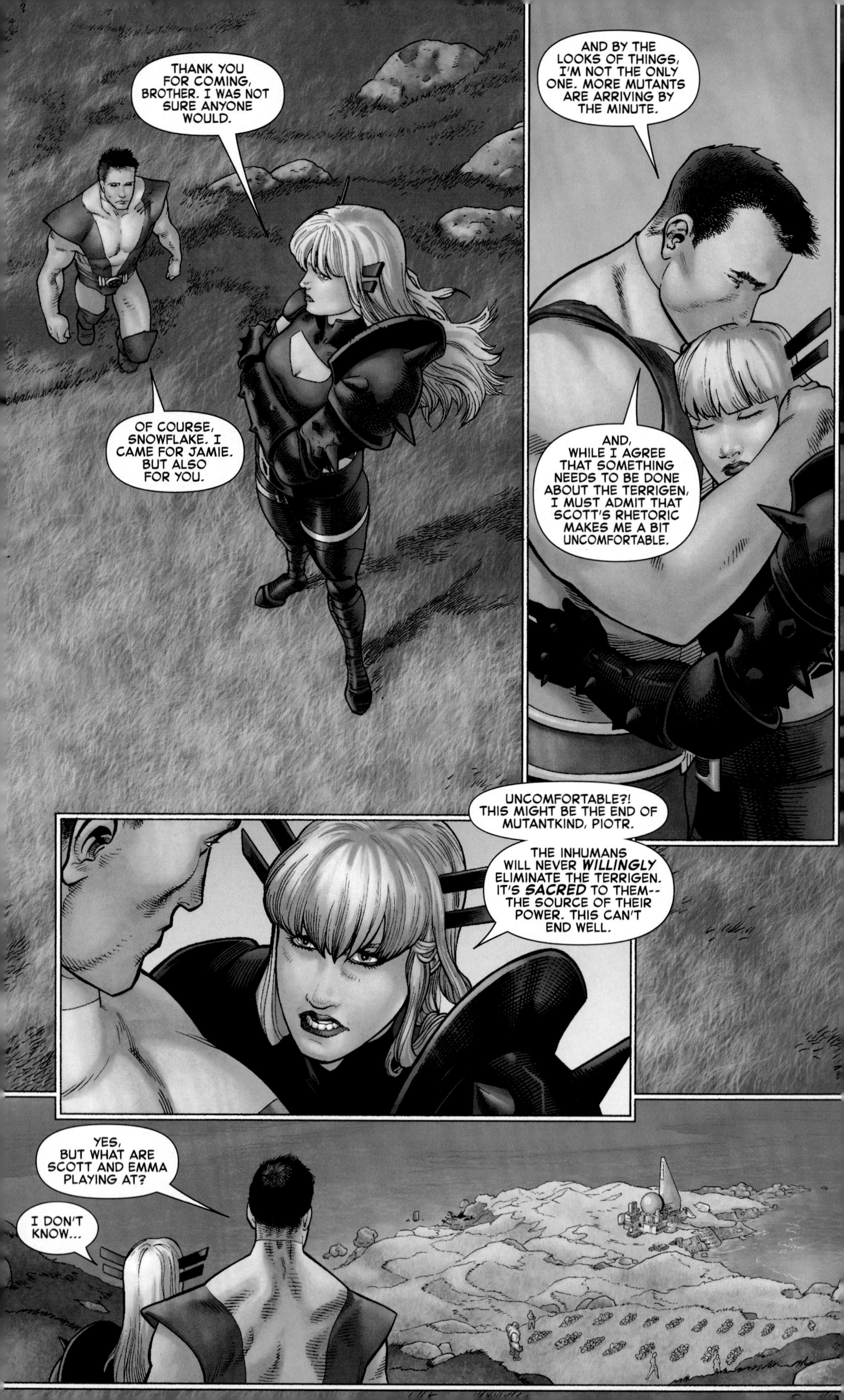
THANK YOU FOR COMING, BROTHER. I WAS NOT SURE ANYONE WOULD.
OF COURSE, SNOWFLAKE. I CAME FOR JAMIE. BUT ALSO FOR YOU.
AND BY THE LOOKS OF THINGS, I'M NOT THE ONLY ONE. MORE MUTANTS ARE ARRIVING BY THE MINUTE.
AND, WHILE I AGREE THAT SOMETHING NEEDS TO BE DONE ABOUT THE TERRIGEN, I MUST ADMIT THAT SCOTT'S RHETORIC MAKES ME A BIT UNCOMFORTABLE.
UNCOMFORTABLE?! THIS MIGHT BE THE END OF MUTANTKIND, PIOTR.
THE INHUMANS WILL NEVER WILLINGLY ELIMINATE THE TERRIGEN. IT'S SACRED TO THEM-- THE SOURCE OF THEIR POWER. THIS CAN'T END WELL.
YES, BUT WHAT ARE SCOTT AND EMMA PLAYING AT?
I DON'T KNOW...

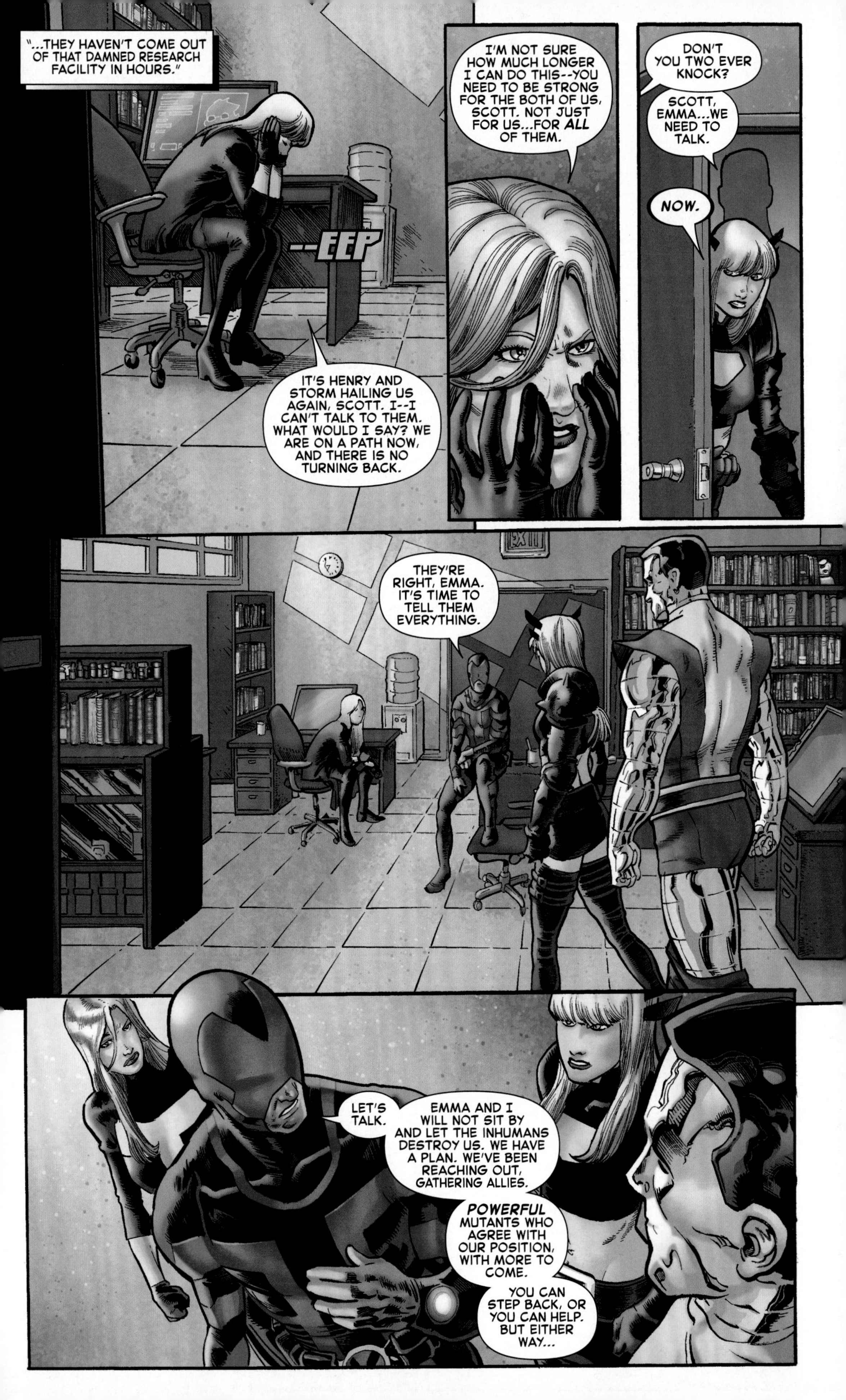
"...THEY HAVEN'T COME OUT OF THAT DAMNED RESEARCH FACILITY IN HOURS."
--EEP
IT'S HENRY AND STORM HAILING US AGAIN, SCOTT. I--I CAN'T TALK TO THEM. WHAT WOULD I SAY? WE ARE ON A PATH NOW, AND THERE IS NO TURNING BACK.
I'M NOT SURE HOW MUCH LONGER I CAN DO THIS--YOU NEED TO BE STRONG FOR THE BOTH OF US, SCOTT. NOT JUST FOR US...FOR ALL OF THEM.
DON'T YOU TWO EVER KNOCK?
SCOTT, EMMA...WE NEED TO TALK.
NOW.
THEY'RE RIGHT, EMMA. IT'S TIME TO TELL THEM EVERYTHING.
LET'S TALK.
EMMA AND I WILL NOT SIT BY AND LET THE INHUMANS DESTROY US. WE HAVE A PLAN. WE'VE BEEN REACHING OUT, GATHERING ALLIES.
POWERFUL MUTANTS WHO AGREE WITH OUR POSITION, WITH MORE TO COME.
YOU CAN STEP BACK, OR YOU CAN HELP. BUT EITHER WAY...

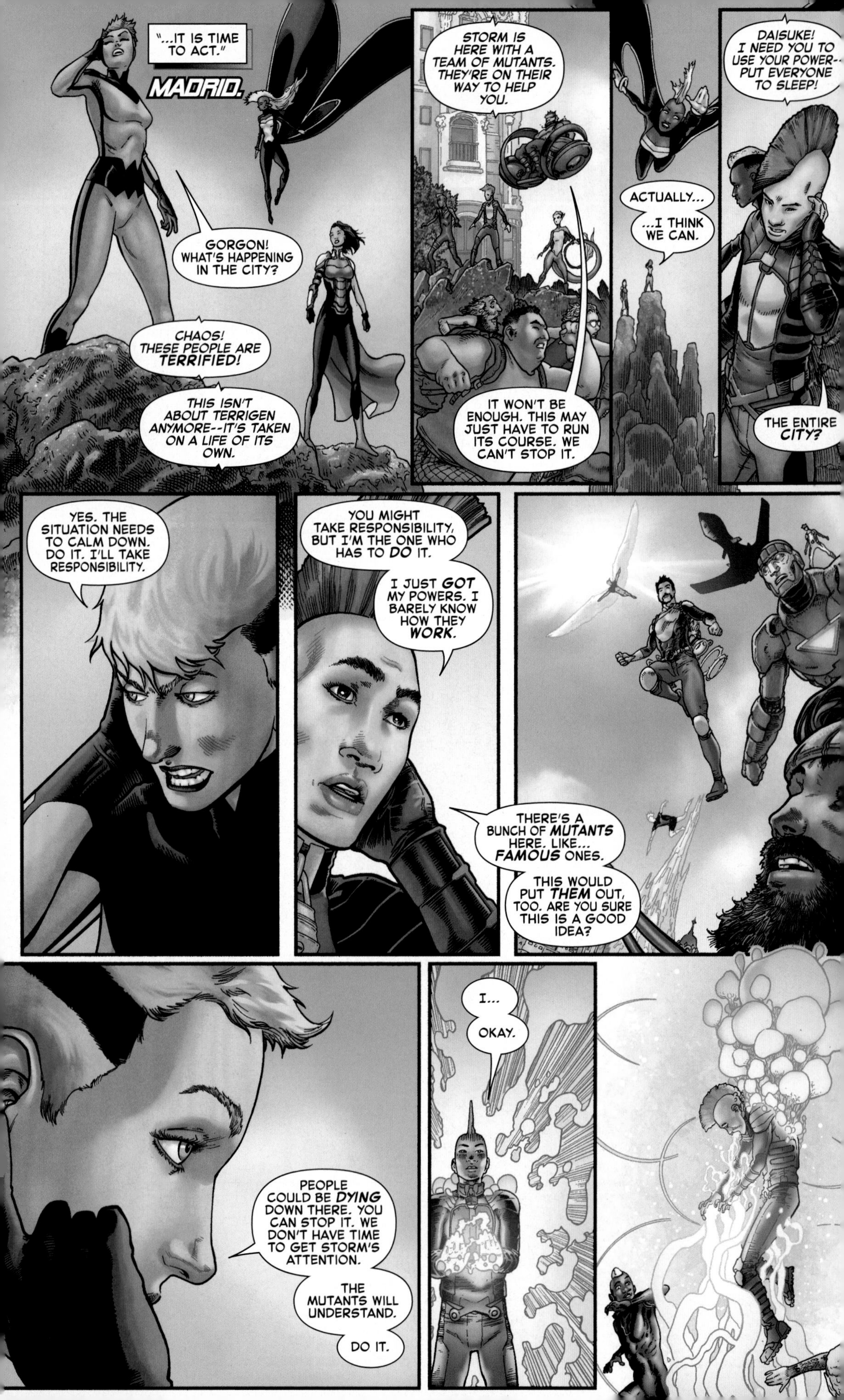

"...IT IS TIME TO ACT."
MADRID.
GORGON! WHAT'S HAPPENING IN THE CITY?
CHAOS! THESE PEOPLE ARE TERRIFIED!
THIS ISN'T ABOUT TERRIGEN ANYMORE--IT'S TAKEN ON A LIFE OF ITS OWN.
STORM IS HERE WITH A TEAM OF MUTANTS. THEY'RE ON THEIR WAY TO HELP YOU.
IT WON'T BE ENOUGH. THIS MAY JUST HAVE TO RUN ITS COURSE. WE CAN'T STOP IT.
ACTUALLY...
...I THINK WE CAN.
DAISUKE! I NEED YOU TO USE YOUR POWER--PUT EVERYONE TO SLEEP!
THE ENTIRE CITY?
YES. THE SITUATION NEEDS TO CALM DOWN. DO IT. I'LL TAKE RESPONSIBILITY.
YOU MIGHT TAKE RESPONSIBILITY, BUT I'M THE ONE WHO HAS TO DO IT.
I JUST GOT MY POWERS. I BARELY KNOW HOW THEY WORK.
THERE'S A BUNCH OF MUTANTS HERE. LIKE... FAMOUS ONES.
THIS WOULD PUT THEM OUT, TOO. ARE YOU SURE THIS IS A GOOD IDEA?
PEOPLE COULD BE DYING DOWN THERE. YOU CAN STOP IT. WE DON'T HAVE TIME TO GET STORM'S ATTENTION.
THE MUTANTS WILL UNDERSTAND.
DO IT.
I...
OKAY.

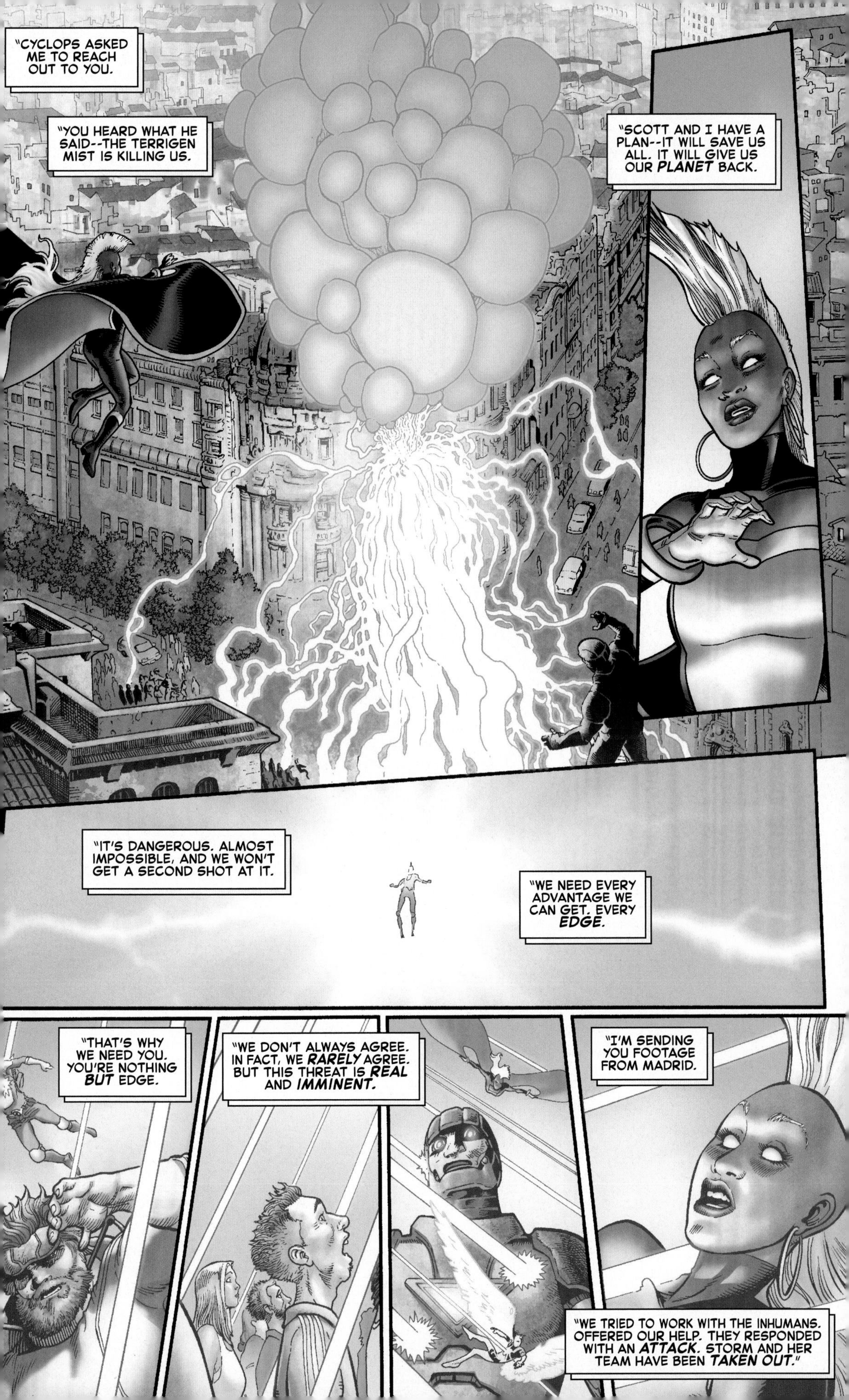
"CYCLOPS ASKED ME TO REACH OUT TO YOU.
"YOU HEARD WHAT HE SAID--THE TERRIGEN MIST IS KILLING US.
"SCOTT AND I HAVE A PLAN--IT WILL SAVE US ALL. IT WILL GIVE US OUR PLANET BACK.
"IT'S DANGEROUS. ALMOST IMPOSSIBLE, AND WE WON'T GET A SECOND SHOT AT IT.
"WE NEED EVERY ADVANTAGE WE CAN GET. EVERY EDGE.
"THAT'S WHY WE NEED YOU. YOU'RE NOTHING BUT EDGE.
"WE DON'T ALWAYS AGREE. IN FACT, WE RARELY AGREE. BUT THIS THREAT IS REAL AND IMMINENT.
"I'M SENDING YOU FOOTAGE FROM MADRID.
"WE TRIED TO WORK WITH THE INHUMANS. OFFERED OUR HELP. THEY RESPONDED WITH AN ATTACK. STORM AND HER TEAM HAVE BEEN TAKEN OUT."

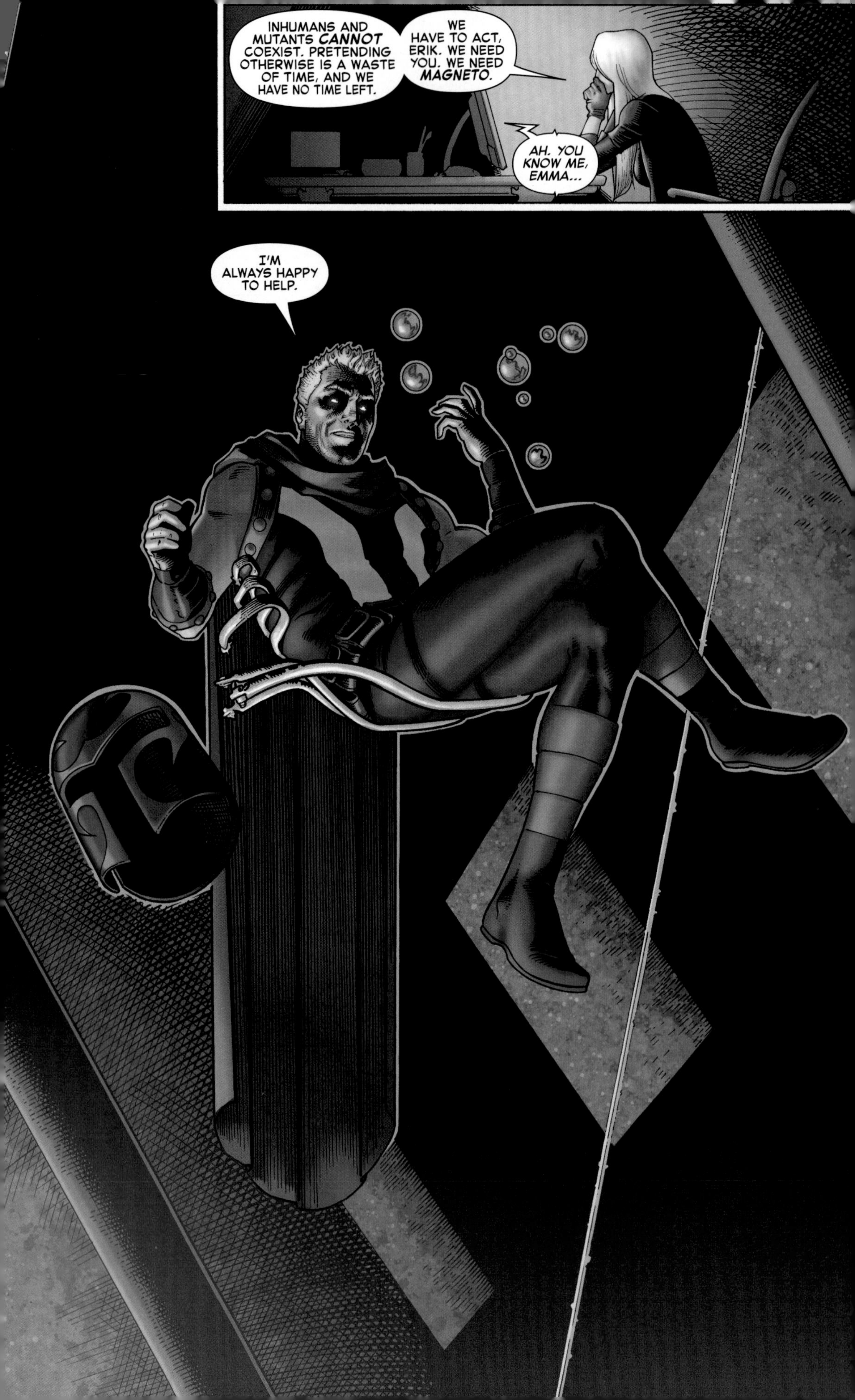
INHUMANS AND MUTANTS CANNOT COEXIST. PRETENDING OTHERWISE IS A WASTE OF TIME, AND WE HAVE NO TIME LEFT.
WE HAVE TO ACT, ERIK. WE NEED YOU. WE NEED MAGNETO.
AH. YOU KNOW ME, EMMA...
I'M ALWAYS HAPPY TO HELP.

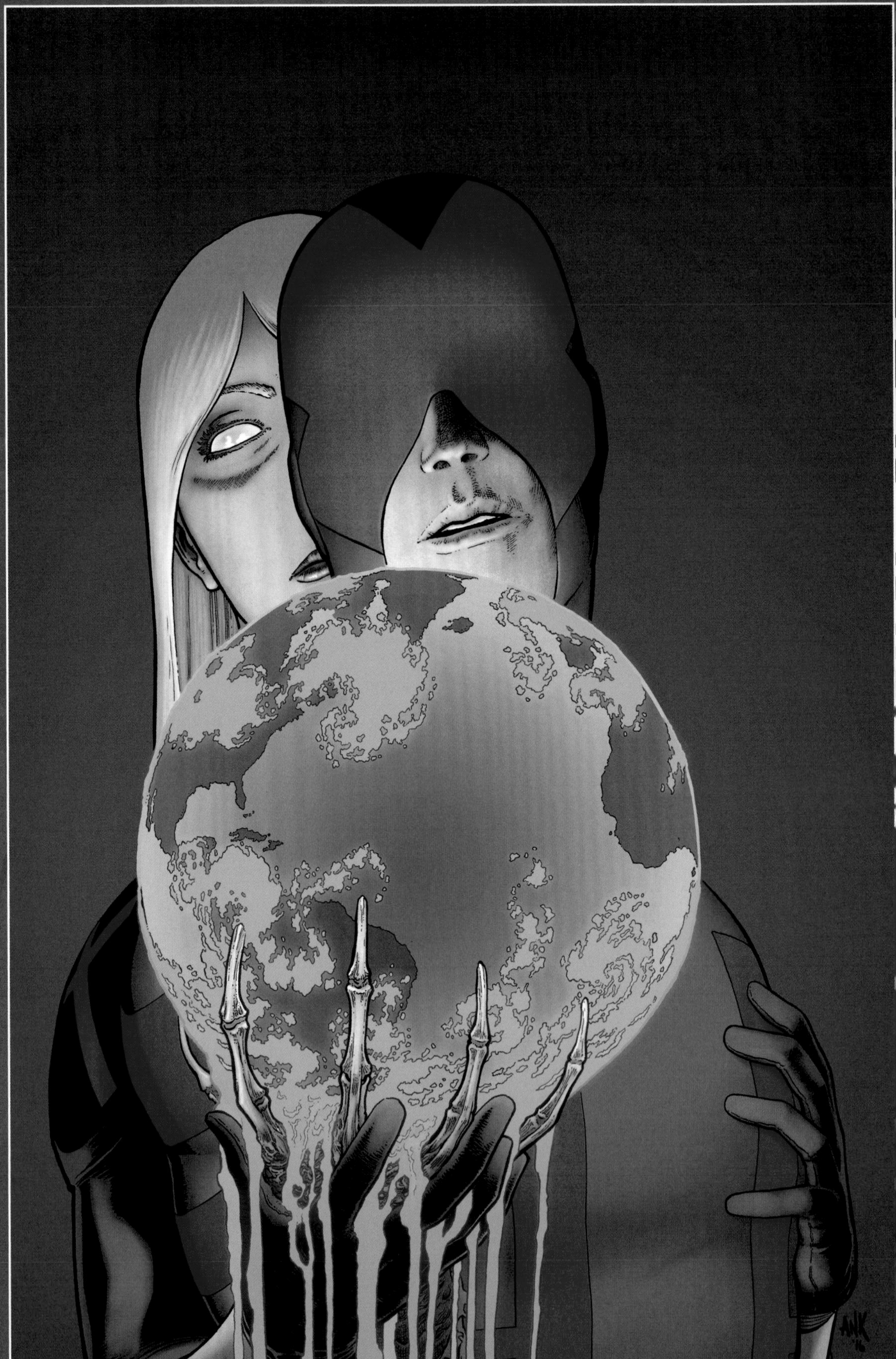

3

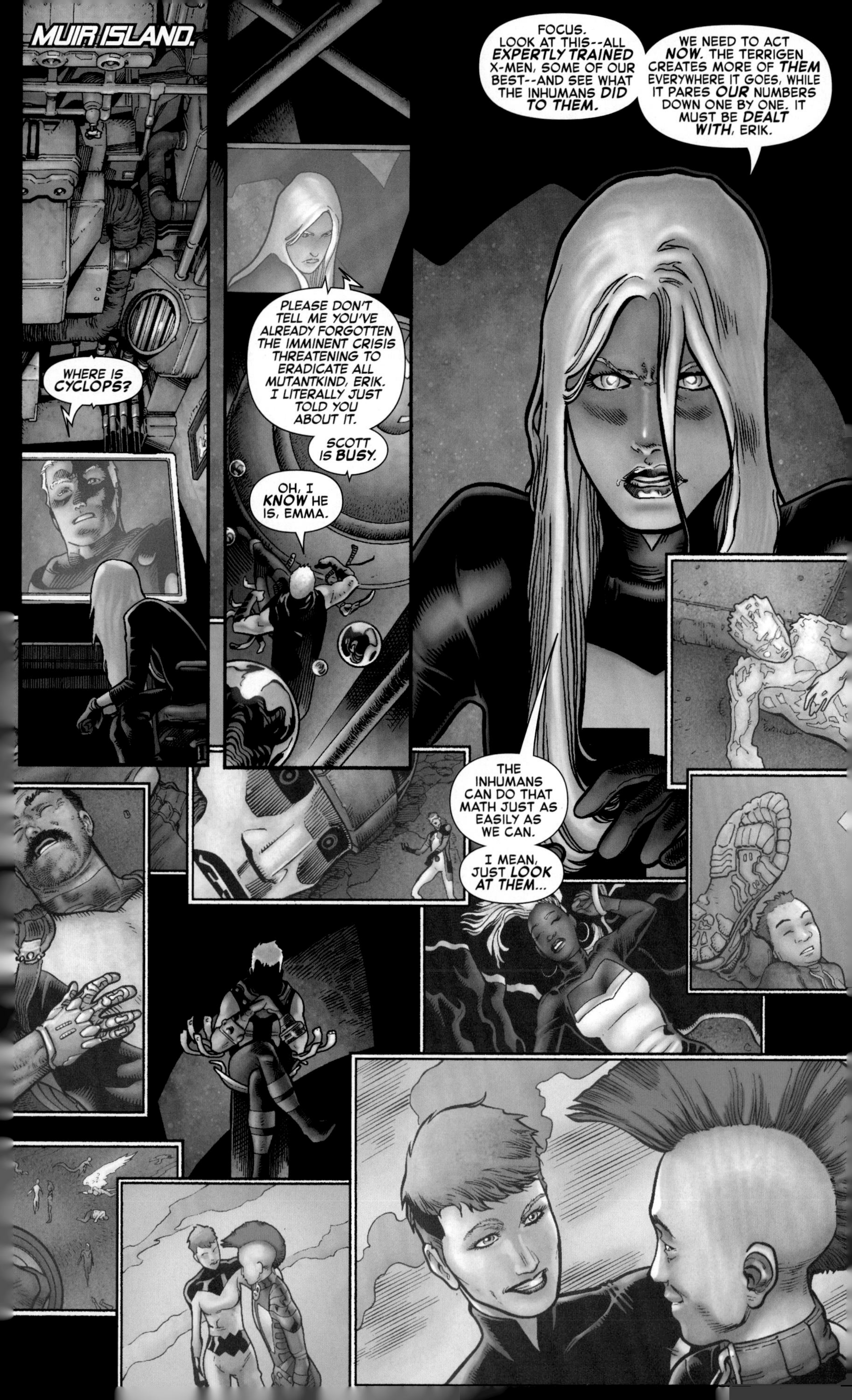
MUIR ISLAND.
FOCUS. LOOK AT THIS--ALL EXPERTLY TRAINED X-MEN, SOME OF OUR BEST--AND SEE WHAT THE INHUMANS DID TO THEM.
WE NEED TO ACT NOW. THE TERRIGEN CREATES MORE OF THEM EVERYWHERE IT GOES, WHILE IT PARES OUR NUMBERS DOWN ONE BY ONE. IT MUST BE DEALT WITH, ERIK.
WHERE IS CYCLOPS?
PLEASE DON'T TELL ME YOU'VE ALREADY FORGOTTEN THE IMMINENT CRISIS THREATENING TO ERADICATE ALL MUTANTKIND, ERIK. I LITERALLY JUST TOLD YOU ABOUT IT.
SCOTT IS BUSY.
OH, I KNOW HE IS, EMMA.
THE INHUMANS CAN DO THAT MATH JUST AS EASILY AS WE CAN.
I MEAN, JUST LOOK AT THEM...

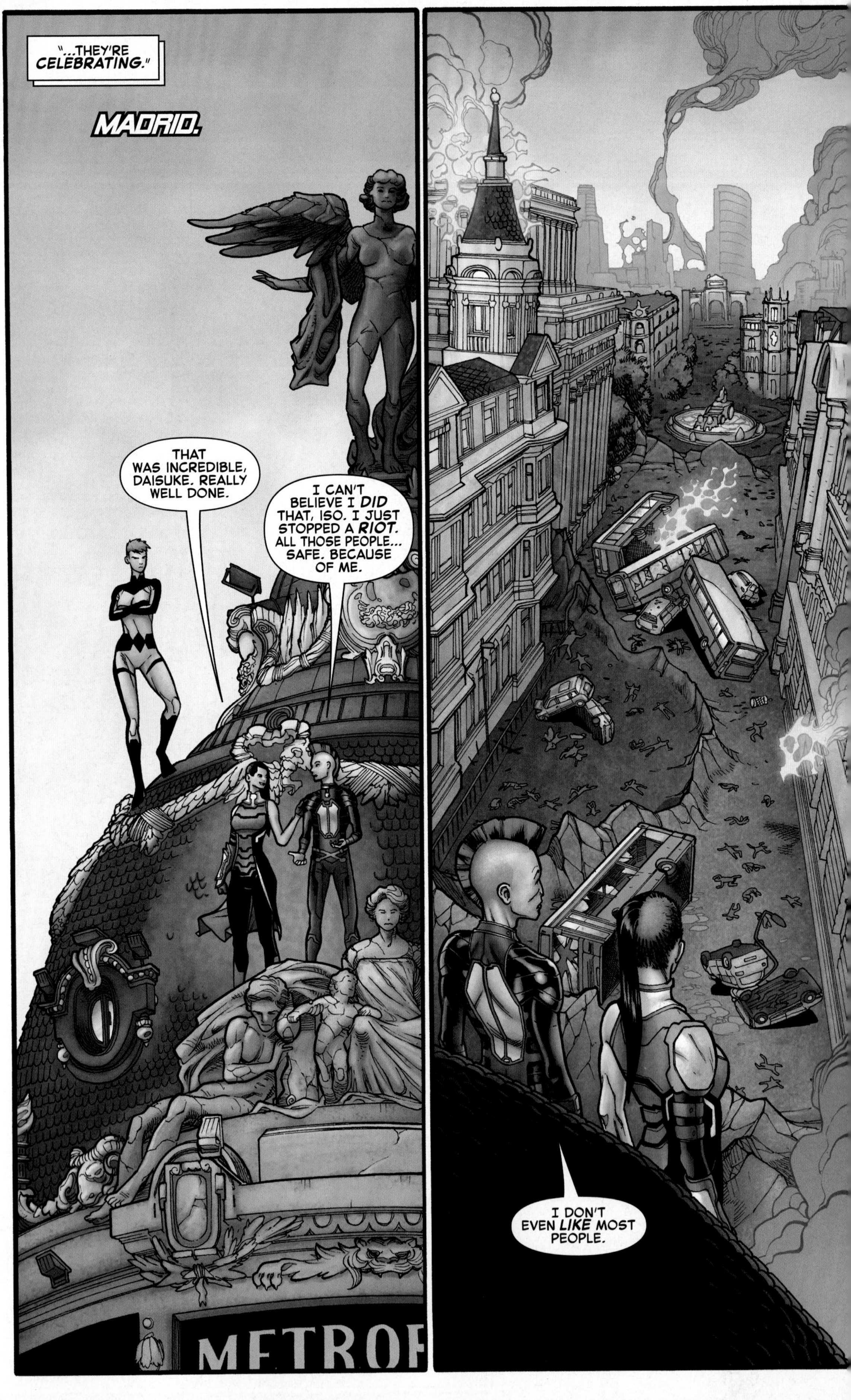
"...THEY'RE CELEBRATING."
MADRID.
THAT WAS INCREDIBLE, DAISUKE. REALLY WELL DONE.
I CAN'T BELIEVE I DID THAT, ISO. I JUST STOPPED A RIOT. ALL THOSE PEOPLE... SAFE. BECAUSE OF ME.
METROP
I DON'T EVEN LIKE MOST PEOPLE.

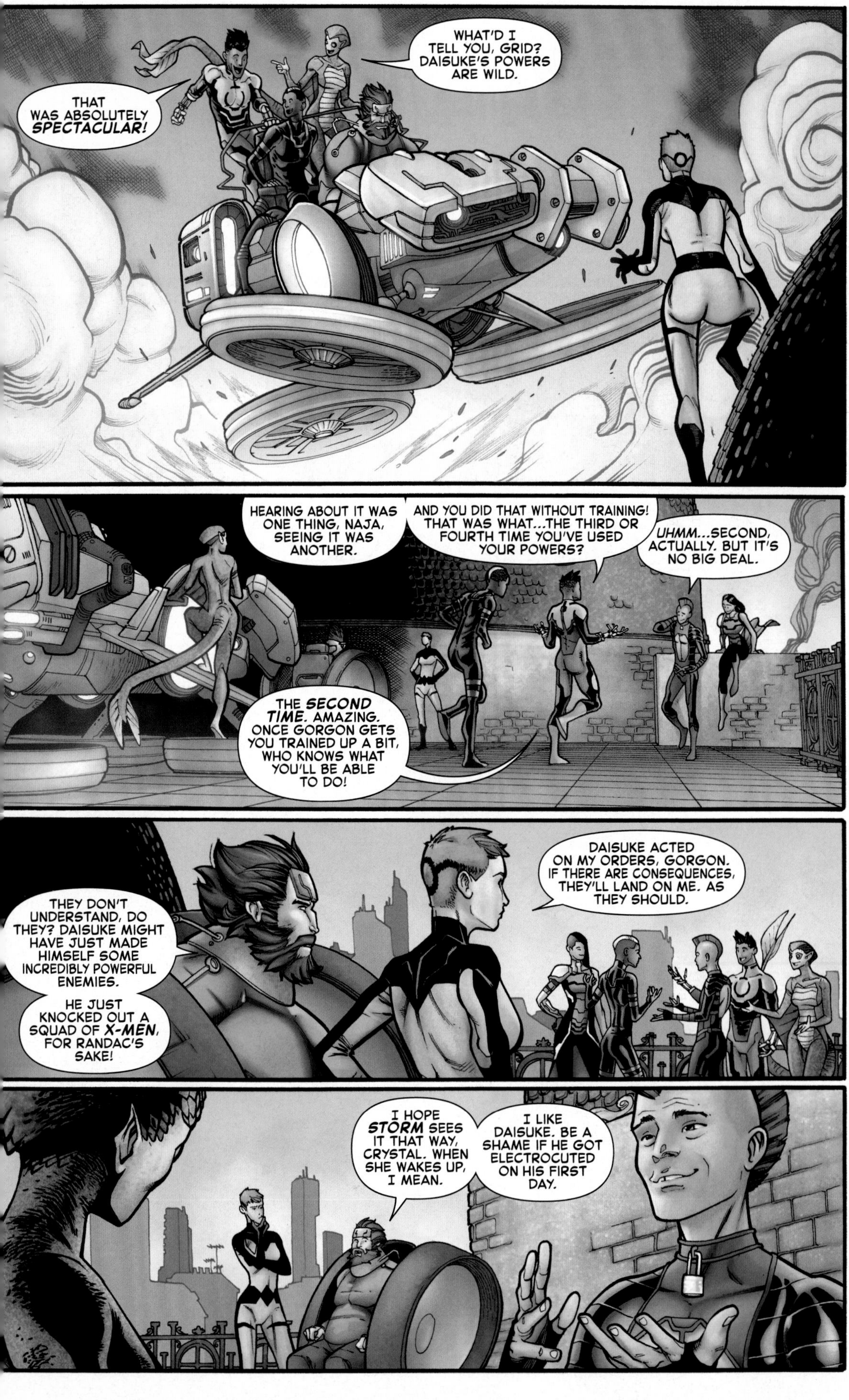
THAT WAS ABSOLUTELY SPECTACULAR!
WHAT'D I TELL YOU, GRID? DAISUKE'S POWERS ARE WILD.
HEARING ABOUT IT WAS ONE THING, NAJA, SEEING IT WAS ANOTHER.
AND YOU DID THAT WITHOUT TRAINING! THAT WAS WHAT...THE THIRD OR FOURTH TIME YOU'VE USED YOUR POWERS?
UHMM...SECOND, ACTUALLY. BUT IT'S NO BIG DEAL.
THE SECOND TIME. AMAZING. ONCE GORGON GETS YOU TRAINED UP A BIT, WHO KNOWS WHAT YOU'LL BE ABLE TO DO!
DAISUKE ACTED ON MY ORDERS, GORGON. IF THERE ARE CONSEQUENCES, THEY'LL LAND ON ME. AS THEY SHOULD.
THEY DON'T UNDERSTAND, DO THEY? DAISUKE MIGHT HAVE JUST MADE HIMSELF SOME INCREDIBLY POWERFUL ENEMIES.
HE JUST KNOCKED OUT A SQUAD OF X-MEN, FOR RANDAC'S SAKE!
I HOPE STORM SEES IT THAT WAY, CRYSTAL. WHEN SHE WAKES UP, I MEAN.
I LIKE DAISUKE. BE A SHAME IF HE GOT ELECTROCUTED ON HIS FIRST DAY.

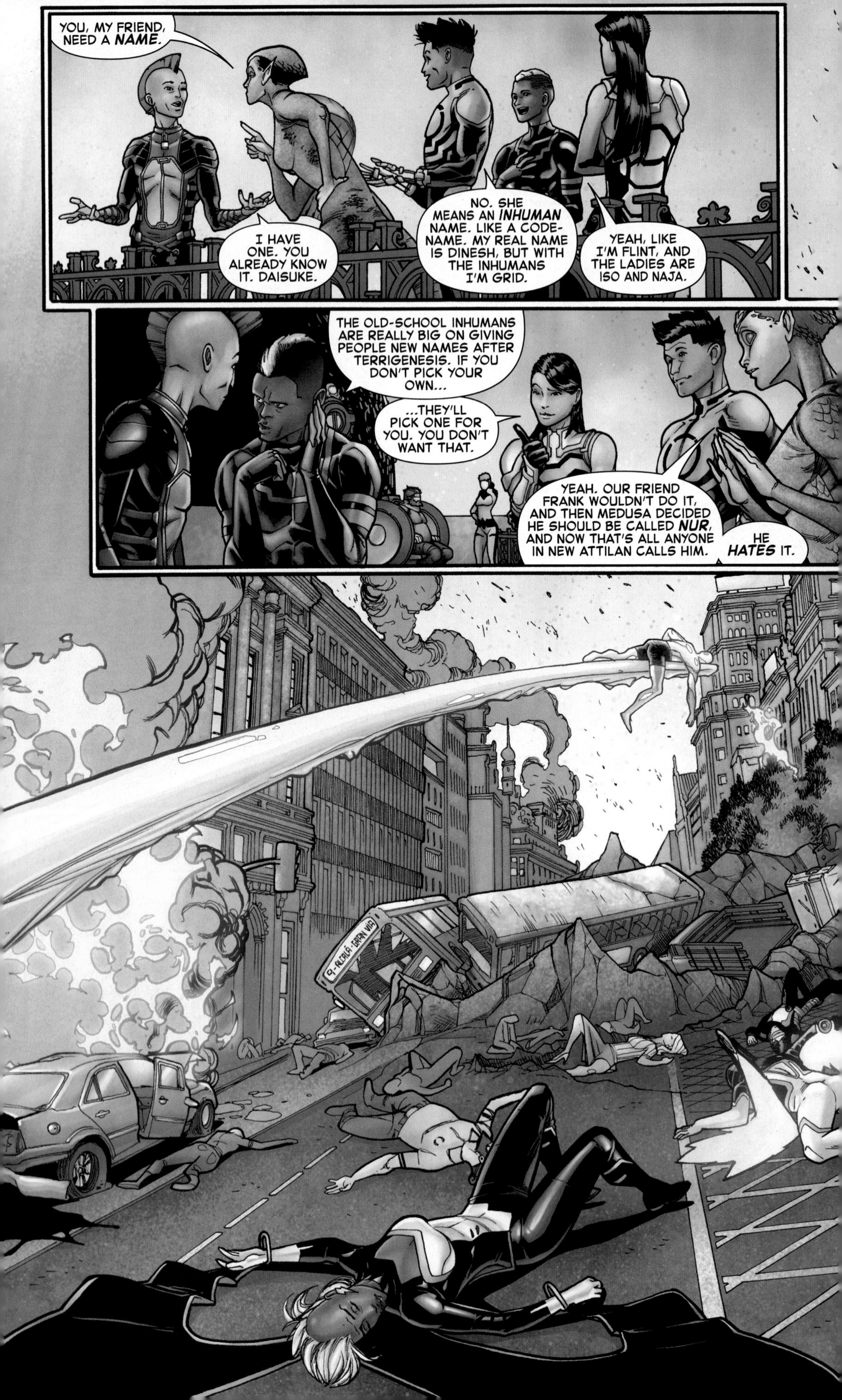
YOU, MY FRIEND, NEED A *NAME.*
I HAVE ONE. YOU ALREADY KNOW IT. DAISUKE.
NO. SHE MEANS AN *INHUMAN* NAME. LIKE A CODE-NAME. MY REAL NAME IS DINESH, BUT WITH THE INHUMANS I'M GRID.
YEAH, LIKE I'M FLINT, AND THE LADIES ARE ISO AND NAJA.
THE OLD-SCHOOL INHUMANS ARE REALLY BIG ON GIVING PEOPLE NEW NAMES AFTER TERRIGENESIS. IF YOU DON'T PICK YOUR OWN...
...THEY'LL PICK ONE FOR YOU. YOU DON'T WANT THAT.
YEAH. OUR FRIEND FRANK WOULDN'T DO IT, AND THEN MEDUSA DECIDED HE SHOULD BE CALLED *NUR*, AND NOW THAT'S ALL ANYONE IN NEW ATTILAN CALLS HIM.
HE *HATES* IT.

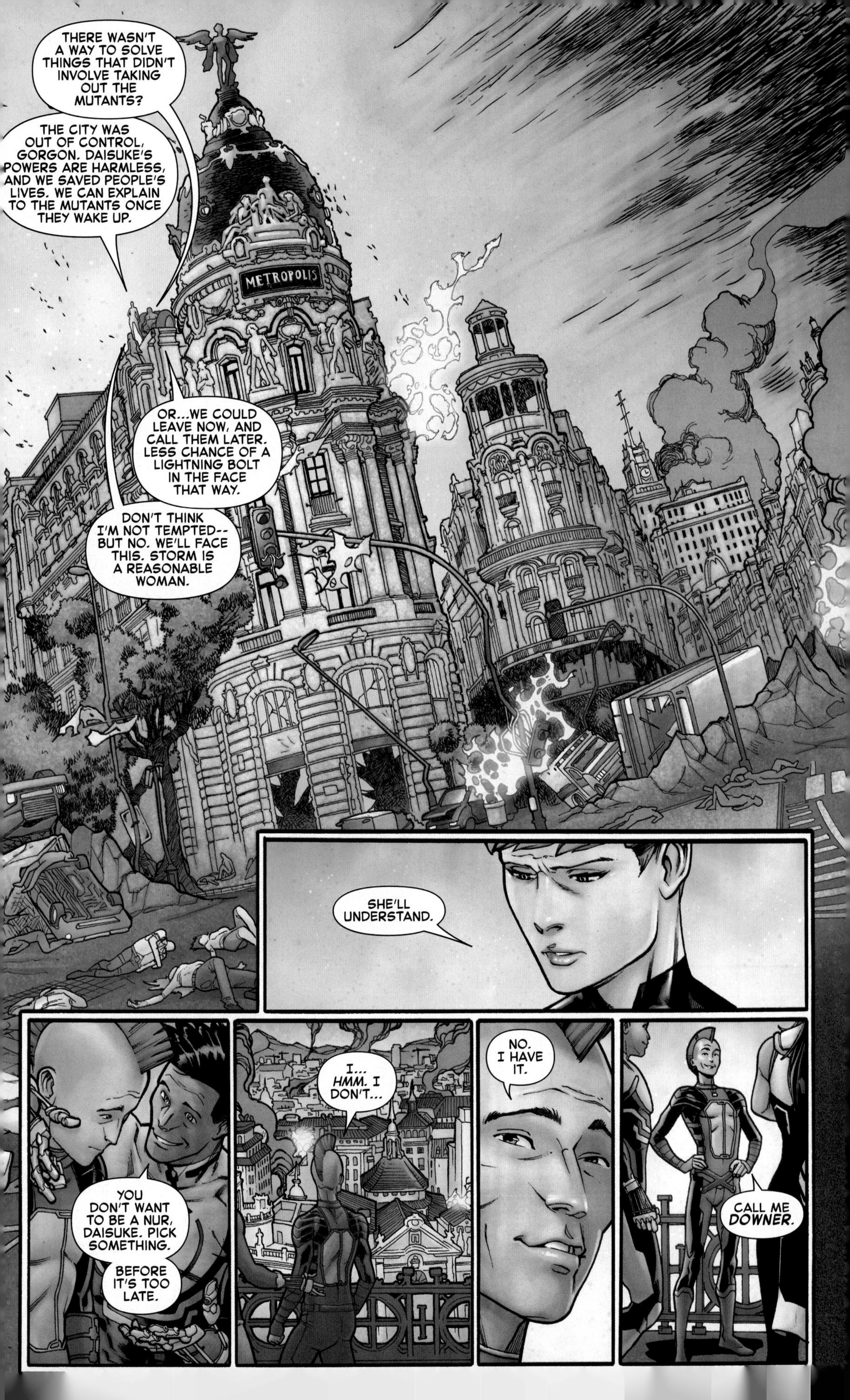
THERE WASN'T A WAY TO SOLVE THINGS THAT DIDN'T INVOLVE TAKING OUT THE MUTANTS?
THE CITY WAS OUT OF CONTROL, GORGON. DAISUKE'S POWERS ARE HARMLESS, AND WE SAVED PEOPLE'S LIVES. WE CAN EXPLAIN TO THE MUTANTS ONCE THEY WAKE UP.
METROPOLIS
OR...WE COULD LEAVE NOW, AND CALL THEM LATER. LESS CHANCE OF A LIGHTNING BOLT IN THE FACE THAT WAY.
DON'T THINK I'M NOT TEMPTED-- BUT NO. WE'LL FACE THIS. STORM IS A REASONABLE WOMAN.
SHE'LL UNDERSTAND.
YOU DON'T WANT TO BE A NUR, DAISUKE. PICK SOMETHING.
BEFORE IT'S TOO LATE.
I... *HMM.* I DON'T...
NO. I HAVE IT.
CALL ME ***DOWNER.***

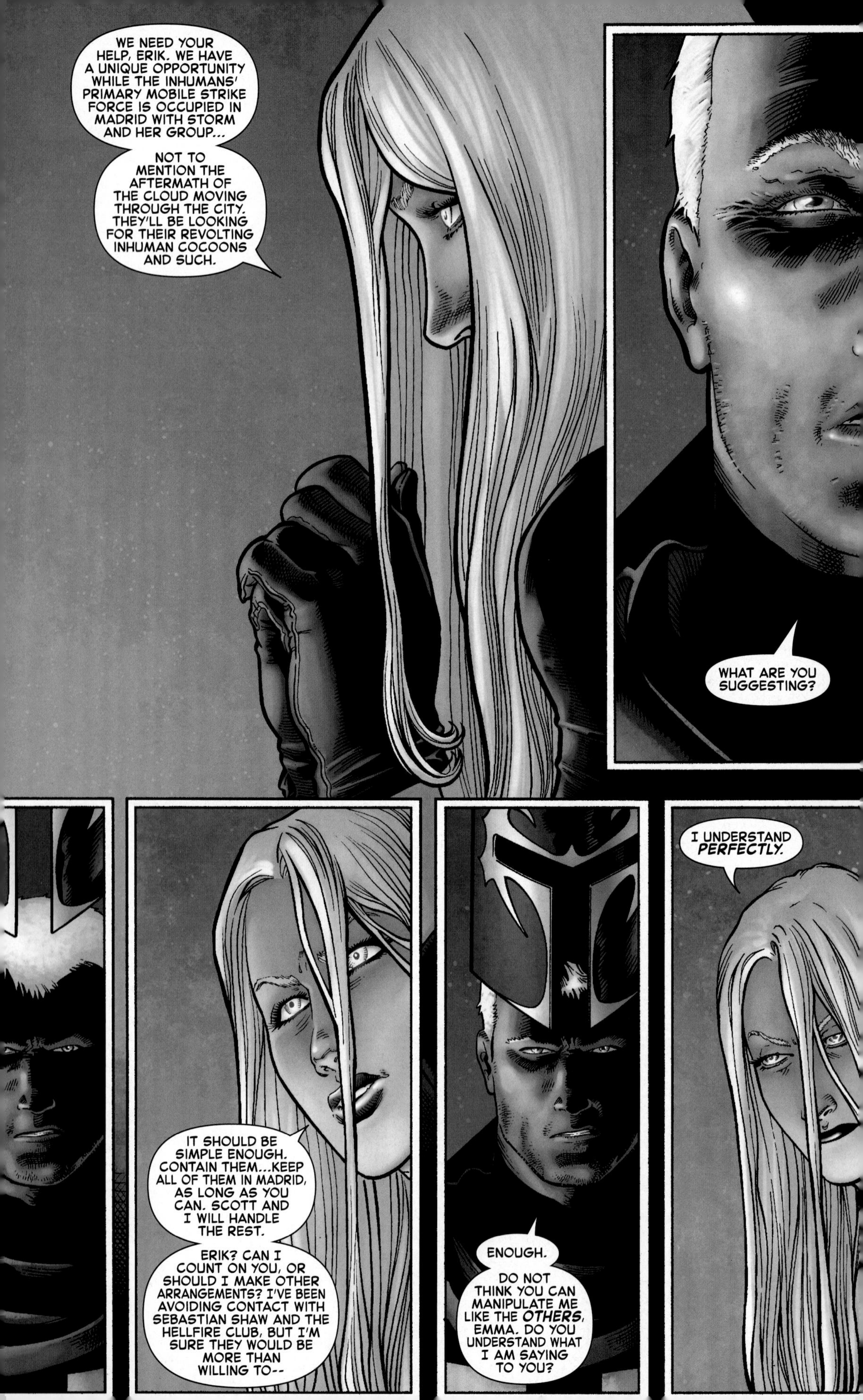
WE NEED YOUR HELP, ERIK. WE HAVE A UNIQUE OPPORTUNITY WHILE THE INHUMANS' PRIMARY MOBILE STRIKE FORCE IS OCCUPIED IN MADRID WITH STORM AND HER GROUP...
NOT TO MENTION THE AFTERMATH OF THE CLOUD MOVING THROUGH THE CITY. THEY'LL BE LOOKING FOR THEIR REVOLTING INHUMAN COCOONS AND SUCH.
WHAT ARE YOU SUGGESTING?
IT SHOULD BE SIMPLE ENOUGH. CONTAIN THEM...KEEP ALL OF THEM IN MADRID, AS LONG AS YOU CAN. SCOTT AND I WILL HANDLE THE REST.
ERIK? CAN I COUNT ON YOU, OR SHOULD I MAKE OTHER ARRANGEMENTS? I'VE BEEN AVOIDING CONTACT WITH SEBASTIAN SHAW AND THE HELLFIRE CLUB, BUT I'M SURE THEY WOULD BE MORE THAN WILLING TO--
ENOUGH.
DO NOT THINK YOU CAN MANIPULATE ME LIKE THE *OTHERS*, EMMA. DO YOU UNDERSTAND WHAT I AM SAYING TO YOU?
I UNDERSTAND *PERFECTLY.*

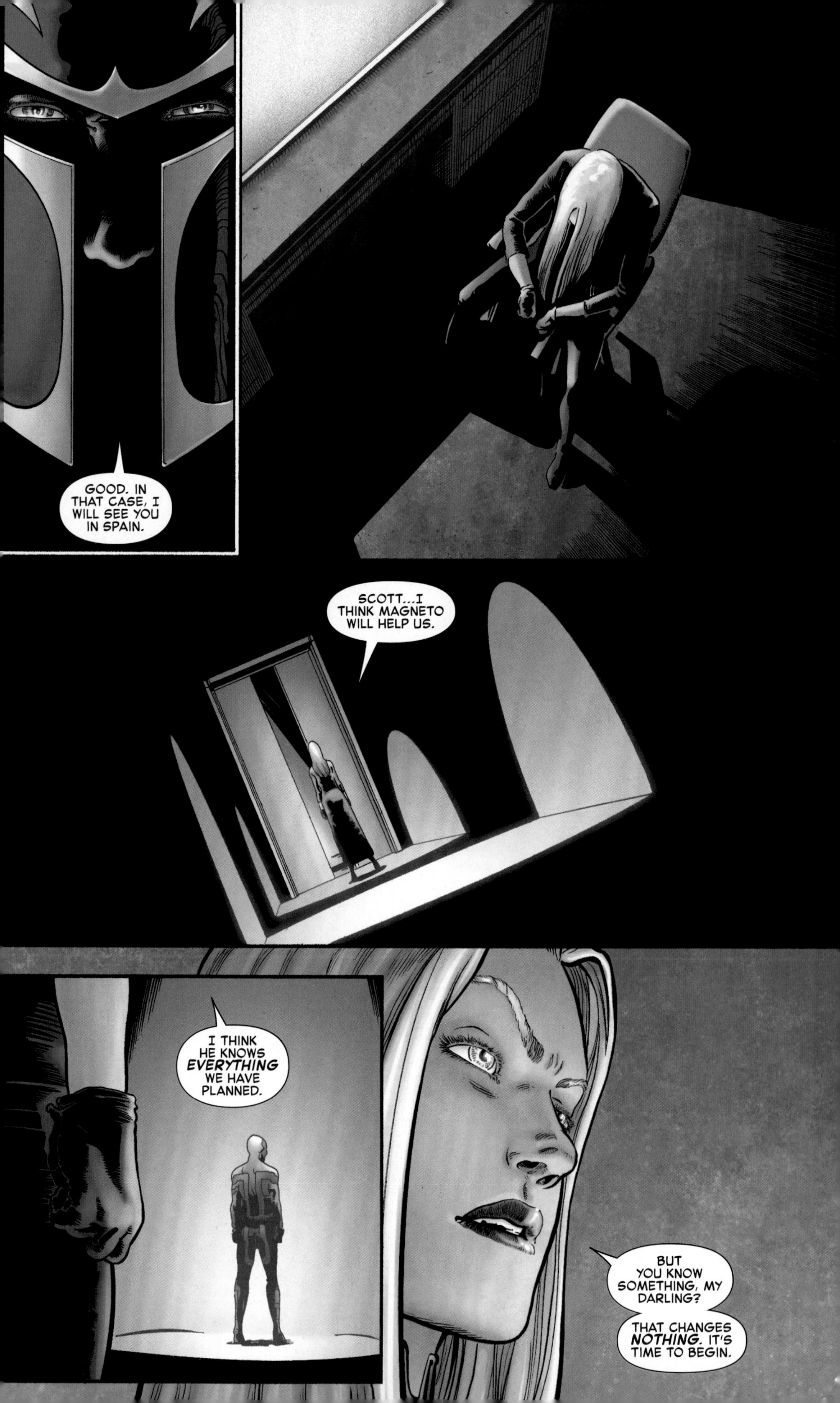
GOOD. IN THAT CASE, I WILL SEE YOU IN SPAIN.
SCOTT...I THINK MAGNETO WILL HELP US.
I THINK HE KNOWS *EVERYTHING* WE HAVE PLANNED.
BUT YOU KNOW SOMETHING, MY DARLING?
THAT CHANGES *NOTHING*. IT'S TIME TO BEGIN.

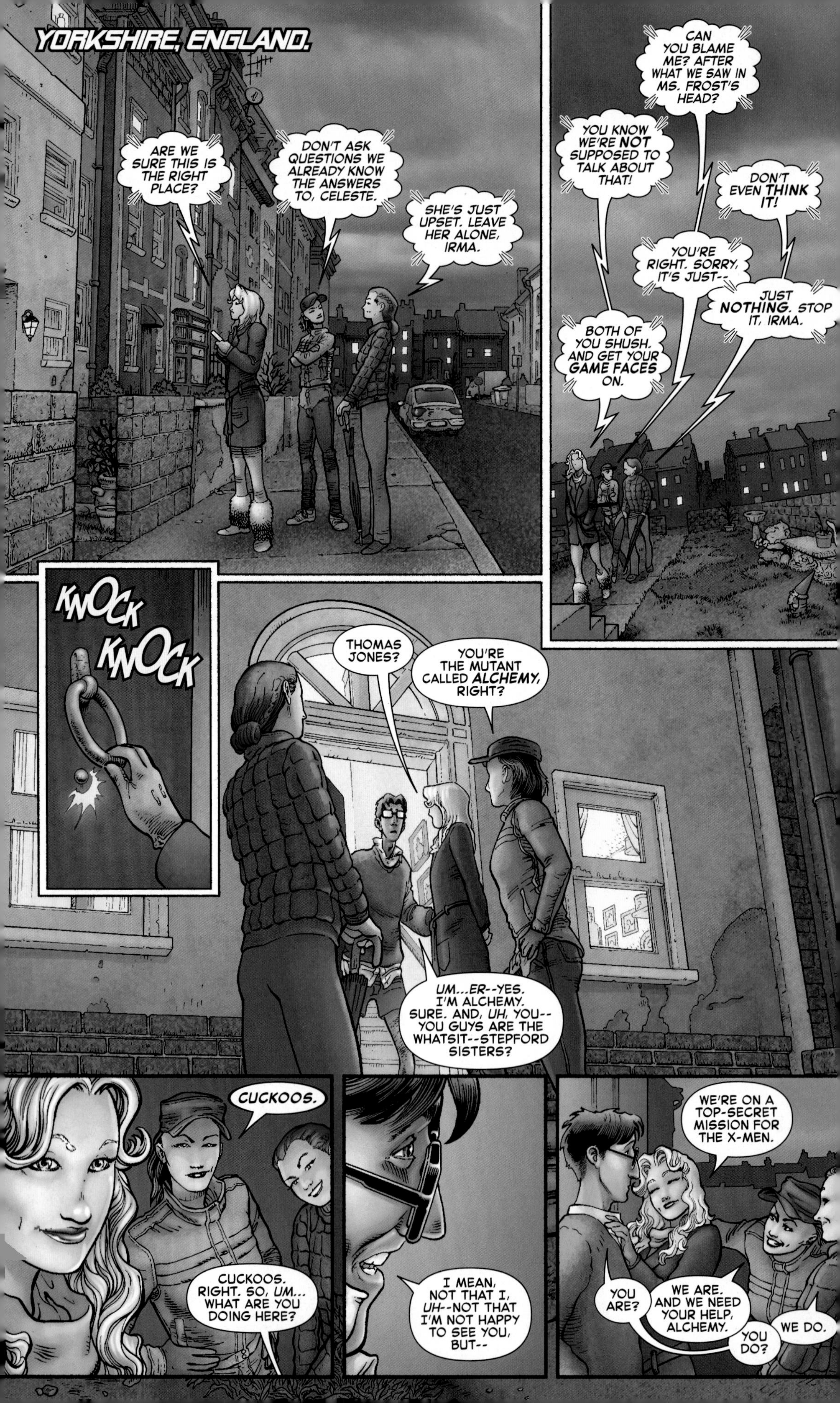
YORKSHIRE, ENGLAND.
ARE WE SURE THIS IS THE RIGHT PLACE?
DON'T ASK QUESTIONS WE ALREADY KNOW THE ANSWERS TO, CELESTE.
SHE'S JUST UPSET. LEAVE HER ALONE, IRMA.
CAN YOU BLAME ME? AFTER WHAT WE SAW IN MS. FROST'S HEAD?
YOU KNOW WE'RE NOT SUPPOSED TO TALK ABOUT THAT!
DON'T EVEN THINK IT!
YOU'RE RIGHT. SORRY, IT'S JUST--
JUST NOTHING. STOP IT, IRMA.
BOTH OF YOU SHUSH. AND GET YOUR GAME FACES ON.
KNOCK
KNOCK
THOMAS JONES?
YOU'RE THE MUTANT CALLED ALCHEMY, RIGHT?
UM...ER--YES. I'M ALCHEMY. SURE. AND, UH, YOU-- YOU GUYS ARE THE WHATSIT--STEPFORD SISTERS?
CUCKOOS.
CUCKOOS. RIGHT. SO, UM... WHAT ARE YOU DOING HERE?
I MEAN, NOT THAT I, UH--NOT THAT I'M NOT HAPPY TO SEE YOU, BUT--
WE'RE ON A TOP-SECRET MISSION FOR THE X-MEN.
YOU ARE?
WE ARE. AND WE NEED YOUR HELP, ALCHEMY.
YOU DO?
WE DO.

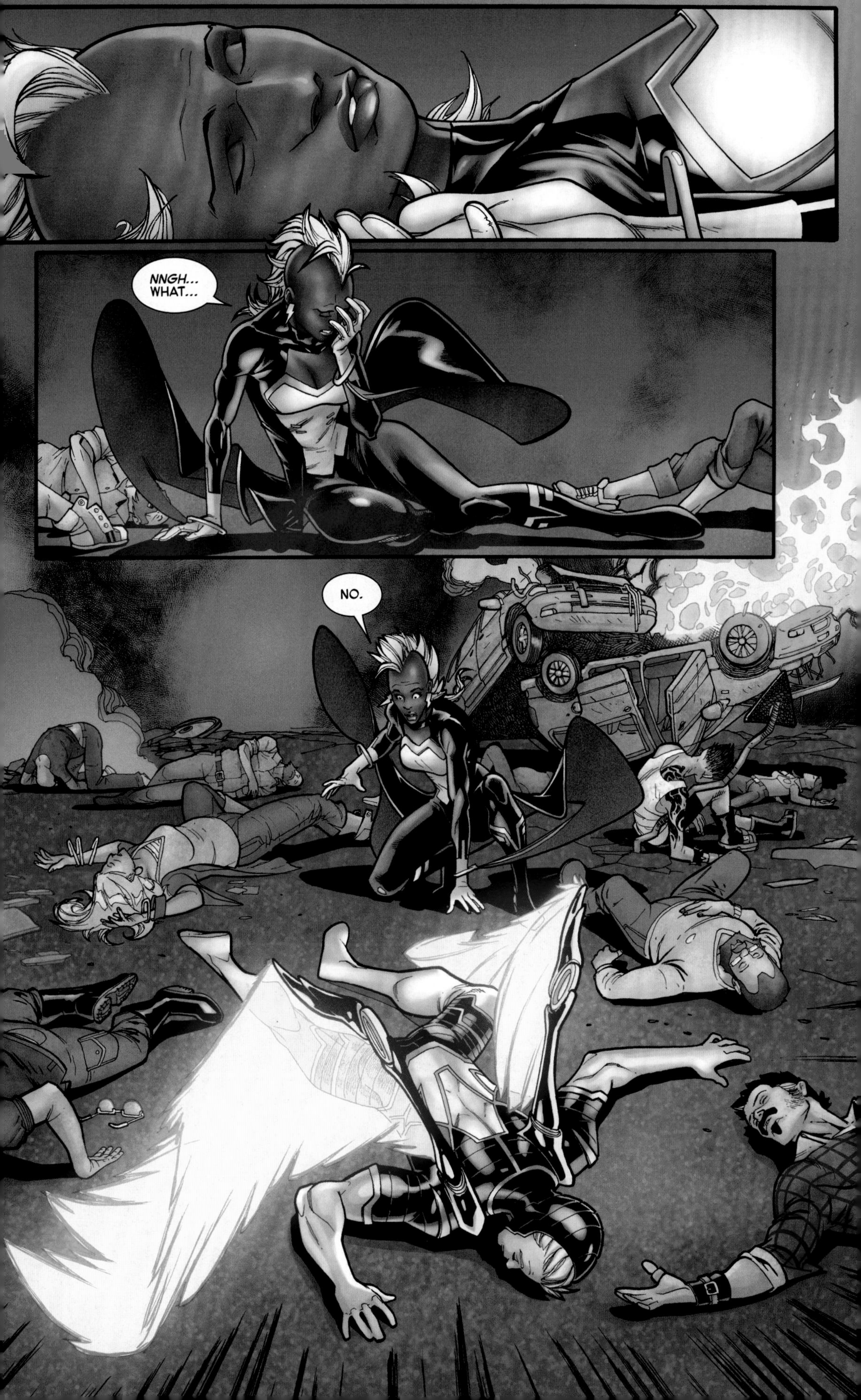
NNGH... WHAT...
NO.

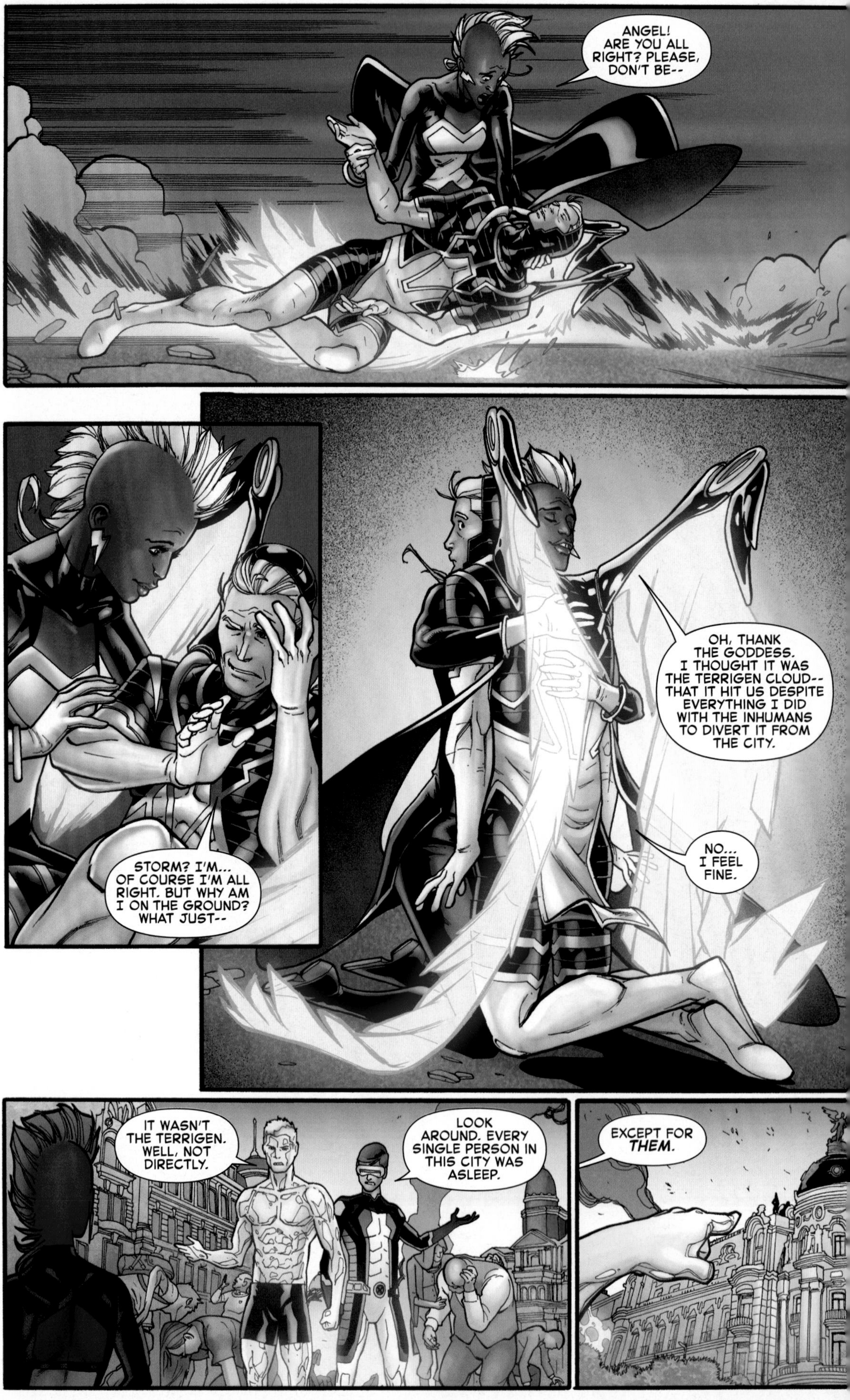
ANGEL! ARE YOU ALL RIGHT? PLEASE, DON'T BE--
STORM? I'M... OF COURSE I'M ALL RIGHT. BUT WHY AM I ON THE GROUND? WHAT JUST--
OH, THANK THE GODDESS. I THOUGHT IT WAS THE TERRIGEN CLOUD--THAT IT HIT US DESPITE EVERYTHING I DID WITH THE INHUMANS TO DIVERT IT FROM THE CITY.
NO... I FEEL FINE.
IT WASN'T THE TERRIGEN. WELL, NOT DIRECTLY.
LOOK AROUND. EVERY SINGLE PERSON IN THIS CITY WAS ASLEEP.
EXCEPT FOR *THEM*.

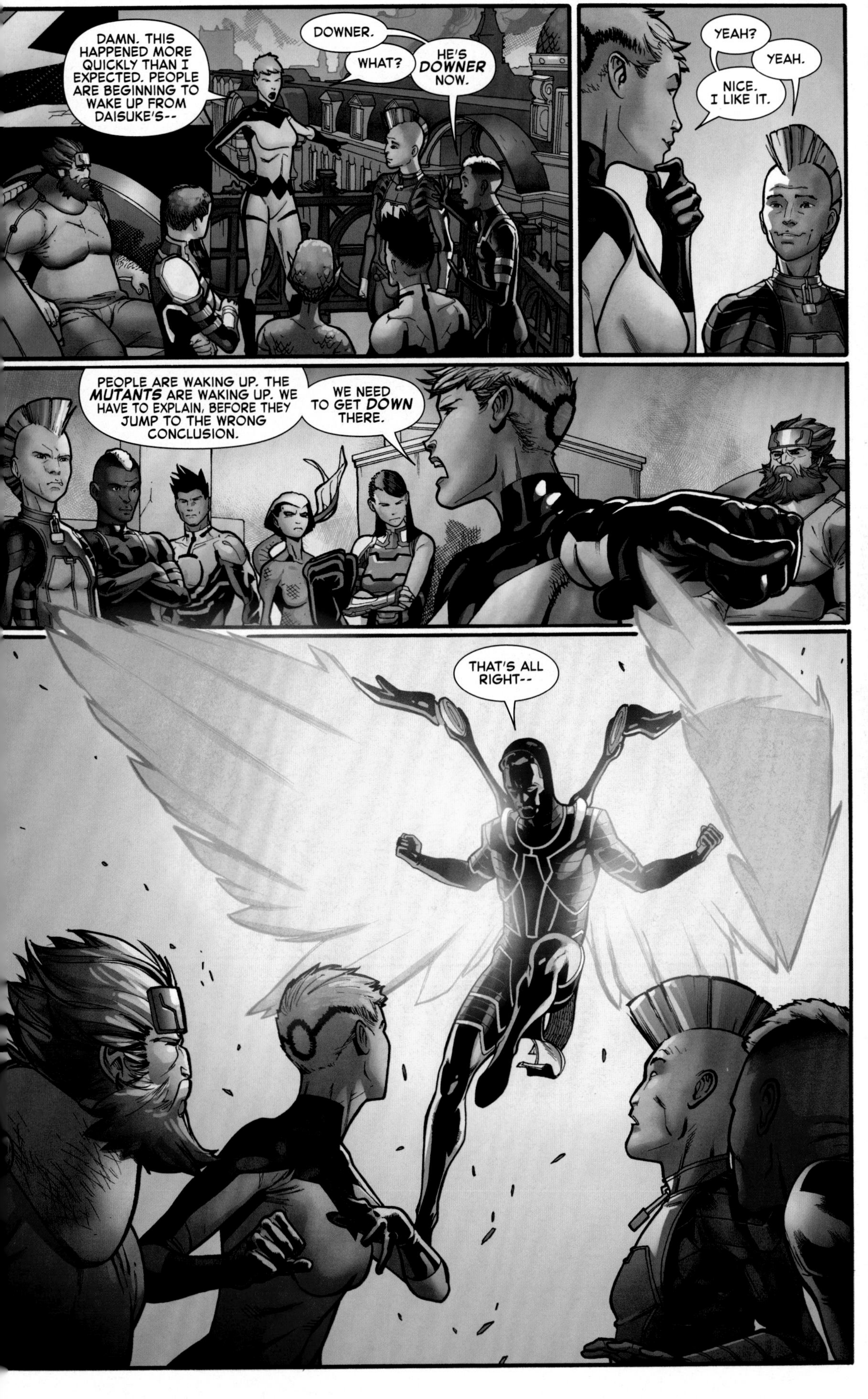
DAMN. THIS HAPPENED MORE QUICKLY THAN I EXPECTED. PEOPLE ARE BEGINNING TO WAKE UP FROM DAISUKE'S--
DOWNER.
WHAT?
HE'S DOWNER NOW.
YEAH?
YEAH.
NICE. I LIKE IT.
PEOPLE ARE WAKING UP. THE MUTANTS ARE WAKING UP. WE HAVE TO EXPLAIN, BEFORE THEY JUMP TO THE WRONG CONCLUSION.
WE NEED TO GET DOWN THERE.
THAT'S ALL RIGHT--

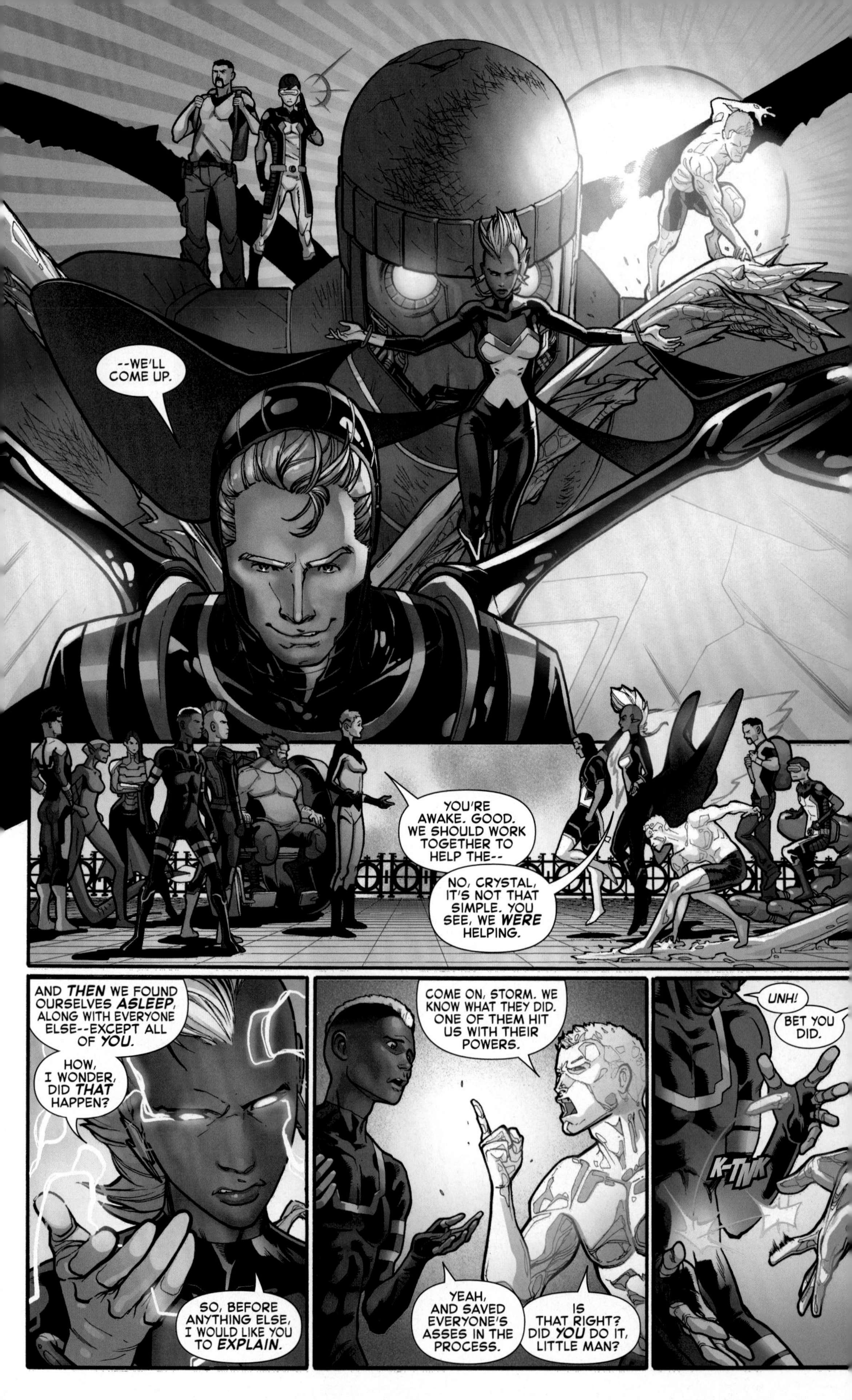
--WE'LL COME UP.
YOU'RE AWAKE. GOOD. WE SHOULD WORK TOGETHER TO HELP THE--
NO, CRYSTAL, IT'S NOT THAT SIMPLE. YOU SEE, WE *WERE* HELPING.
AND *THEN* WE FOUND OURSELVES *ASLEEP*, ALONG WITH EVERYONE ELSE--EXCEPT ALL OF *YOU.*
HOW, I WONDER, DID *THAT* HAPPEN?
SO, BEFORE ANYTHING ELSE, I WOULD LIKE YOU TO *EXPLAIN.*
COME ON, STORM. WE KNOW WHAT THEY DID. ONE OF THEM HIT US WITH THEIR POWERS.
YEAH, AND SAVED EVERYONE'S ASSES IN THE PROCESS.
IS THAT RIGHT? DID *YOU* DO IT, LITTLE MAN?
UNH!
BET YOU DID.
K-TNK

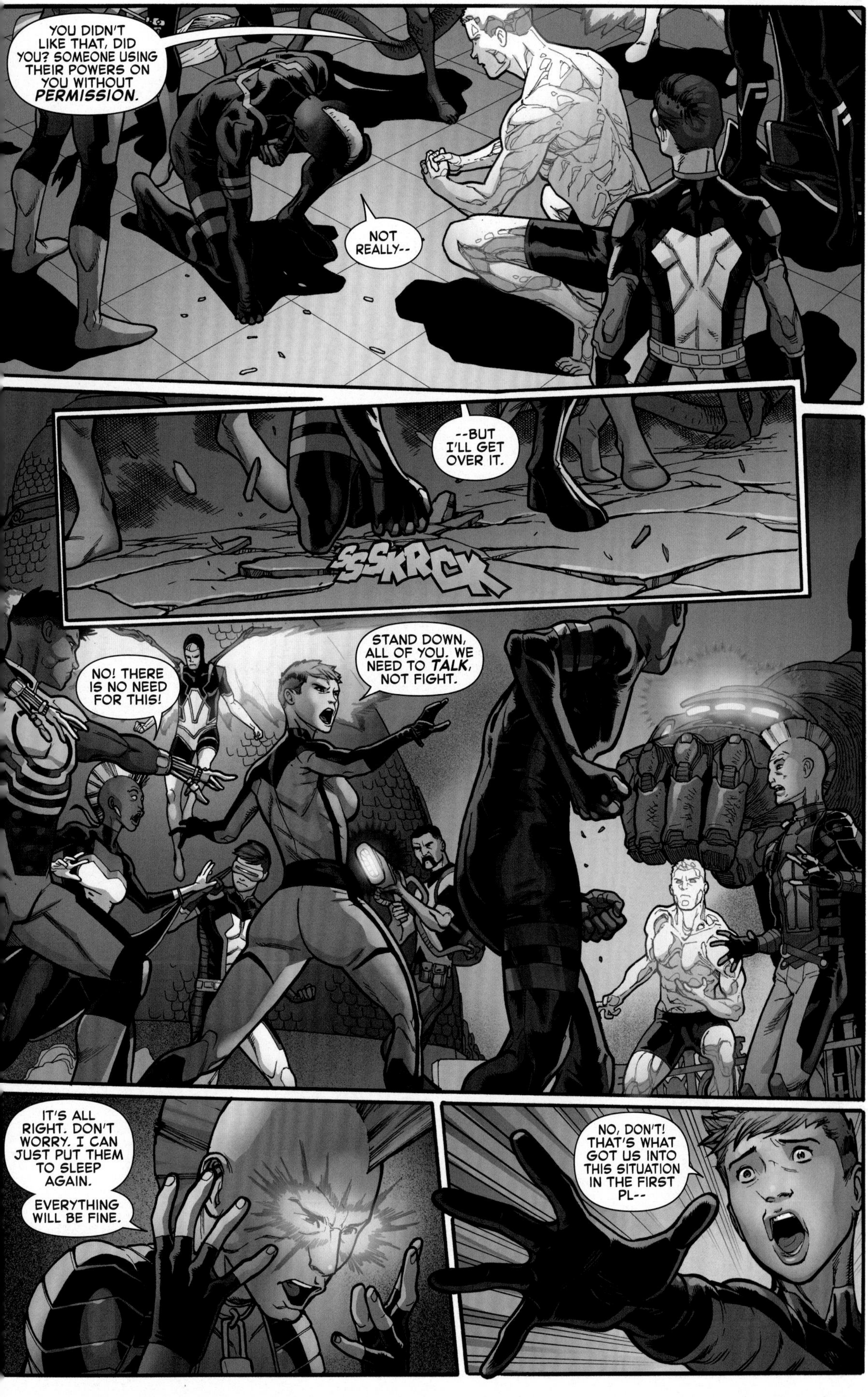
YOU DIDN'T LIKE THAT, DID YOU? SOMEONE USING THEIR POWERS ON YOU WITHOUT PERMISSION.
NOT REALLY--
--BUT I'LL GET OVER IT.
SSSKRCK
NO! THERE IS NO NEED FOR THIS!
STAND DOWN, ALL OF YOU. WE NEED TO TALK, NOT FIGHT.
IT'S ALL RIGHT. DON'T WORRY. I CAN JUST PUT THEM TO SLEEP AGAIN.
EVERYTHING WILL BE FINE.
NO, DON'T! THAT'S WHAT GOT US INTO THIS SITUATION IN THE FIRST PL--

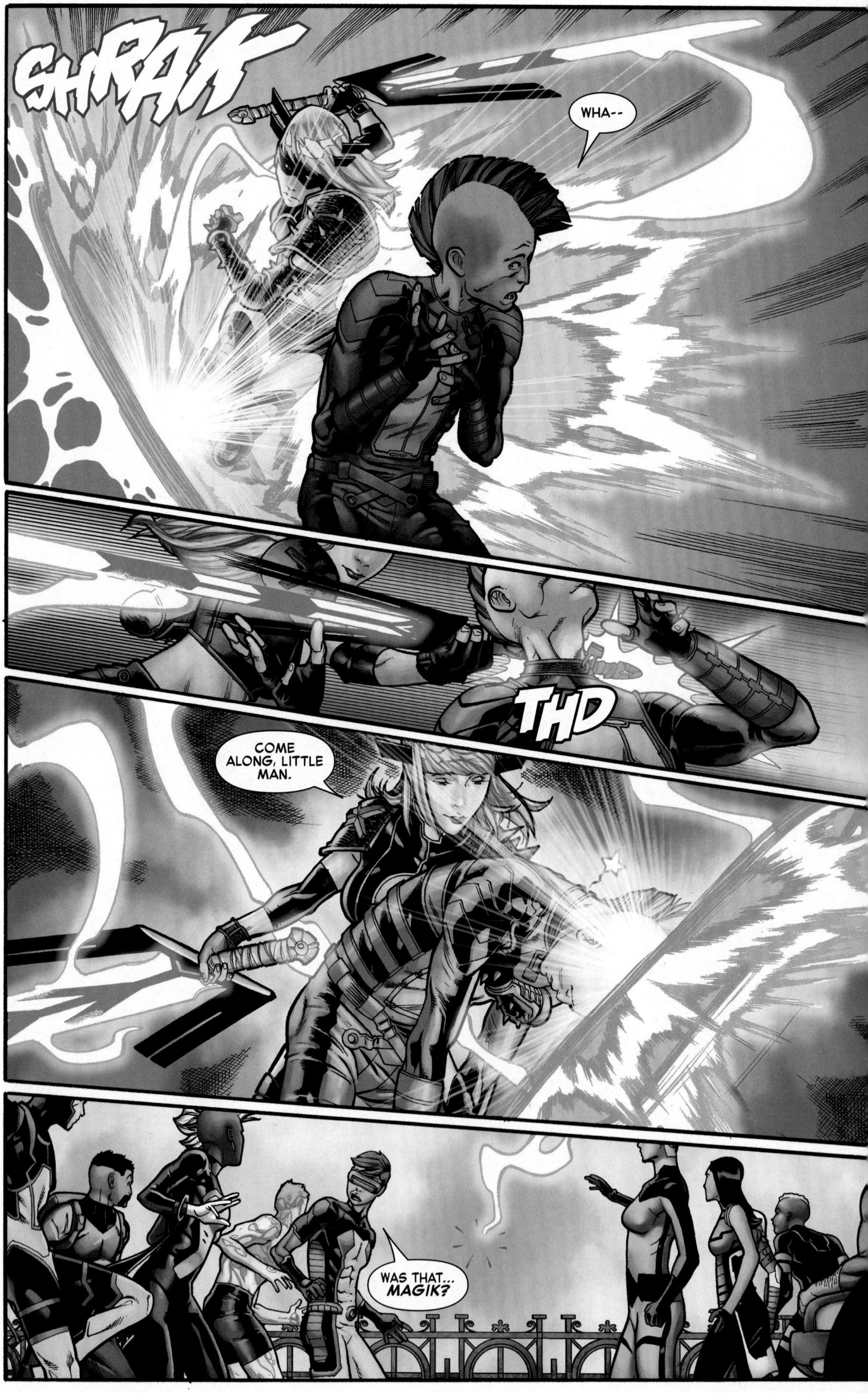
SHRAK
WHA--
THD
COME ALONG, LITTLE MAN.
WAS THAT... MAGIK?

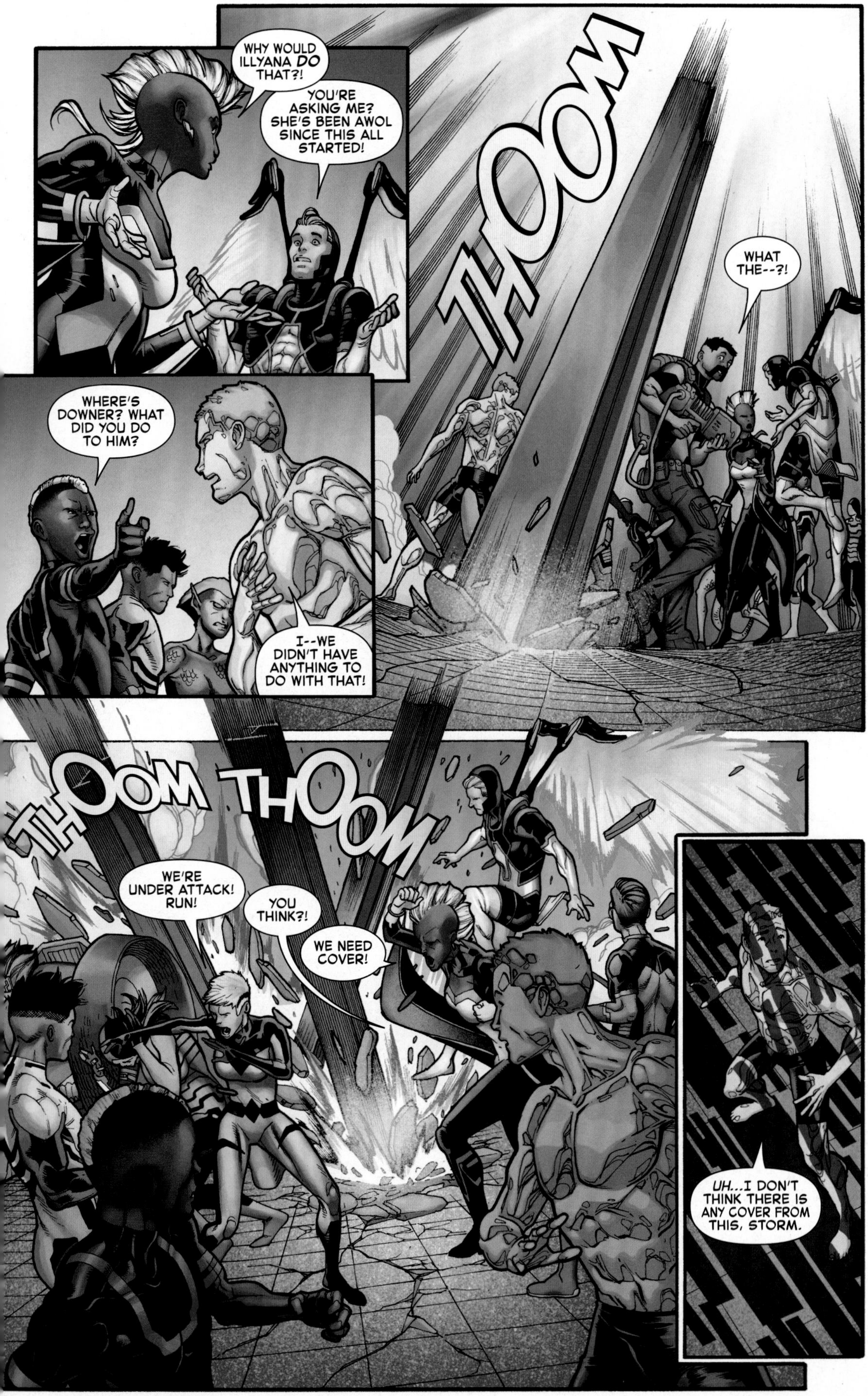

WHY WOULD ILLYANA *DO* THAT?!
YOU'RE ASKING ME? SHE'S BEEN AWOL SINCE THIS ALL STARTED!
THOOM
WHERE'S DOWNER? WHAT DID YOU DO TO HIM?
I--WE DIDN'T HAVE ANYTHING TO DO WITH THAT!
WHAT THE--?!
THOOM THOOM
WE'RE UNDER ATTACK! RUN!
YOU THINK?!
WE NEED COVER!
*UH...*I DON'T THINK THERE IS ANY COVER FROM THIS, STORM.

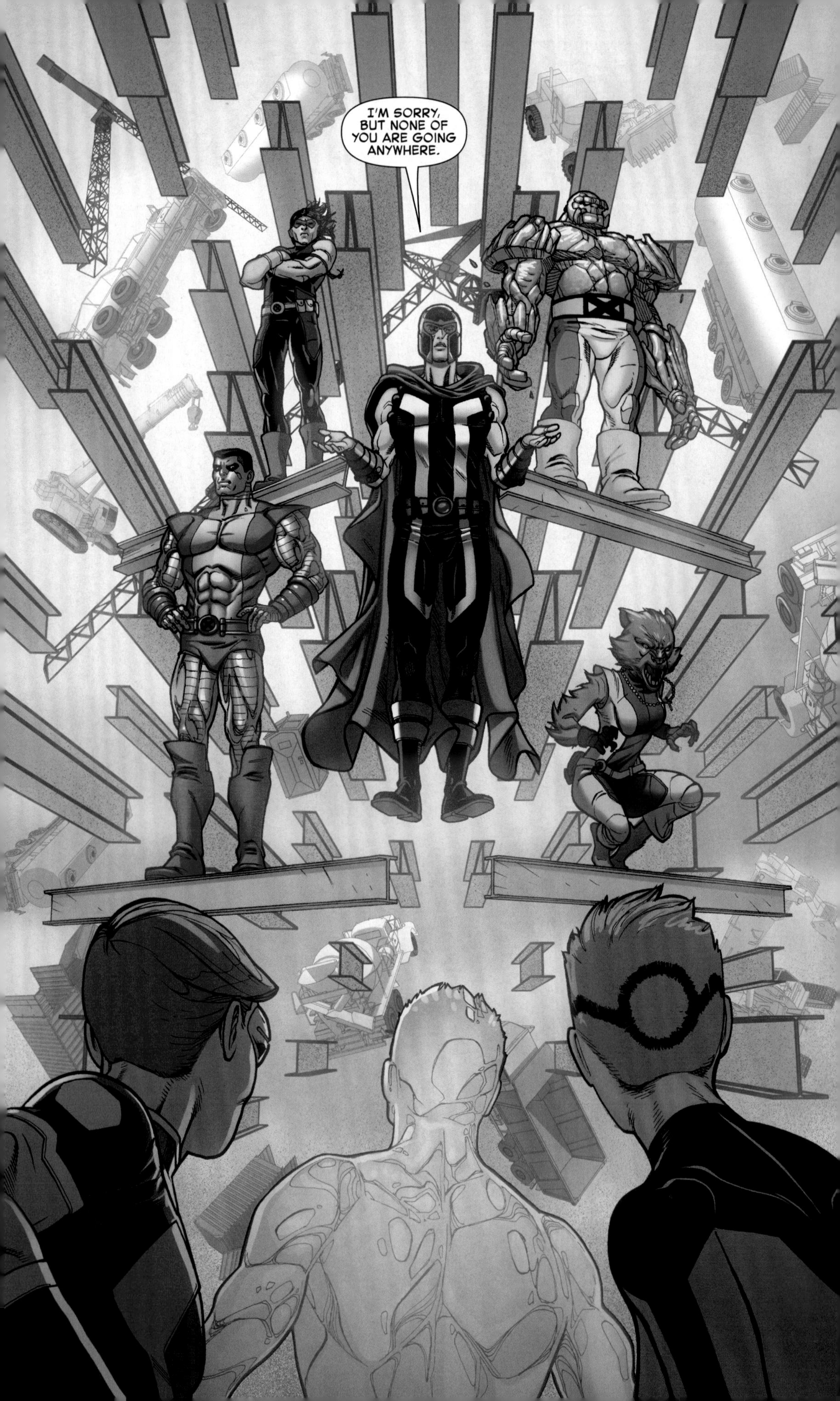
I'M SORRY, BUT NONE OF YOU ARE GOING ANYWHERE.

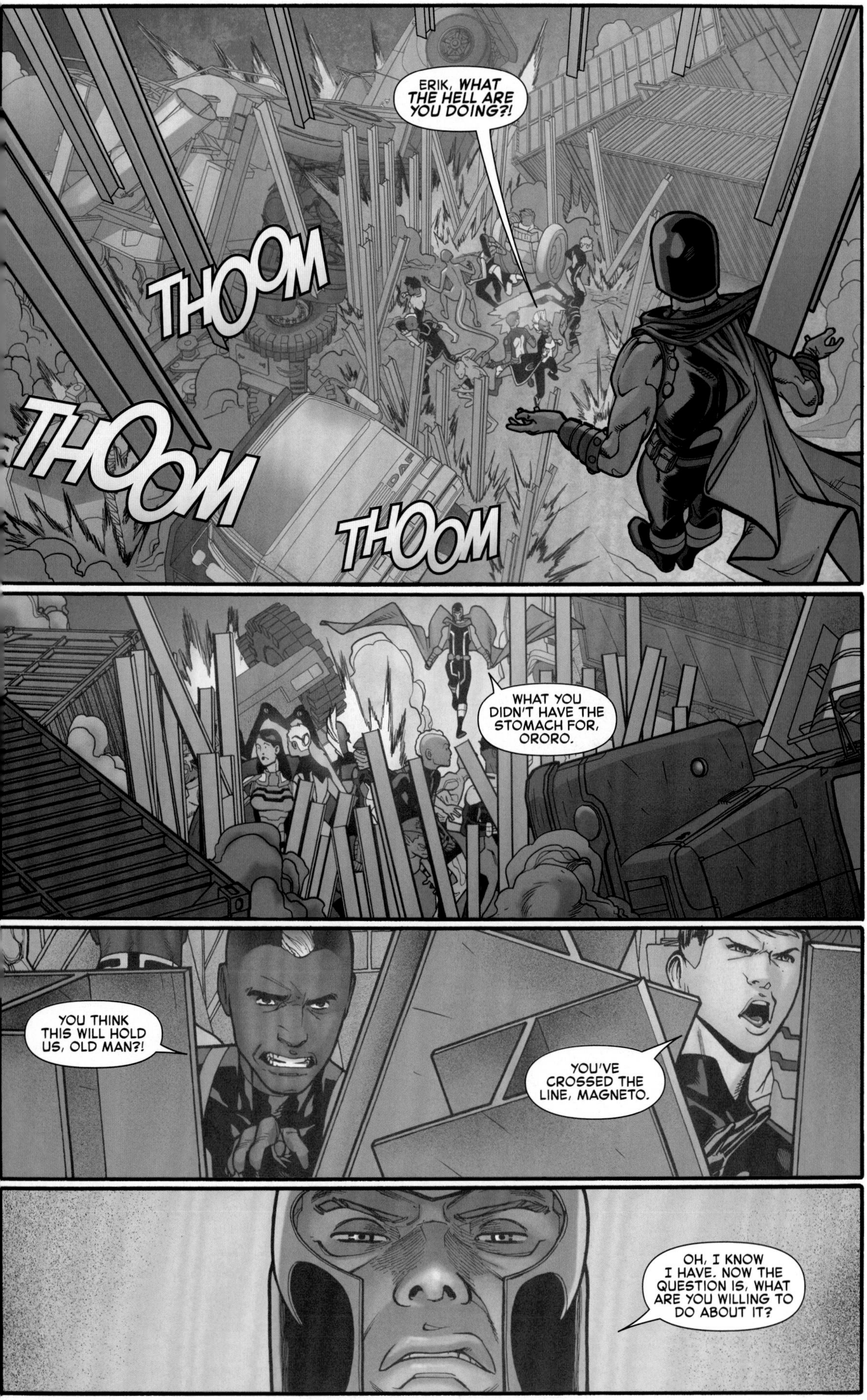
ERIK, WHAT THE HELL ARE YOU DOING?!
THOOM
THOOM
THOOM
WHAT YOU DIDN'T HAVE THE STOMACH FOR, ORORO.
YOU THINK THIS WILL HOLD US, OLD MAN?!
YOU'VE CROSSED THE LINE, MAGNETO.
OH, I KNOW I HAVE. NOW THE QUESTION IS, WHAT ARE YOU WILLING TO DO ABOUT IT?

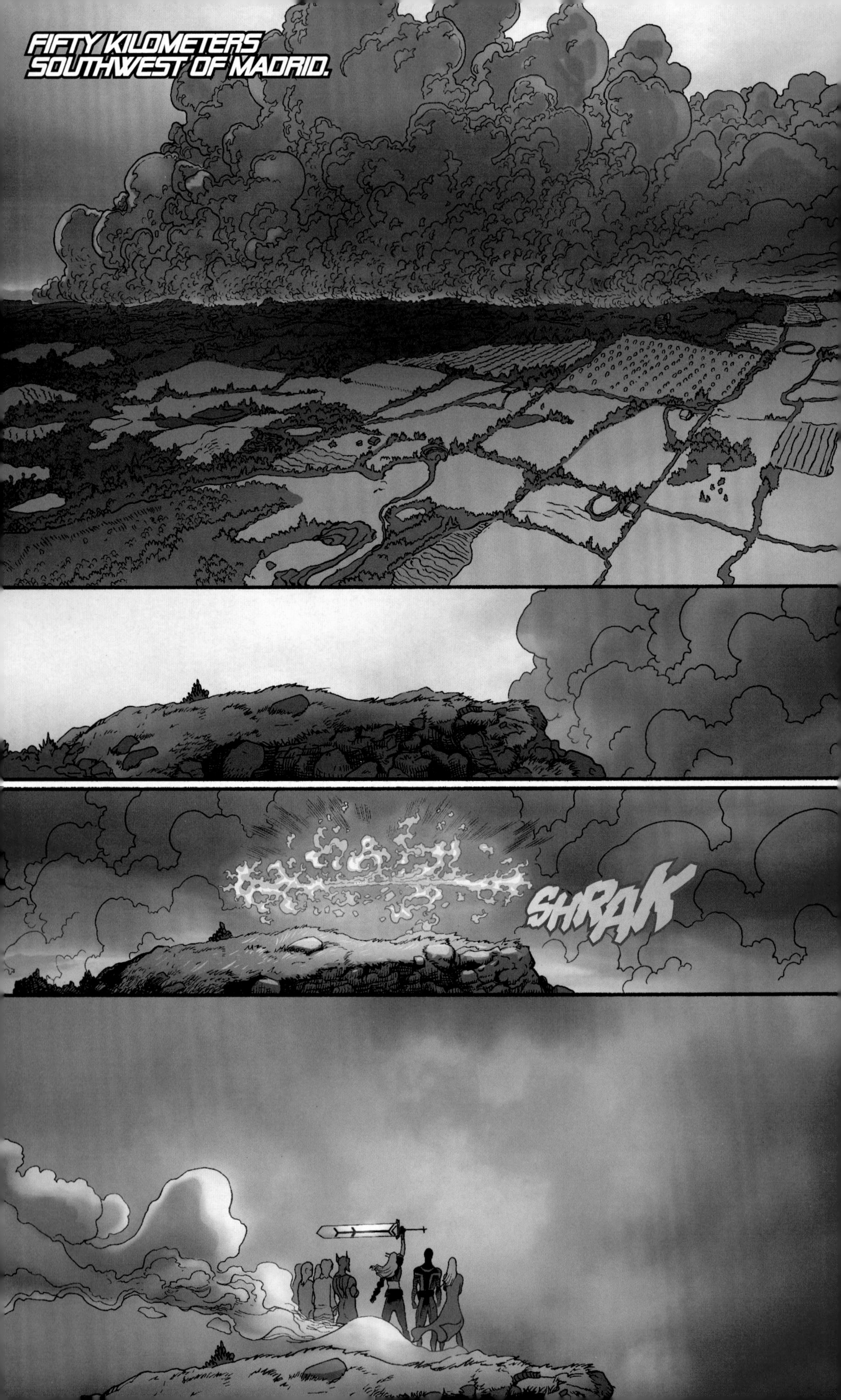
FIFTY KILOMETERS SOUTHWEST OF MADRID.
SHRAK

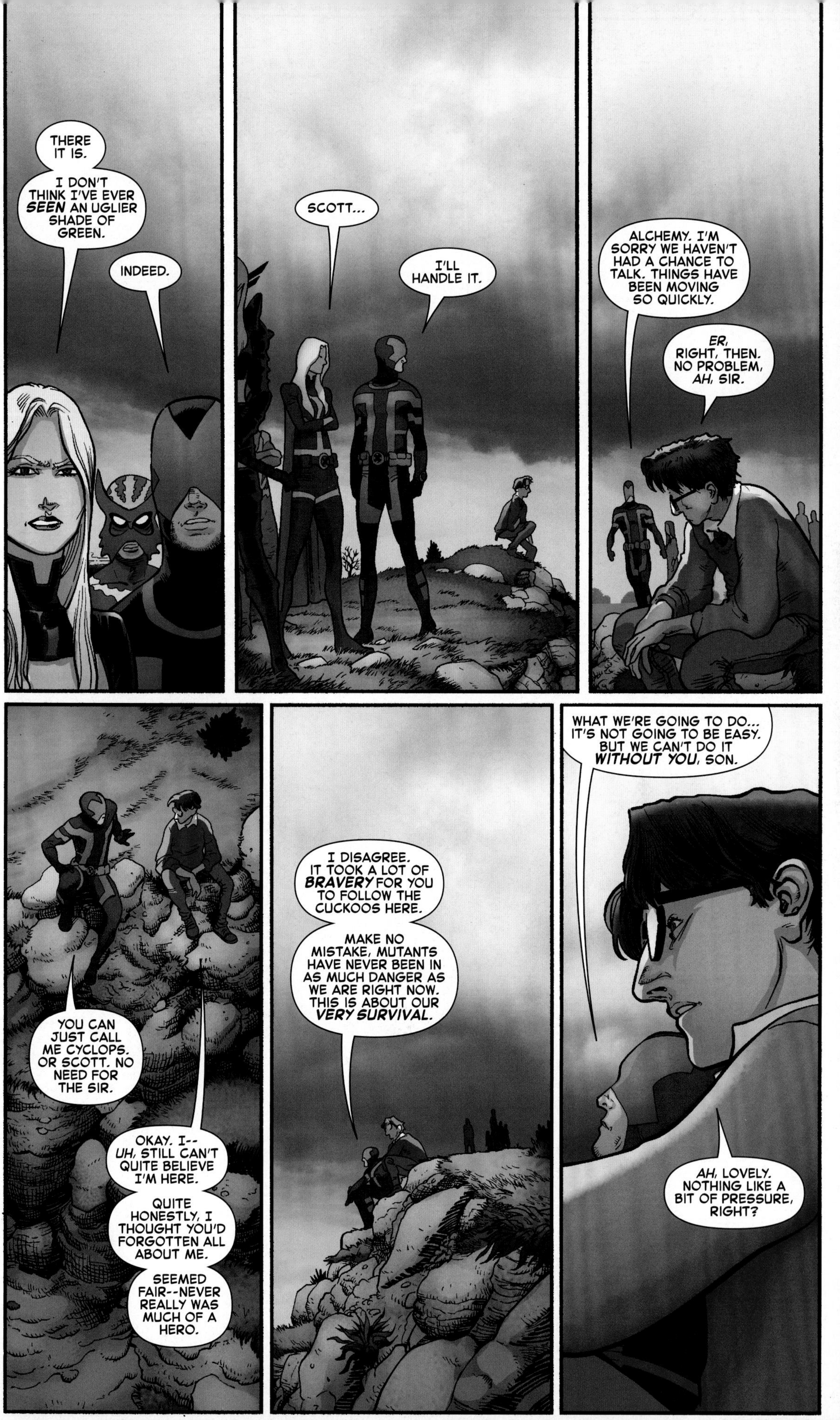
THERE IT IS.
I DON'T THINK I'VE EVER SEEN AN UGLIER SHADE OF GREEN.
INDEED.
SCOTT...
I'LL HANDLE IT.
ALCHEMY. I'M SORRY WE HAVEN'T HAD A CHANCE TO TALK. THINGS HAVE BEEN MOVING SO QUICKLY.
ER, RIGHT, THEN. NO PROBLEM, AH, SIR.
YOU CAN JUST CALL ME CYCLOPS. OR SCOTT. NO NEED FOR THE SIR.
OKAY. I-- UH, STILL CAN'T QUITE BELIEVE I'M HERE.
QUITE HONESTLY, I THOUGHT YOU'D FORGOTTEN ALL ABOUT ME.
SEEMED FAIR--NEVER REALLY WAS MUCH OF A HERO.
I DISAGREE. IT TOOK A LOT OF BRAVERY FOR YOU TO FOLLOW THE CUCKOOS HERE.
MAKE NO MISTAKE, MUTANTS HAVE NEVER BEEN IN AS MUCH DANGER AS WE ARE RIGHT NOW. THIS IS ABOUT OUR VERY SURVIVAL.
WHAT WE'RE GOING TO DO... IT'S NOT GOING TO BE EASY. BUT WE CAN'T DO IT WITHOUT YOU, SON.
AH, LOVELY. NOTHING LIKE A BIT OF PRESSURE, RIGHT?

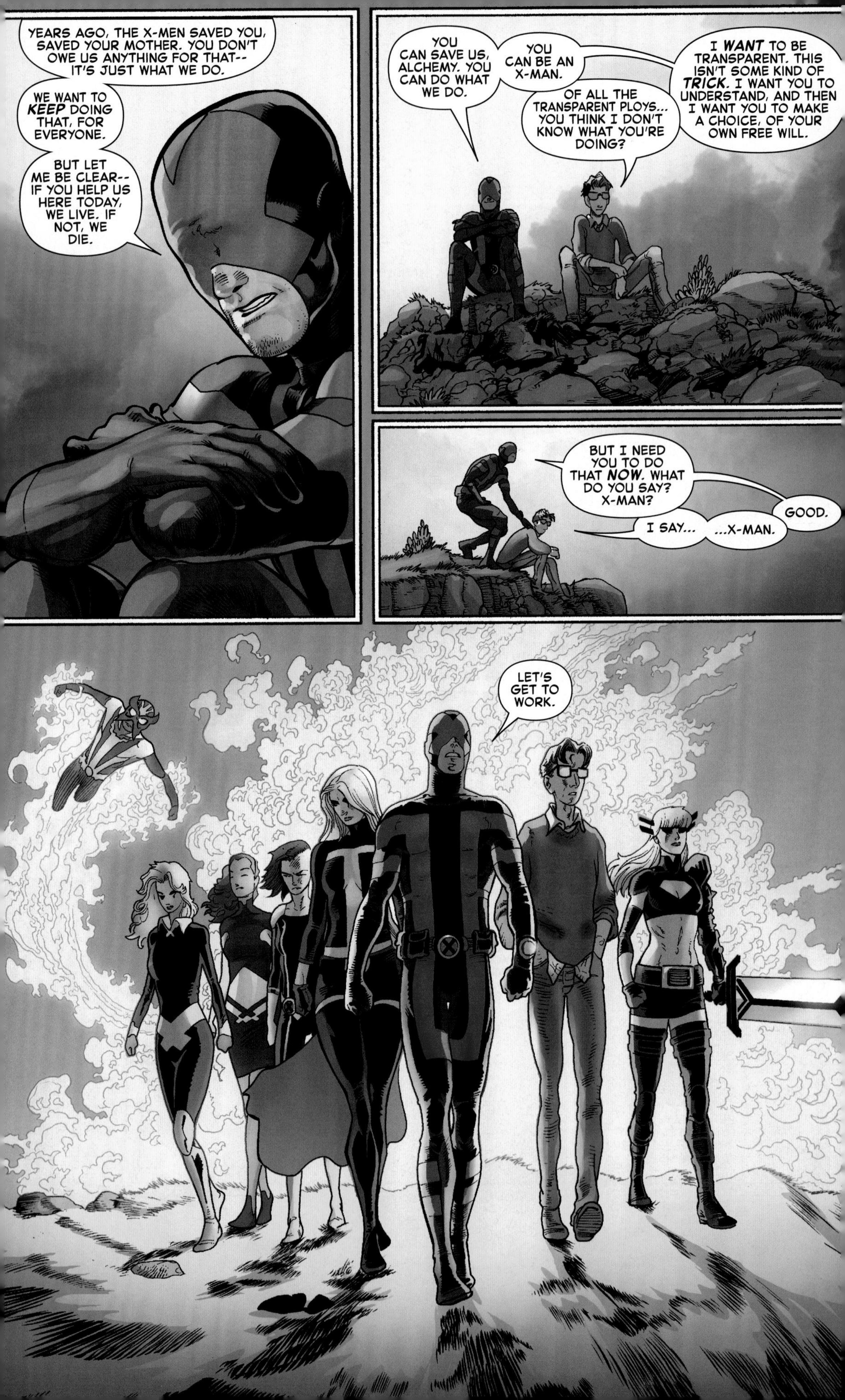
YEARS AGO, THE X-MEN SAVED YOU, SAVED YOUR MOTHER. YOU DON'T OWE US ANYTHING FOR THAT-- IT'S JUST WHAT WE DO.
WE WANT TO KEEP DOING THAT, FOR EVERYONE.
BUT LET ME BE CLEAR-- IF YOU HELP US HERE TODAY, WE LIVE. IF NOT, WE DIE.
YOU CAN SAVE US, ALCHEMY. YOU CAN DO WHAT WE DO.
YOU CAN BE AN X-MAN.
OF ALL THE TRANSPARENT PLOYS... YOU THINK I DON'T KNOW WHAT YOU'RE DOING?
I WANT TO BE TRANSPARENT. THIS ISN'T SOME KIND OF TRICK. I WANT YOU TO UNDERSTAND, AND THEN I WANT YOU TO MAKE A CHOICE, OF YOUR OWN FREE WILL.
BUT I NEED YOU TO DO THAT NOW. WHAT DO YOU SAY? X-MAN?
I SAY...
...X-MAN.
GOOD.
LET'S GET TO WORK.

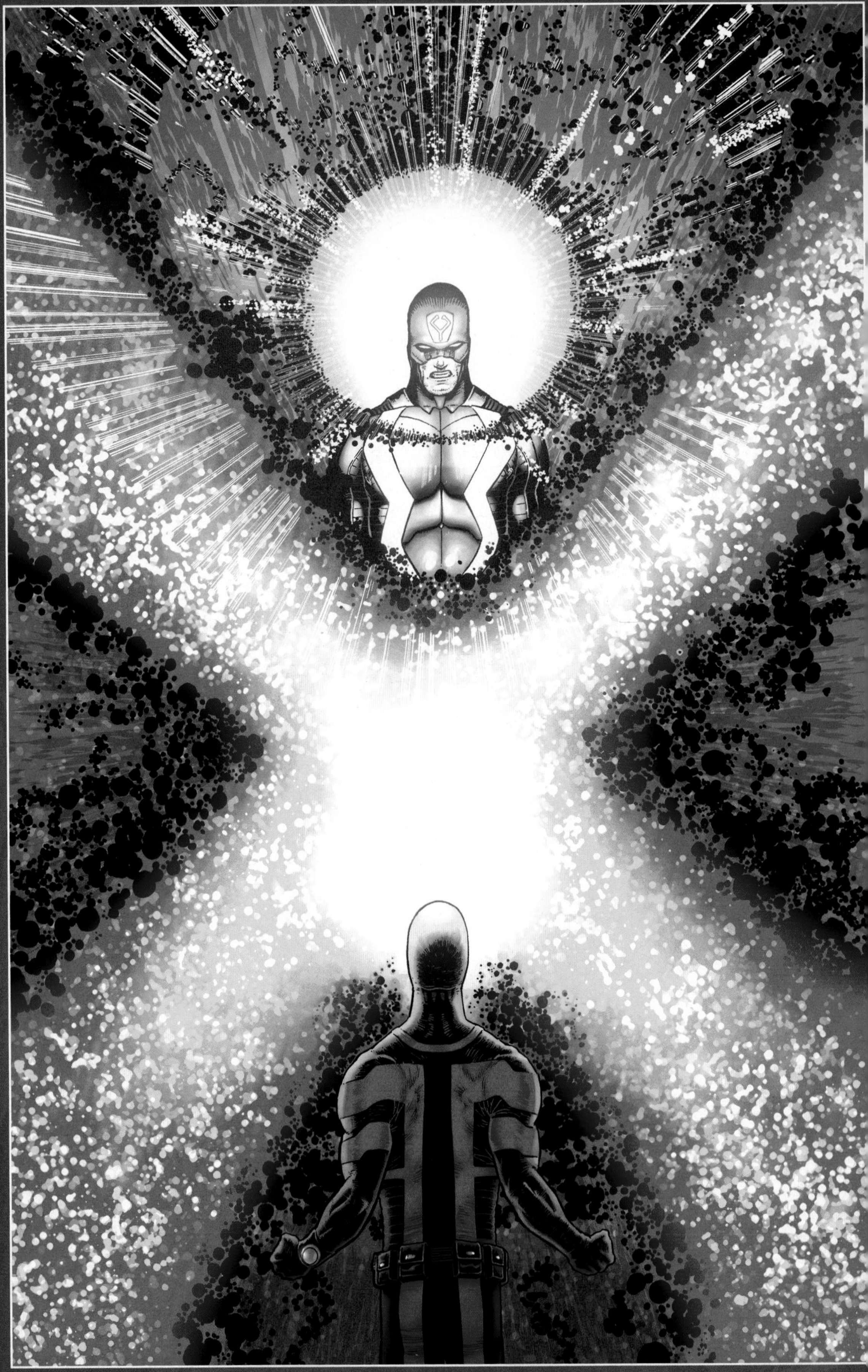

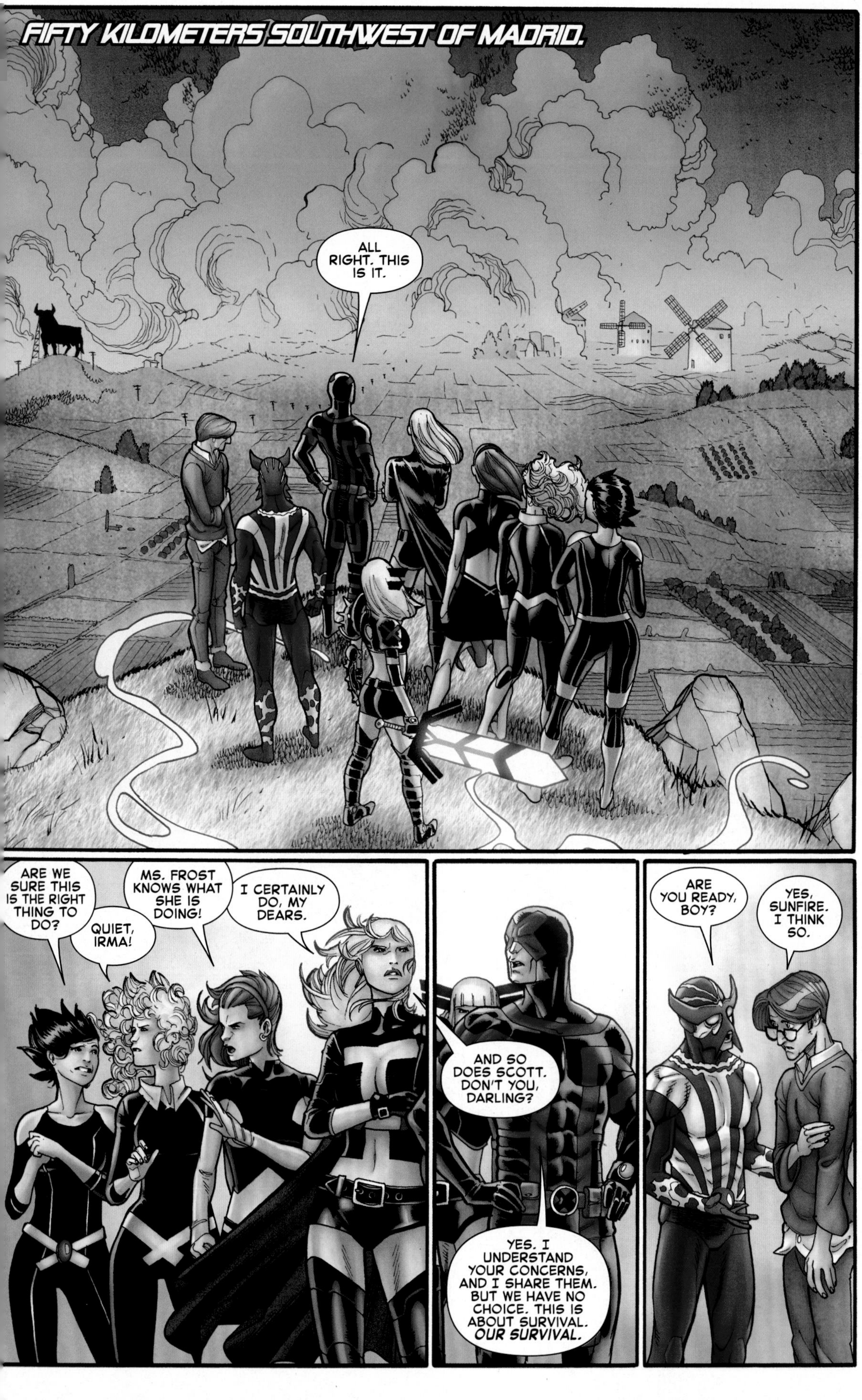

FIFTY KILOMETERS SOUTHWEST OF MADRID.
ALL RIGHT. THIS IS IT.
ARE WE SURE THIS IS THE RIGHT THING TO DO?
QUIET, IRMA!
MS. FROST KNOWS WHAT SHE IS DOING!
I CERTAINLY DO, MY DEARS.
AND SO DOES SCOTT. DON'T YOU, DARLING?
YES. I UNDERSTAND YOUR CONCERNS, AND I SHARE THEM. BUT WE HAVE NO CHOICE. THIS IS ABOUT SURVIVAL. OUR SURVIVAL.
ARE YOU READY, BOY?
YES, SUNFIRE. I THINK SO.

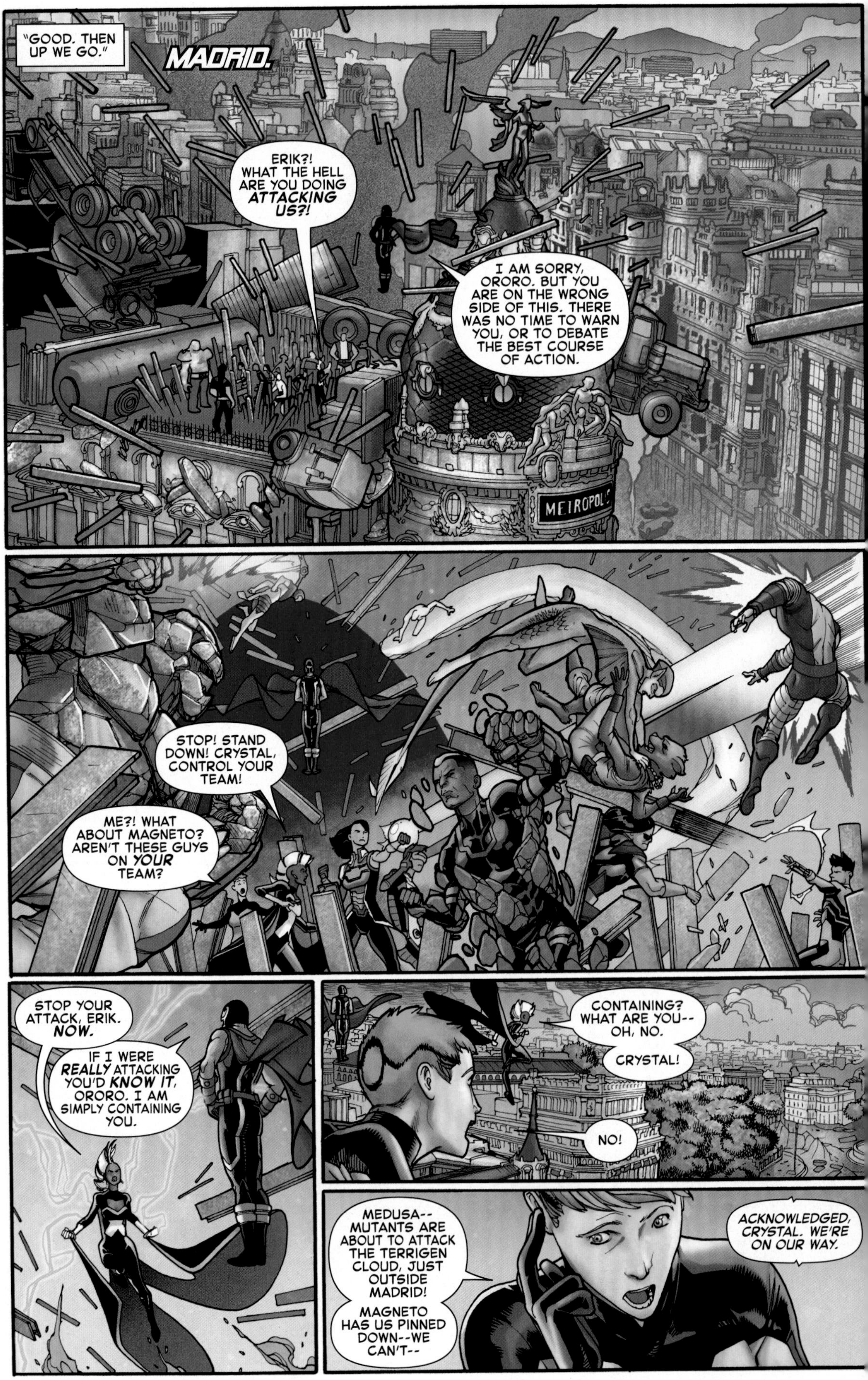
"GOOD. THEN UP WE GO."
MADRID.
ERIK?! WHAT THE HELL ARE YOU DOING ATTACKING US?!
I AM SORRY, ORORO. BUT YOU ARE ON THE WRONG SIDE OF THIS. THERE WAS NO TIME TO WARN YOU, OR TO DEBATE THE BEST COURSE OF ACTION.
METROPOLIS
STOP! STAND DOWN! CRYSTAL, CONTROL YOUR TEAM!
ME?! WHAT ABOUT MAGNETO? AREN'T THESE GUYS ON YOUR TEAM?
STOP YOUR ATTACK, ERIK. NOW.
IF I WERE REALLY ATTACKING YOU'D KNOW IT, ORORO. I AM SIMPLY CONTAINING YOU.
CONTAINING? WHAT ARE YOU-- OH, NO.
CRYSTAL!
NO!
MEDUSA-- MUTANTS ARE ABOUT TO ATTACK THE TERRIGEN CLOUD, JUST OUTSIDE MADRID!
MAGNETO HAS US PINNED DOWN--WE CAN'T--
ACKNOWLEDGED, CRYSTAL. WE'RE ON OUR WAY.

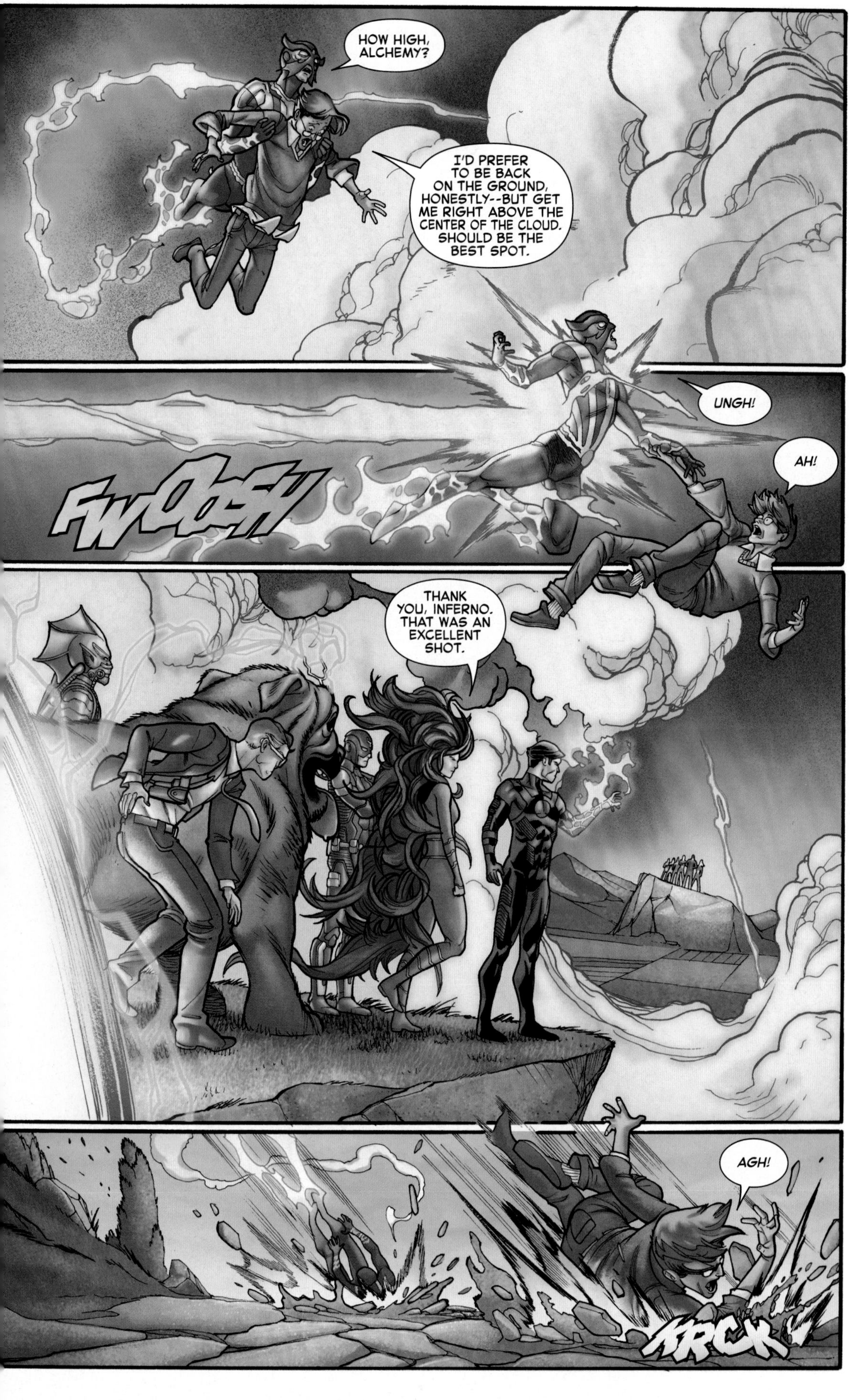
HOW HIGH, ALCHEMY?
I'D PREFER TO BE BACK ON THE GROUND, HONESTLY--BUT GET ME RIGHT ABOVE THE CENTER OF THE CLOUD. SHOULD BE THE BEST SPOT.
UNGH!
AH!
FWOOSH
THANK YOU, INFERNO. THAT WAS AN EXCELLENT SHOT.
AGH!
KRCK

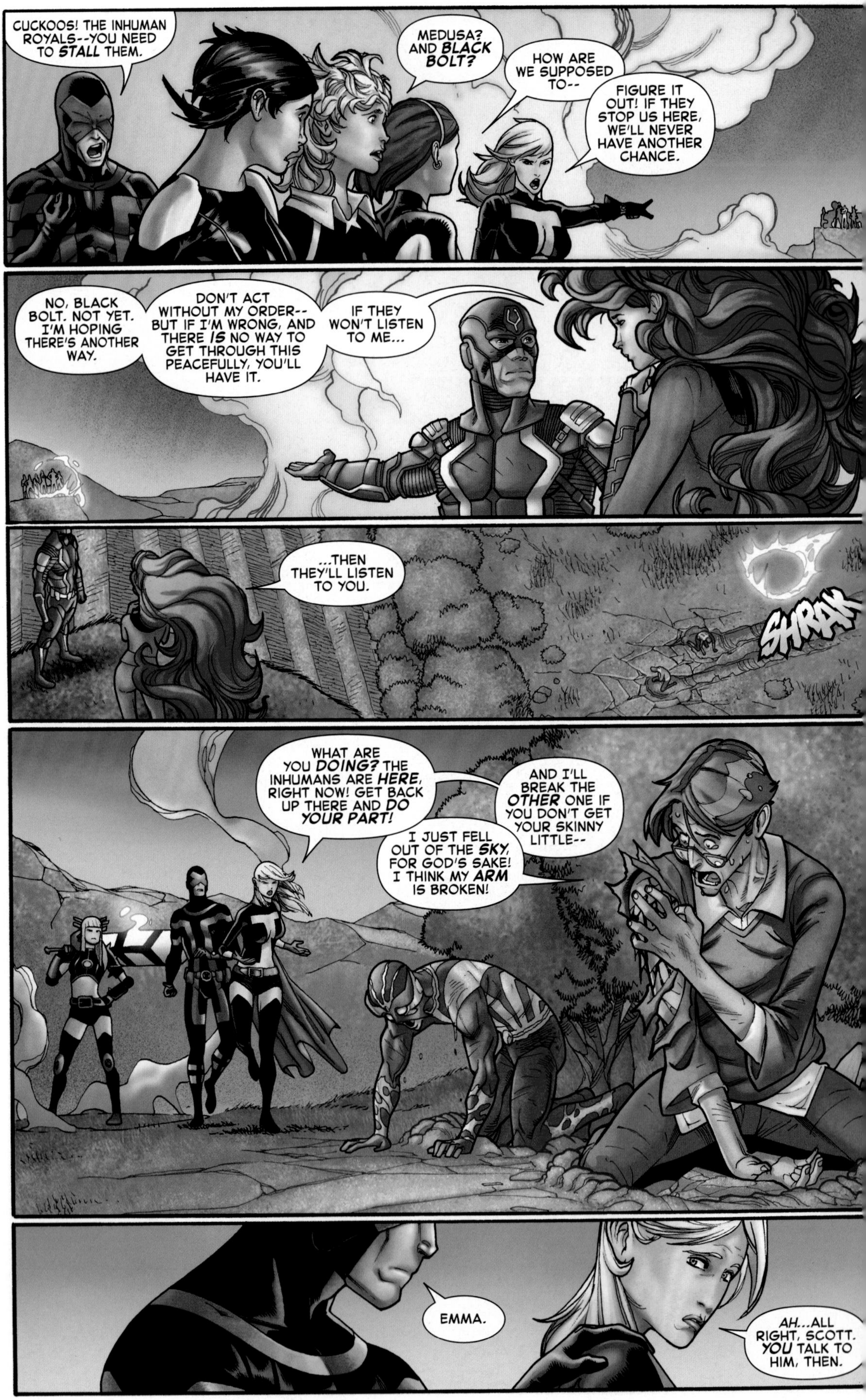

CUCKOOS! THE INHUMAN ROYALS--YOU NEED TO STALL THEM.
MEDUSA? AND BLACK BOLT?
HOW ARE WE SUPPOSED TO--
FIGURE IT OUT! IF THEY STOP US HERE, WE'LL NEVER HAVE ANOTHER CHANCE.
NO, BLACK BOLT. NOT YET. I'M HOPING THERE'S ANOTHER WAY.
DON'T ACT WITHOUT MY ORDER--BUT IF I'M WRONG, AND THERE IS NO WAY TO GET THROUGH THIS PEACEFULLY, YOU'LL HAVE IT.
IF THEY WON'T LISTEN TO ME...
...THEN THEY'LL LISTEN TO YOU.
SHRAK
WHAT ARE YOU DOING? THE INHUMANS ARE HERE, RIGHT NOW! GET BACK UP THERE AND DO YOUR PART!
I JUST FELL OUT OF THE SKY, FOR GOD'S SAKE! I THINK MY ARM IS BROKEN!
AND I'LL BREAK THE OTHER ONE IF YOU DON'T GET YOUR SKINNY LITTLE--
EMMA.
AH...ALL RIGHT, SCOTT. YOU TALK TO HIM, THEN.

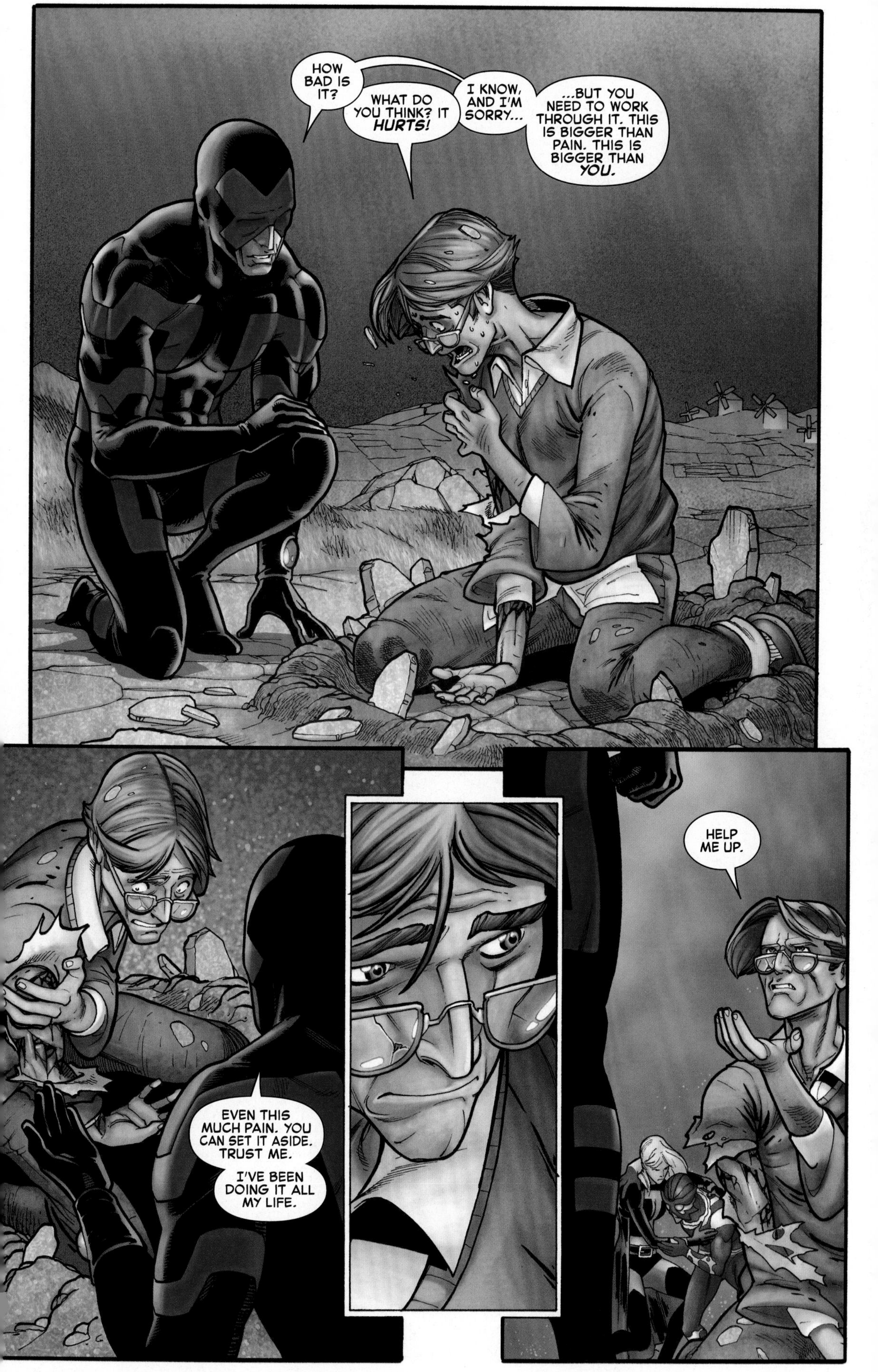
HOW BAD IS IT?
WHAT DO YOU THINK? IT HURTS!
I KNOW, AND I'M SORRY...
...BUT YOU NEED TO WORK THROUGH IT. THIS IS BIGGER THAN PAIN. THIS IS BIGGER THAN YOU.
EVEN THIS MUCH PAIN. YOU CAN SET IT ASIDE. TRUST ME.
I'VE BEEN DOING IT ALL MY LIFE.
HELP ME UP.

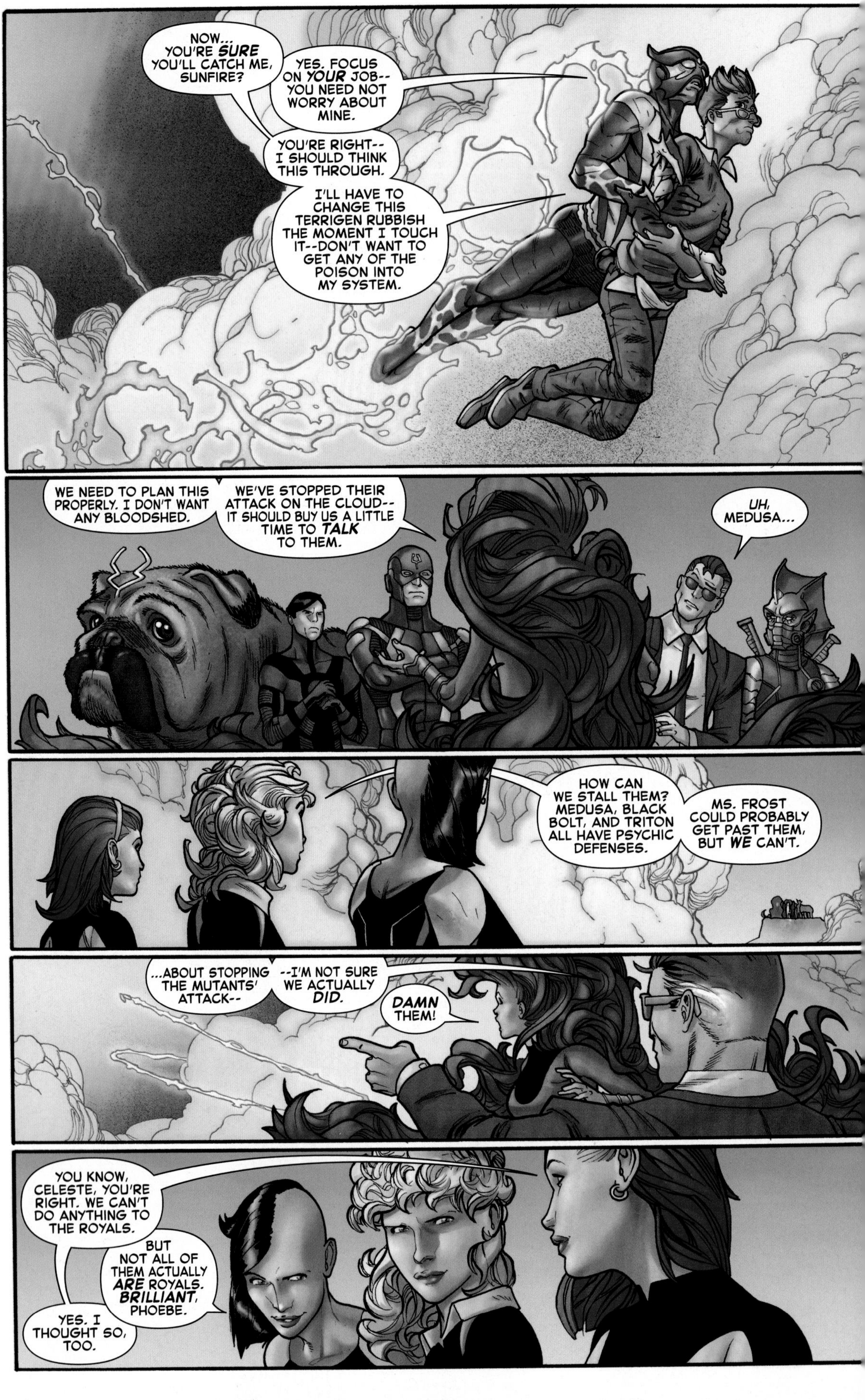
NOW... YOU'RE SURE YOU'LL CATCH ME, SUNFIRE?
YES. FOCUS ON YOUR JOB-- YOU NEED NOT WORRY ABOUT MINE.
YOU'RE RIGHT-- I SHOULD THINK THIS THROUGH.
I'LL HAVE TO CHANGE THIS TERRIGEN RUBBISH THE MOMENT I TOUCH IT--DON'T WANT TO GET ANY OF THE POISON INTO MY SYSTEM.
WE NEED TO PLAN THIS PROPERLY. I DON'T WANT ANY BLOODSHED.
WE'VE STOPPED THEIR ATTACK ON THE CLOUD-- IT SHOULD BUY US A LITTLE TIME TO TALK TO THEM.
UH, MEDUSA...
HOW CAN WE STALL THEM? MEDUSA, BLACK BOLT, AND TRITON ALL HAVE PSYCHIC DEFENSES.
MS. FROST COULD PROBABLY GET PAST THEM, BUT WE CAN'T.
...ABOUT STOPPING THE MUTANTS' ATTACK--
--I'M NOT SURE WE ACTUALLY DID.
DAMN THEM!
YOU KNOW, CELESTE, YOU'RE RIGHT. WE CAN'T DO ANYTHING TO THE ROYALS.
BUT NOT ALL OF THEM ACTUALLY ARE ROYALS. BRILLIANT, PHOEBE.
YES. I THOUGHT SO, TOO.

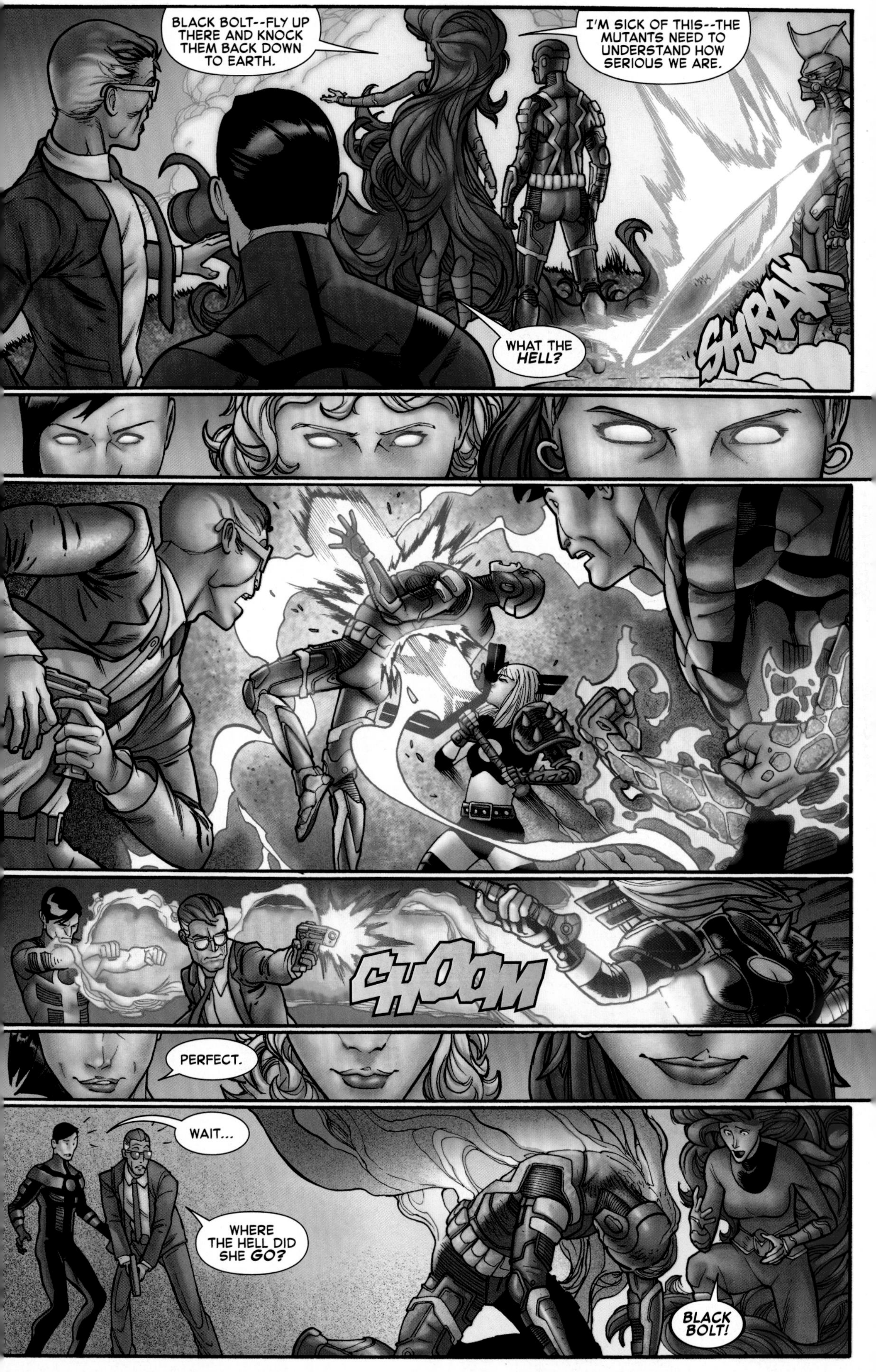
BLACK BOLT--FLY UP THERE AND KNOCK THEM BACK DOWN TO EARTH.
I'M SICK OF THIS--THE MUTANTS NEED TO UNDERSTAND HOW SERIOUS WE ARE.
WHAT THE HELL?
SHRAK
CHOOM
PERFECT.
WAIT...
WHERE THE HELL DID SHE GO?
BLACK BOLT!

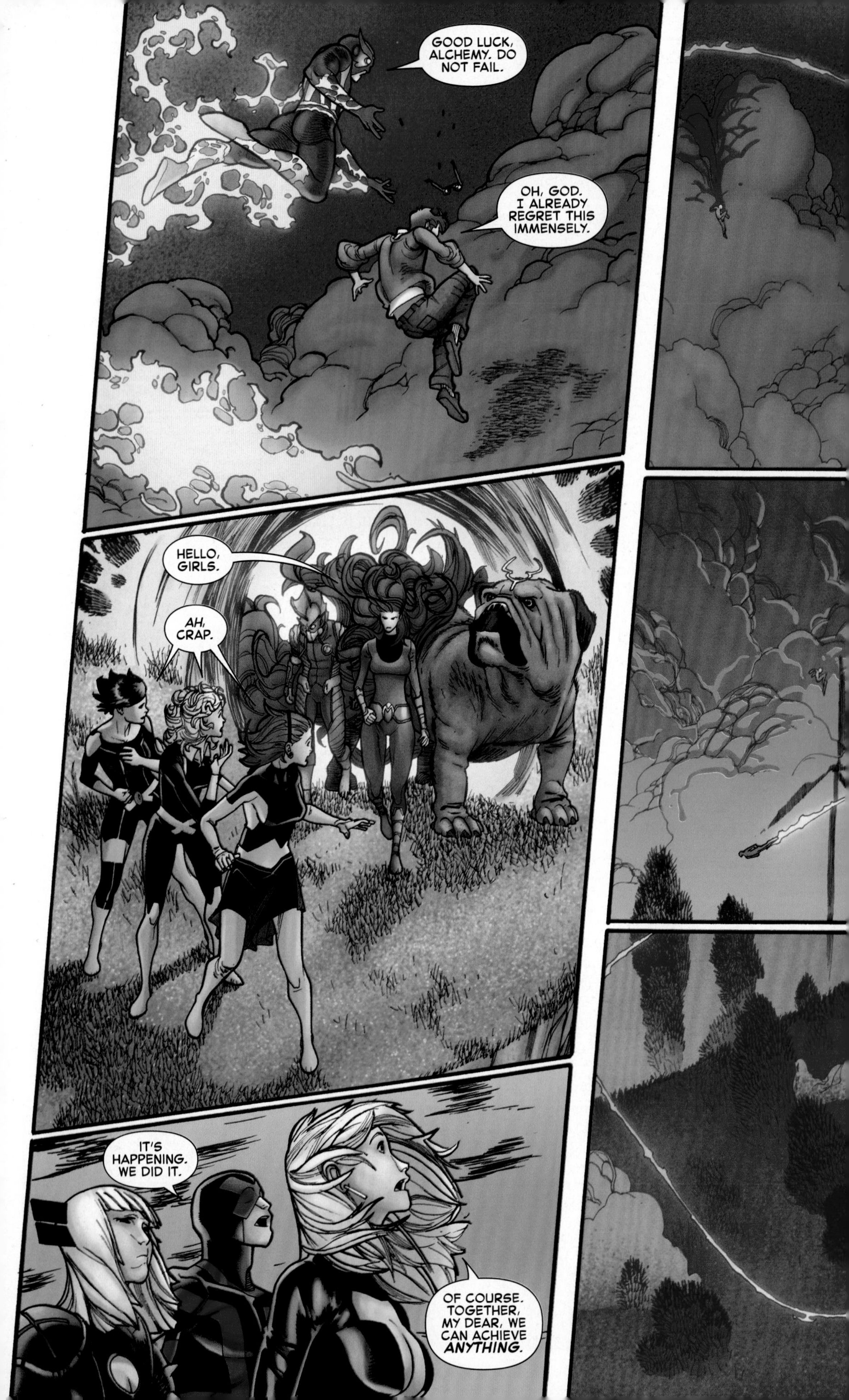
GOOD LUCK, ALCHEMY. DO NOT FAIL.
OH, GOD. I ALREADY REGRET THIS IMMENSELY.
HELLO, GIRLS.
AH, CRAP.
IT'S HAPPENING. WE DID IT.
OF COURSE. TOGETHER, MY DEAR, WE CAN ACHIEVE *ANYTHING*.

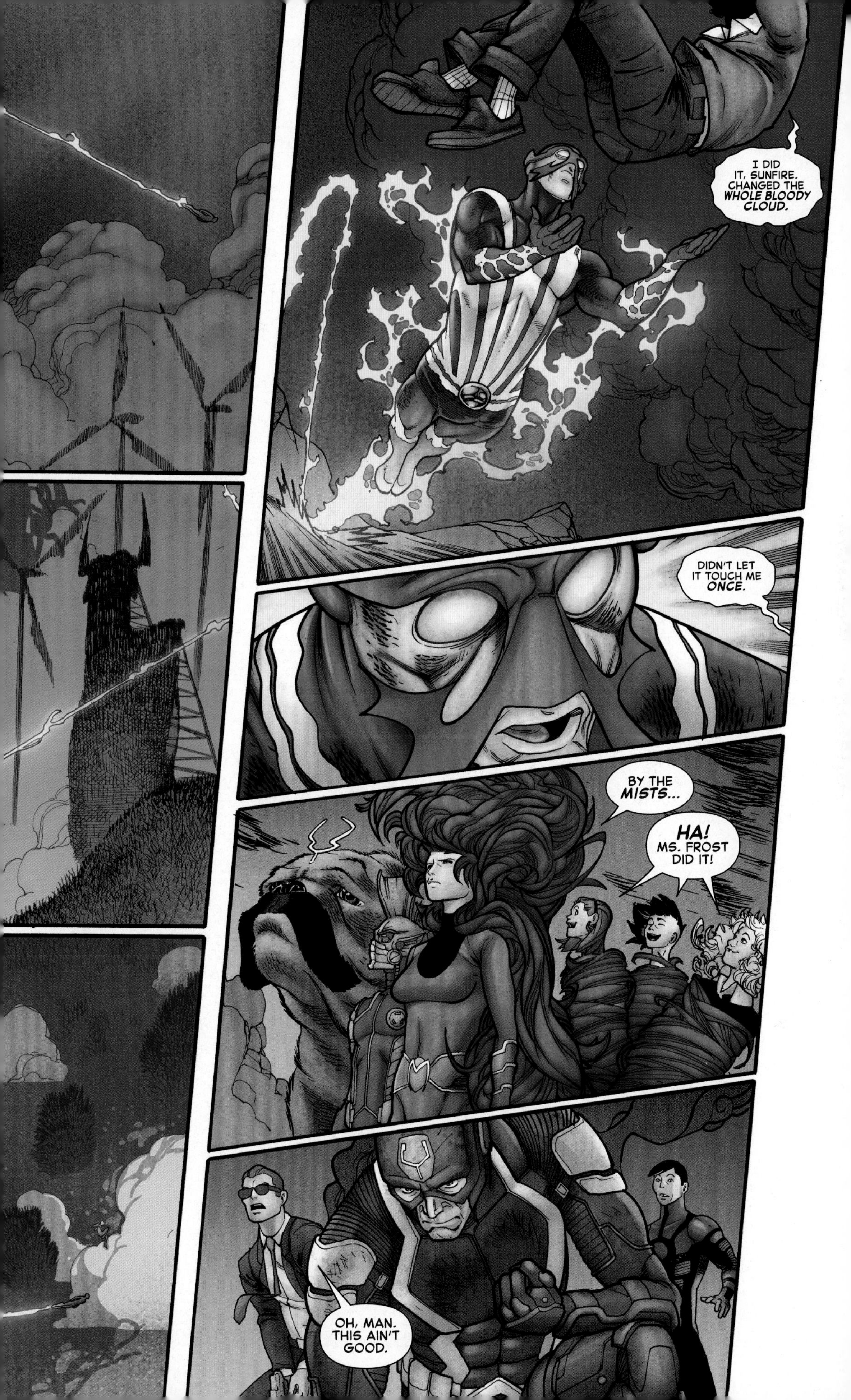
I DID IT, SUNFIRE. CHANGED THE WHOLE BLOODY CLOUD.
DIDN'T LET IT TOUCH ME ONCE.
BY THE MISTS...
HA! MS. FROST DID IT!
OH, MAN. THIS AIN'T GOOD.

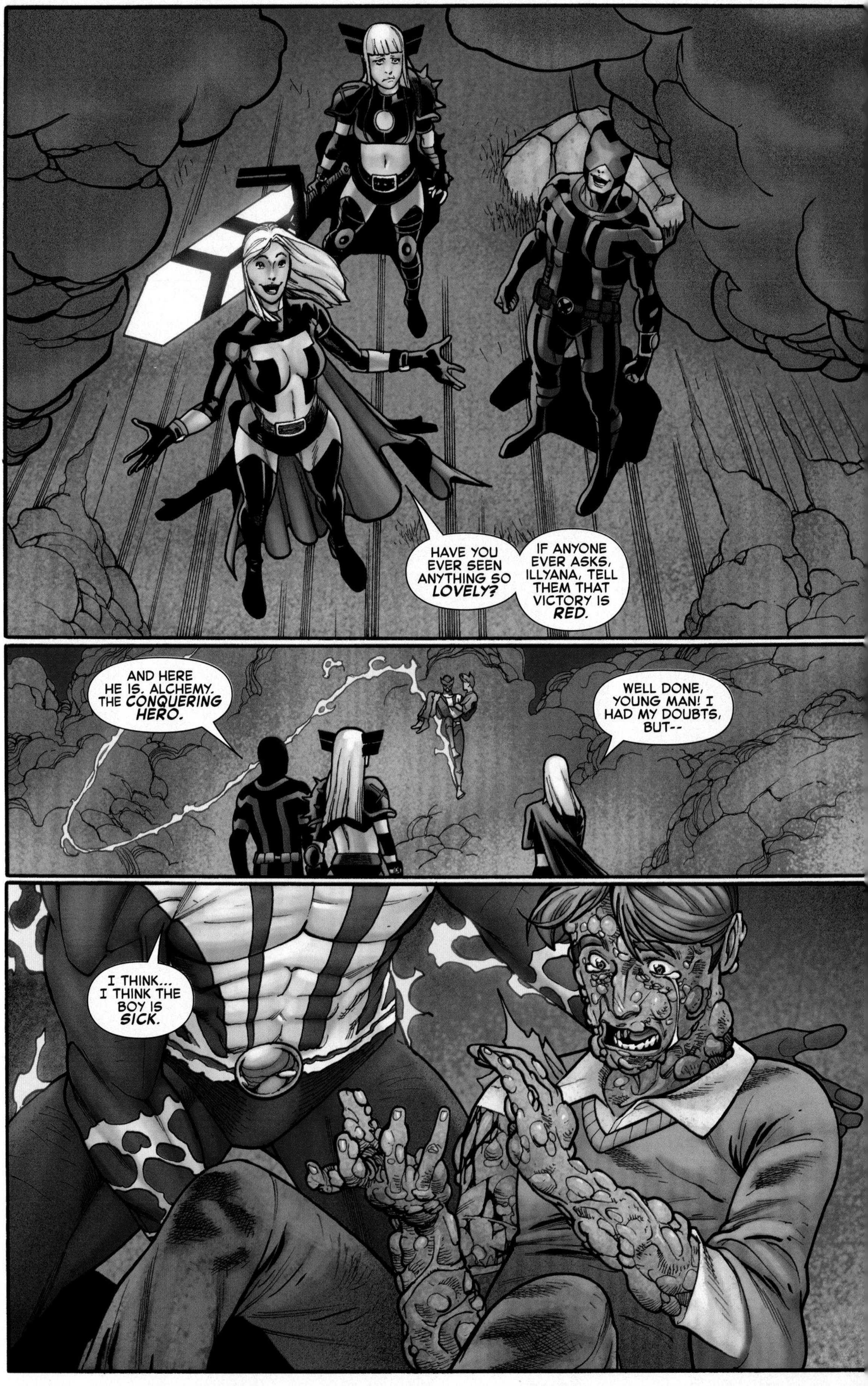
HAVE YOU EVER SEEN ANYTHING SO LOVELY?
IF ANYONE EVER ASKS, ILLYANA, TELL THEM THAT VICTORY IS RED.
AND HERE HE IS. ALCHEMY. THE CONQUERING HERO.
WELL DONE, YOUNG MAN! I HAD MY DOUBTS, BUT--
I THINK... I THINK THE BOY IS SICK.

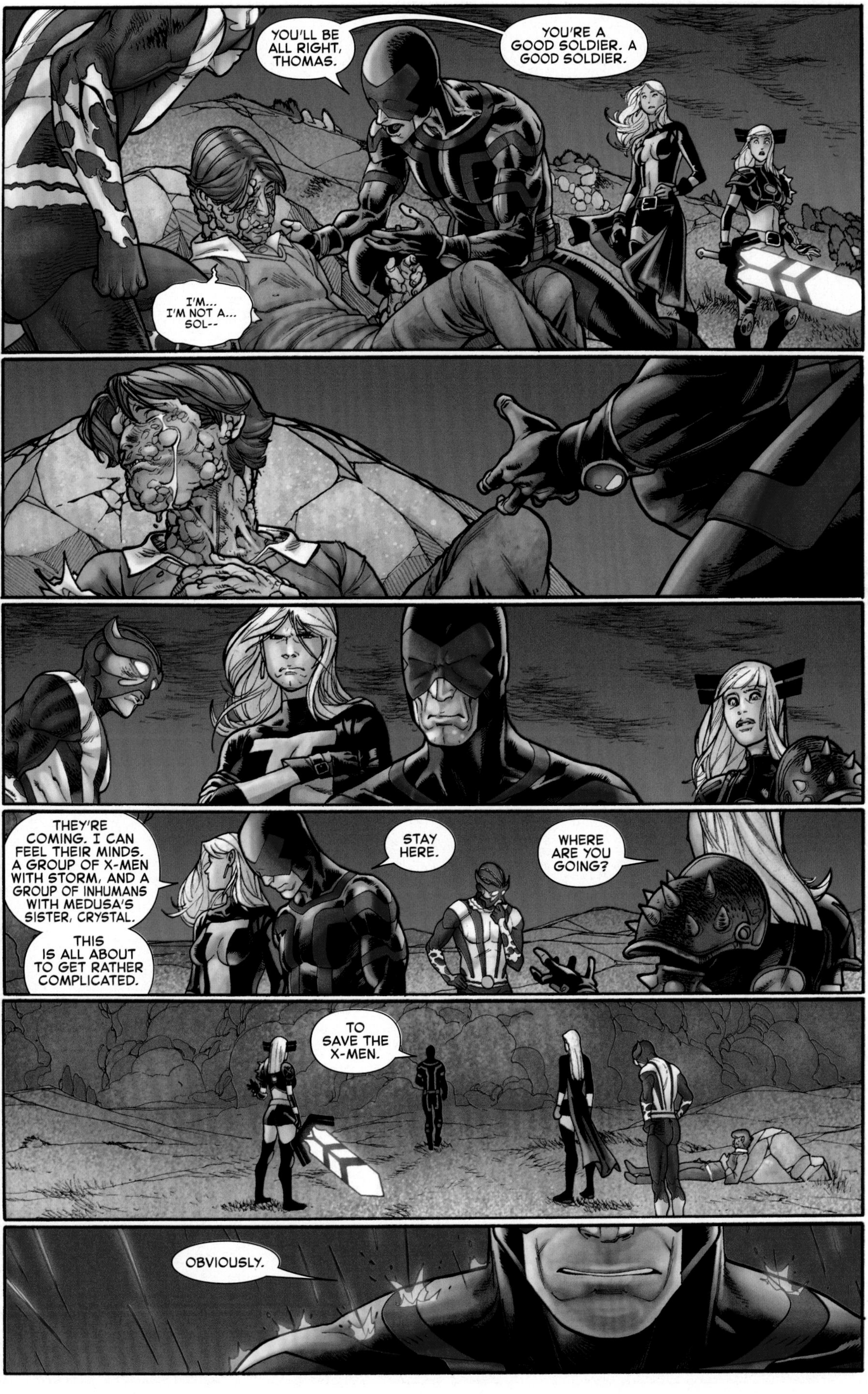
YOU'LL BE ALL RIGHT, THOMAS.
YOU'RE A GOOD SOLDIER. A GOOD SOLDIER.
I'M... I'M NOT A... SOL--
THEY'RE COMING. I CAN FEEL THEIR MINDS. A GROUP OF X-MEN WITH STORM, AND A GROUP OF INHUMANS WITH MEDUSA'S SISTER, CRYSTAL.
THIS IS ALL ABOUT TO GET RATHER COMPLICATED.
STAY HERE.
WHERE ARE YOU GOING?
TO SAVE THE X-MEN.
OBVIOUSLY.

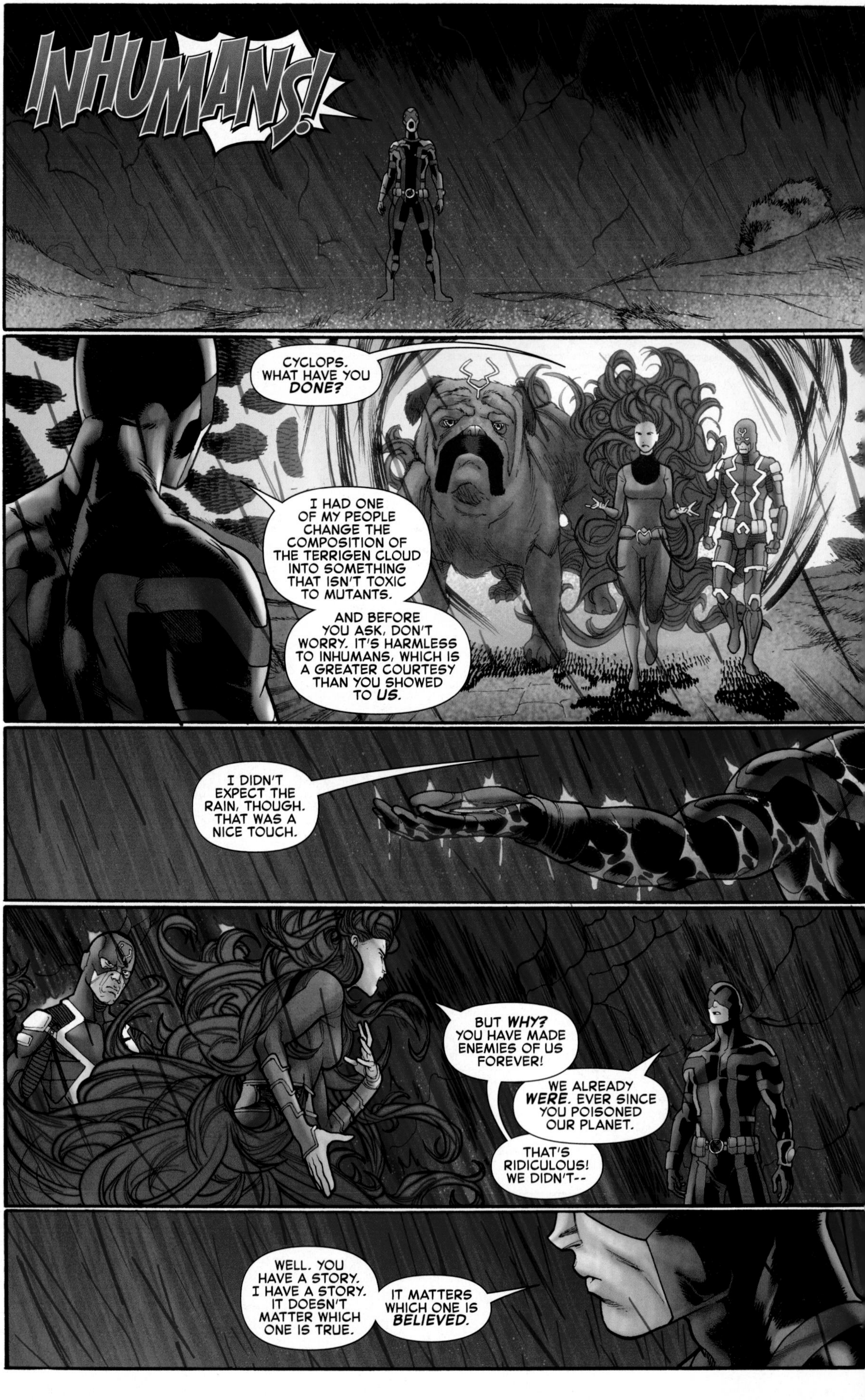
INHUMANS!
CYCLOPS. WHAT HAVE YOU DONE?
I HAD ONE OF MY PEOPLE CHANGE THE COMPOSITION OF THE TERRIGEN CLOUD INTO SOMETHING THAT ISN'T TOXIC TO MUTANTS.
AND BEFORE YOU ASK, DON'T WORRY. IT'S HARMLESS TO INHUMANS, WHICH IS A GREATER COURTESY THAN YOU SHOWED TO US.
I DIDN'T EXPECT THE RAIN, THOUGH. THAT WAS A NICE TOUCH.
BUT WHY? YOU HAVE MADE ENEMIES OF US FOREVER!
WE ALREADY WERE. EVER SINCE YOU POISONED OUR PLANET.
THAT'S RIDICULOUS! WE DIDN'T--
WELL. YOU HAVE A STORY. I HAVE A STORY. IT DOESN'T MATTER WHICH ONE IS TRUE.
IT MATTERS WHICH ONE IS BELIEVED.

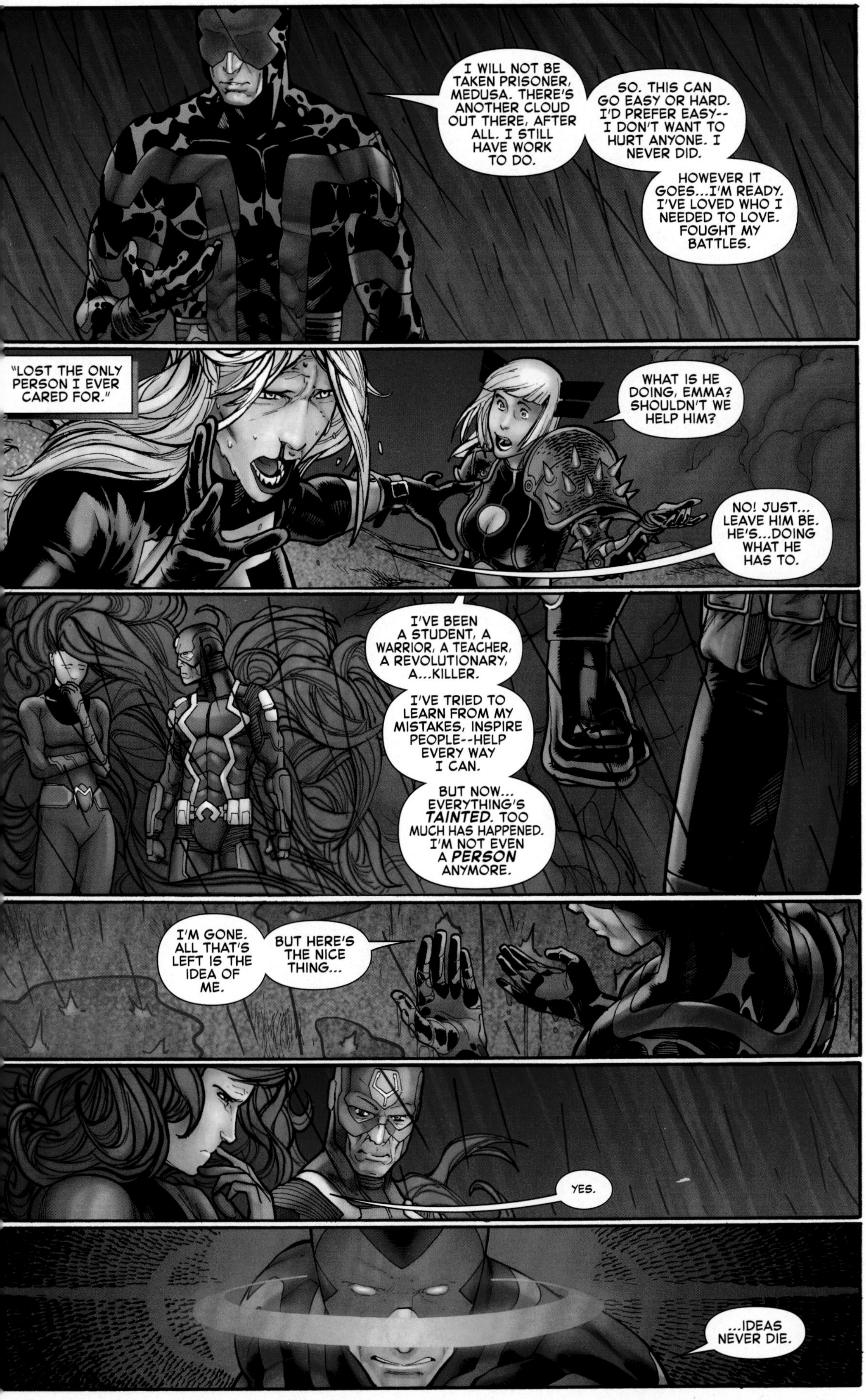
I WILL NOT BE TAKEN PRISONER, MEDUSA. THERE'S ANOTHER CLOUD OUT THERE, AFTER ALL. I STILL HAVE WORK TO DO.
SO. THIS CAN GO EASY OR HARD. I'D PREFER EASY-- I DON'T WANT TO HURT ANYONE. I NEVER DID.
HOWEVER IT GOES...I'M READY. I'VE LOVED WHO I NEEDED TO LOVE. FOUGHT MY BATTLES.
"LOST THE ONLY PERSON I EVER CARED FOR."
WHAT IS HE DOING, EMMA? SHOULDN'T WE HELP HIM?
NO! JUST... LEAVE HIM BE. HE'S...DOING WHAT HE HAS TO.
I'VE BEEN A STUDENT, A WARRIOR, A TEACHER, A REVOLUTIONARY, A...KILLER.
I'VE TRIED TO LEARN FROM MY MISTAKES, INSPIRE PEOPLE--HELP EVERY WAY I CAN.
BUT NOW... EVERYTHING'S TAINTED. TOO MUCH HAS HAPPENED. I'M NOT EVEN A PERSON ANYMORE.
I'M GONE. ALL THAT'S LEFT IS THE IDEA OF ME.
BUT HERE'S THE NICE THING...
YES.
...IDEAS NEVER DIE.

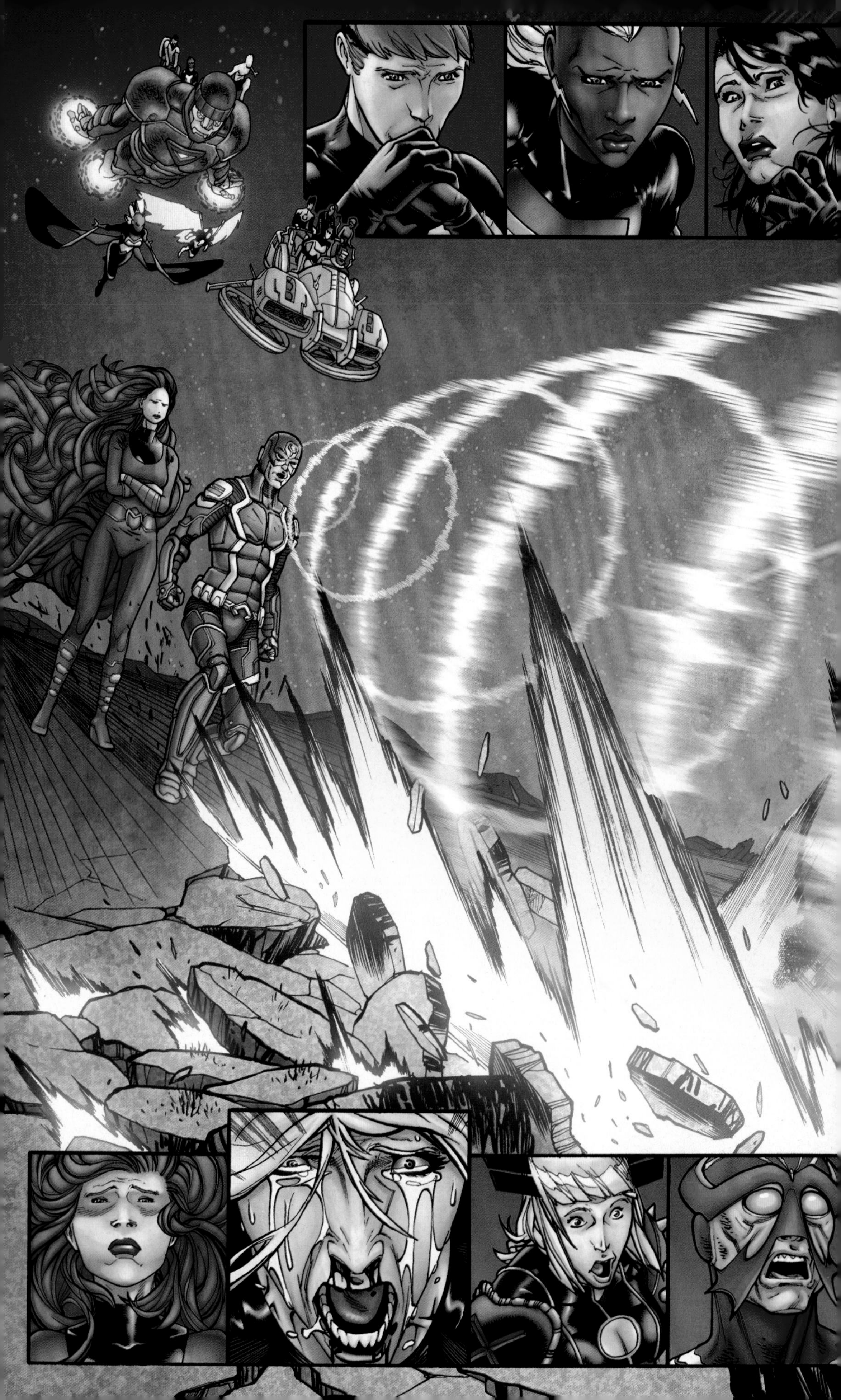

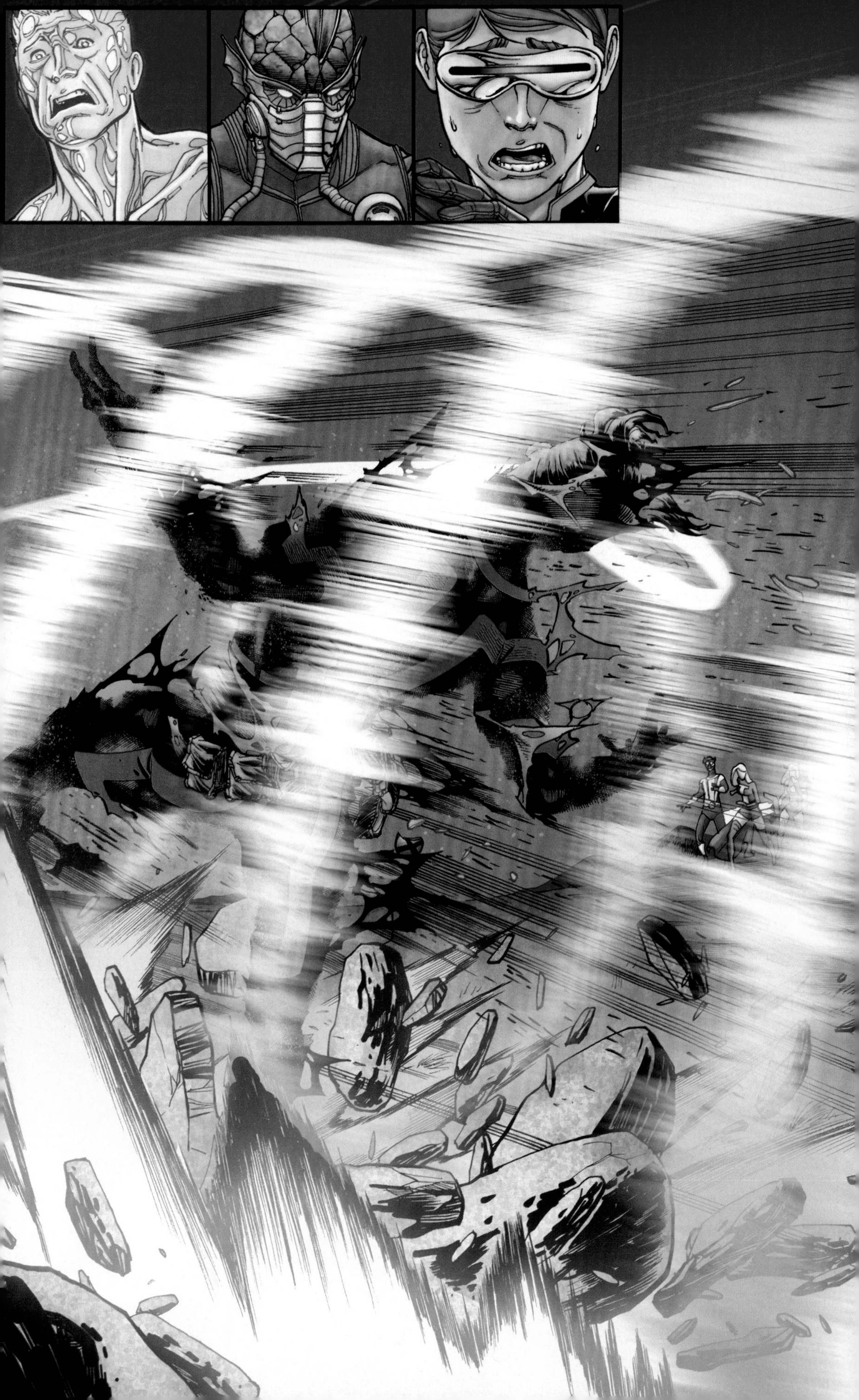

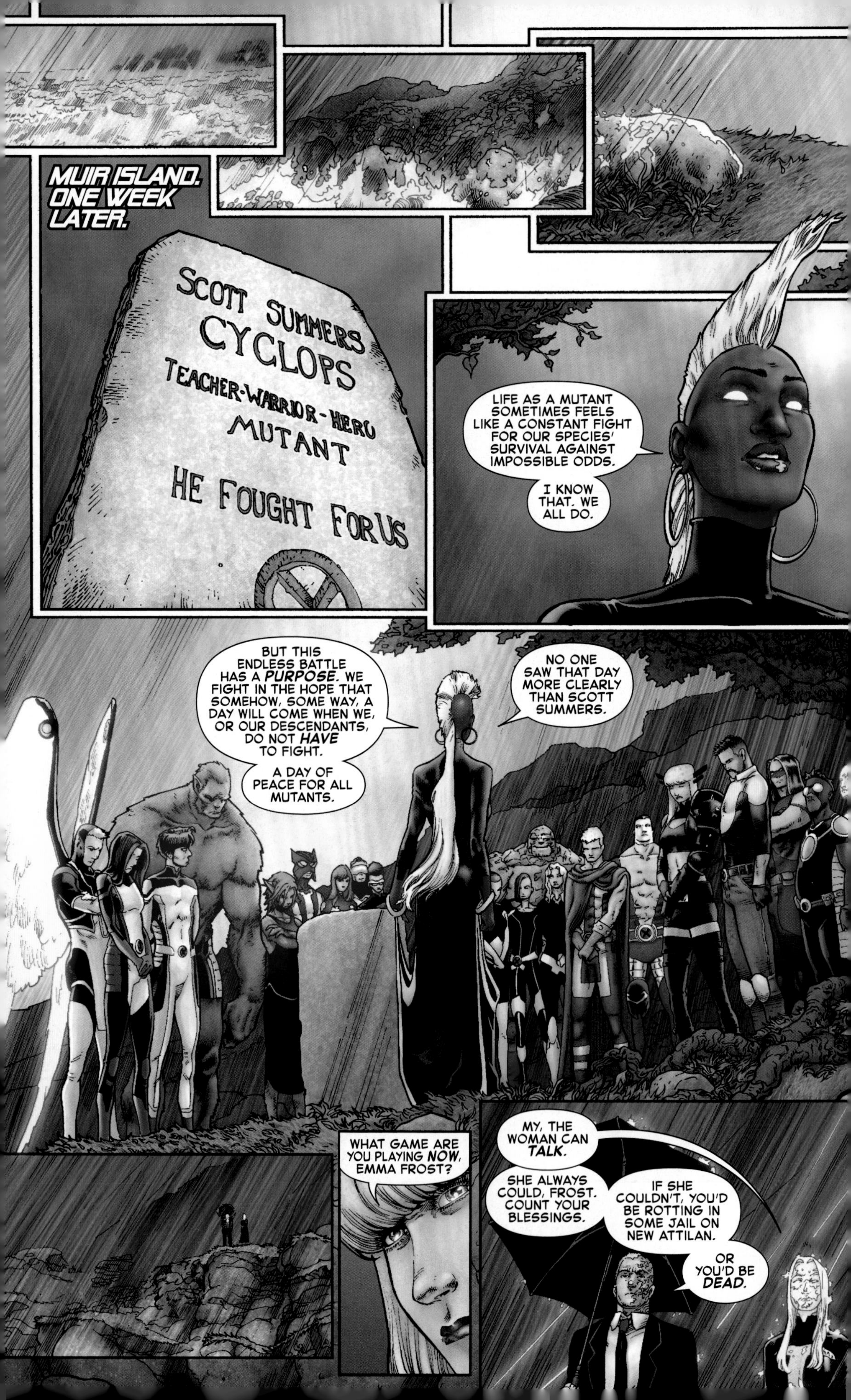
MUIR ISLAND. ONE WEEK LATER.
SCOTT SUMMERS
CYCLOPS
TEACHER-WARRIOR-HERO
MUTANT
HE FOUGHT FOR US
LIFE AS A MUTANT SOMETIMES FEELS LIKE A CONSTANT FIGHT FOR OUR SPECIES' SURVIVAL AGAINST IMPOSSIBLE ODDS.
I KNOW THAT. WE ALL DO.
BUT THIS ENDLESS BATTLE HAS A PURPOSE. WE FIGHT IN THE HOPE THAT SOMEHOW, SOME WAY, A DAY WILL COME WHEN WE, OR OUR DESCENDANTS, DO NOT HAVE TO FIGHT.
A DAY OF PEACE FOR ALL MUTANTS.
NO ONE SAW THAT DAY MORE CLEARLY THAN SCOTT SUMMERS.
WHAT GAME ARE YOU PLAYING NOW, EMMA FROST?
MY, THE WOMAN CAN TALK.
SHE ALWAYS COULD, FROST. COUNT YOUR BLESSINGS.
IF SHE COULDN'T, YOU'D BE ROTTING IN SOME JAIL ON NEW ATTILAN.
OR YOU'D BE DEAD.

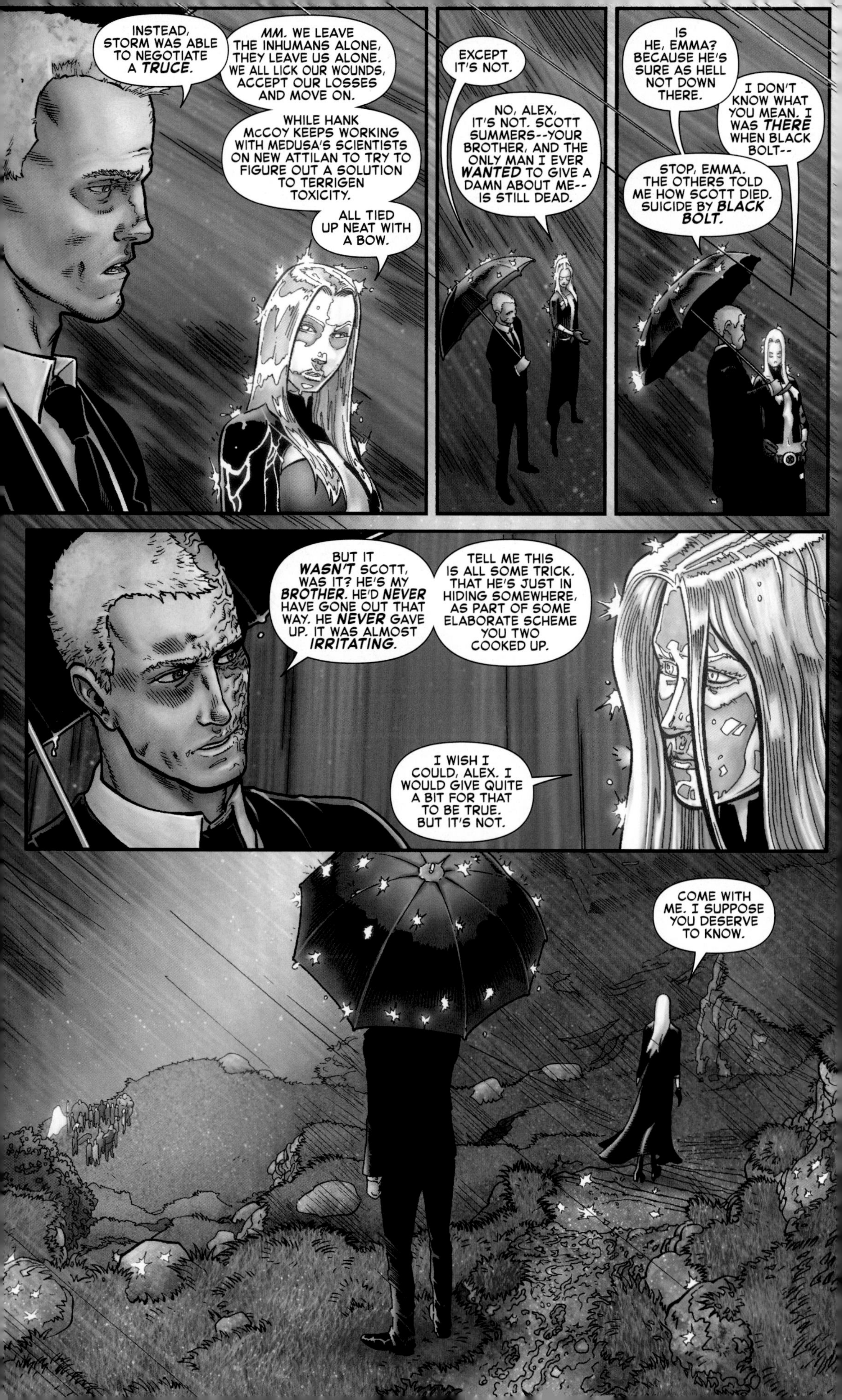
INSTEAD, STORM WAS ABLE TO NEGOTIATE A TRUCE.
MM. WE LEAVE THE INHUMANS ALONE, THEY LEAVE US ALONE. WE ALL LICK OUR WOUNDS, ACCEPT OUR LOSSES AND MOVE ON.
WHILE HANK McCOY KEEPS WORKING WITH MEDUSA'S SCIENTISTS ON NEW ATTILAN TO TRY TO FIGURE OUT A SOLUTION TO TERRIGEN TOXICITY.
ALL TIED UP NEAT WITH A BOW.
EXCEPT IT'S NOT.
NO, ALEX, IT'S NOT. SCOTT SUMMERS--YOUR BROTHER, AND THE ONLY MAN I EVER WANTED TO GIVE A DAMN ABOUT ME--IS STILL DEAD.
IS HE, EMMA? BECAUSE HE'S SURE AS HELL NOT DOWN THERE.
I DON'T KNOW WHAT YOU MEAN. I WAS THERE WHEN BLACK BOLT--
STOP, EMMA. THE OTHERS TOLD ME HOW SCOTT DIED. SUICIDE BY BLACK BOLT.
BUT IT WASN'T SCOTT, WAS IT? HE'S MY BROTHER. HE'D NEVER HAVE GONE OUT THAT WAY. HE NEVER GAVE UP. IT WAS ALMOST IRRITATING.
TELL ME THIS IS ALL SOME TRICK. THAT HE'S JUST IN HIDING SOMEWHERE, AS PART OF SOME ELABORATE SCHEME YOU TWO COOKED UP.
I WISH I COULD, ALEX. I WOULD GIVE QUITE A BIT FOR THAT TO BE TRUE. BUT IT'S NOT.
COME WITH ME. I SUPPOSE YOU DESERVE TO KNOW.

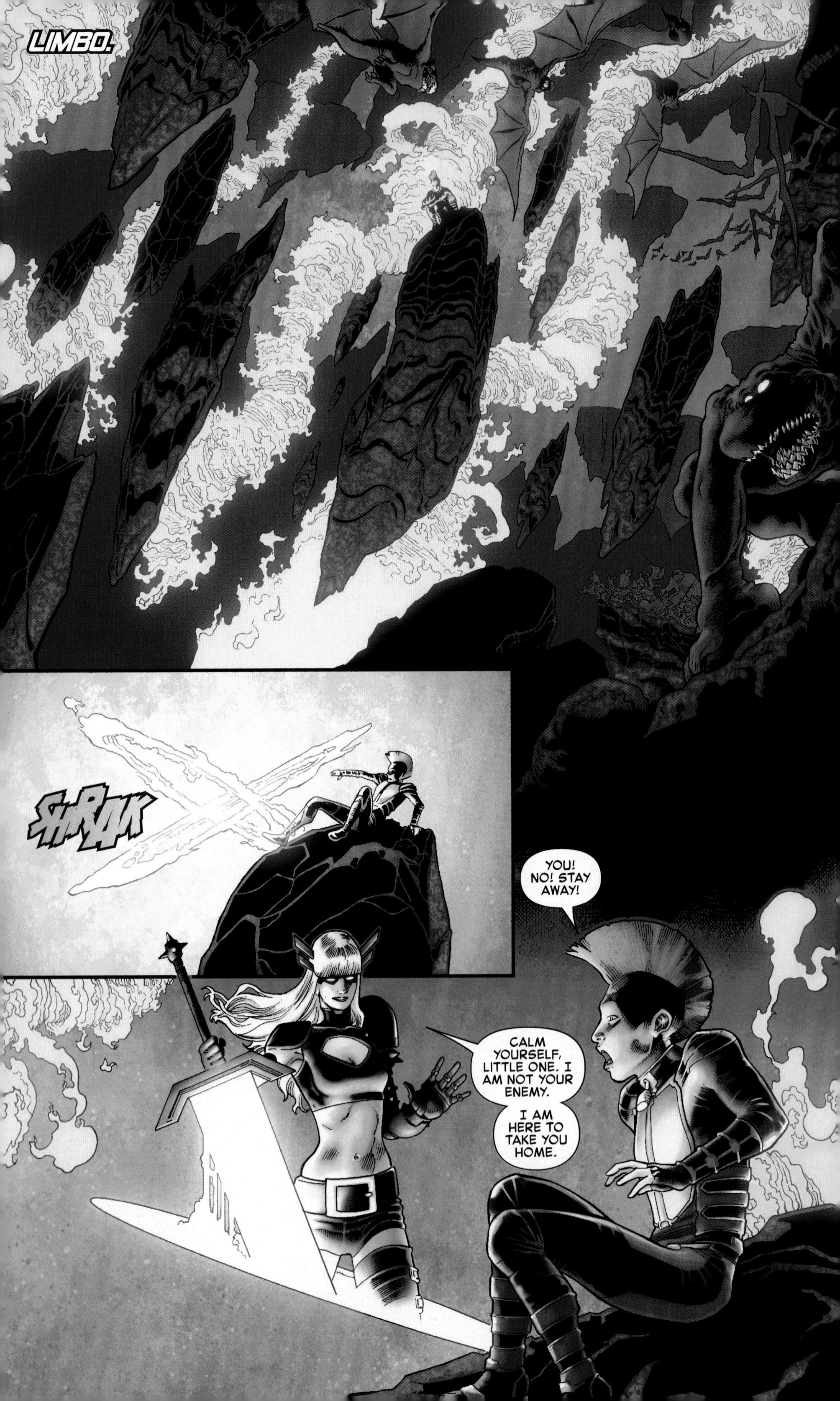
LIMBO.
SHRAAK
YOU! NO! STAY AWAY!
CALM YOURSELF, LITTLE ONE. I AM NOT YOUR ENEMY.
I AM HERE TO TAKE YOU HOME.

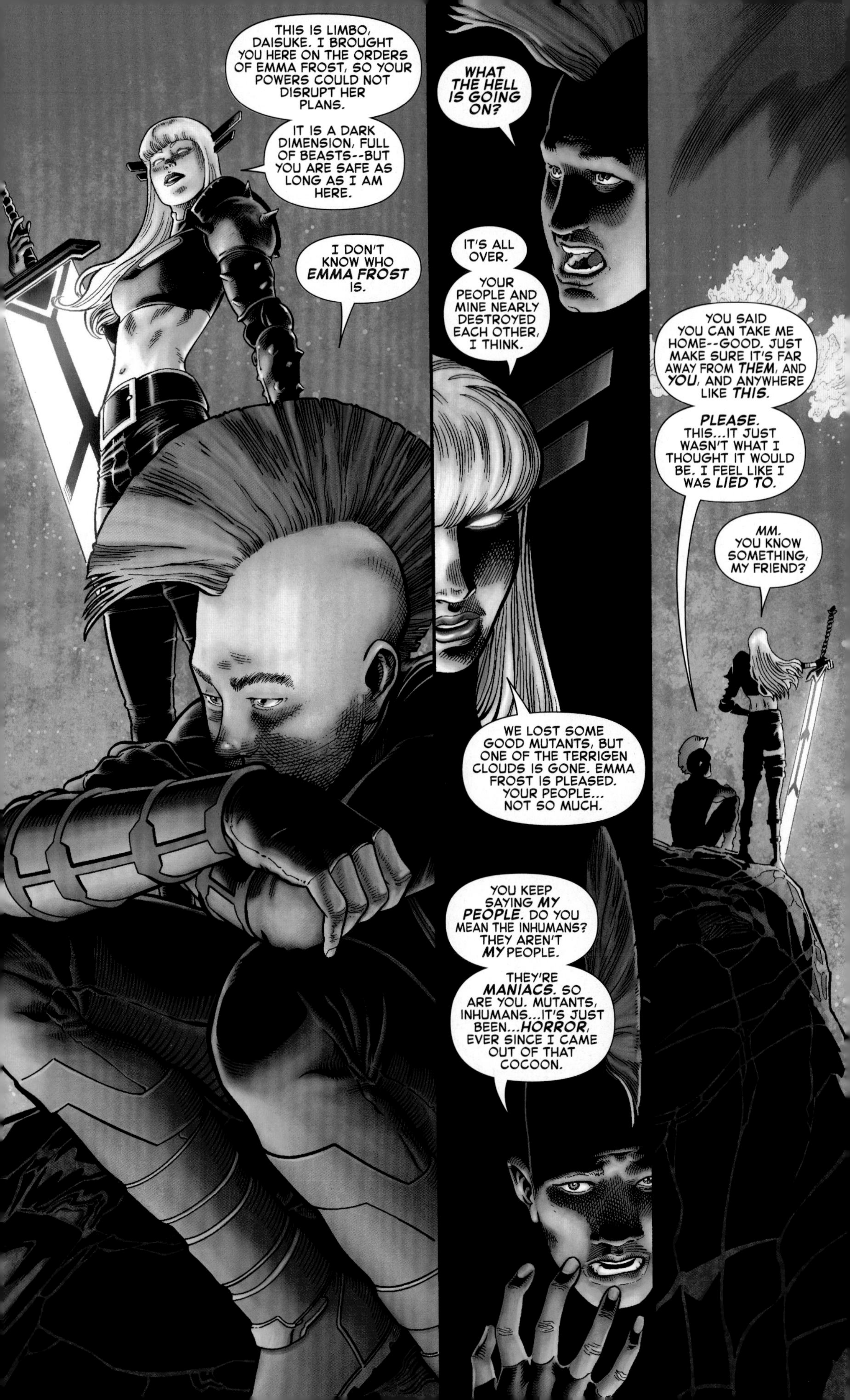
THIS IS LIMBO, DAISUKE. I BROUGHT YOU HERE ON THE ORDERS OF EMMA FROST, SO YOUR POWERS COULD NOT DISRUPT HER PLANS.
IT IS A DARK DIMENSION, FULL OF BEASTS--BUT YOU ARE SAFE AS LONG AS I AM HERE.
I DON'T KNOW WHO EMMA FROST IS.
WHAT THE HELL IS GOING ON?
IT'S ALL OVER.
YOUR PEOPLE AND MINE NEARLY DESTROYED EACH OTHER, I THINK.
WE LOST SOME GOOD MUTANTS, BUT ONE OF THE TERRIGEN CLOUDS IS GONE. EMMA FROST IS PLEASED. YOUR PEOPLE... NOT SO MUCH.
YOU KEEP SAYING MY PEOPLE. DO YOU MEAN THE INHUMANS? THEY AREN'T MY PEOPLE.
THEY'RE MANIACS. SO ARE YOU. MUTANTS, INHUMANS...IT'S JUST BEEN...HORROR, EVER SINCE I CAME OUT OF THAT COCOON.
YOU SAID YOU CAN TAKE ME HOME--GOOD. JUST MAKE SURE IT'S FAR AWAY FROM THEM, AND YOU, AND ANYWHERE LIKE THIS.
PLEASE. THIS...IT JUST WASN'T WHAT I THOUGHT IT WOULD BE. I FEEL LIKE I WAS LIED TO.
MM. YOU KNOW SOMETHING, MY FRIEND?

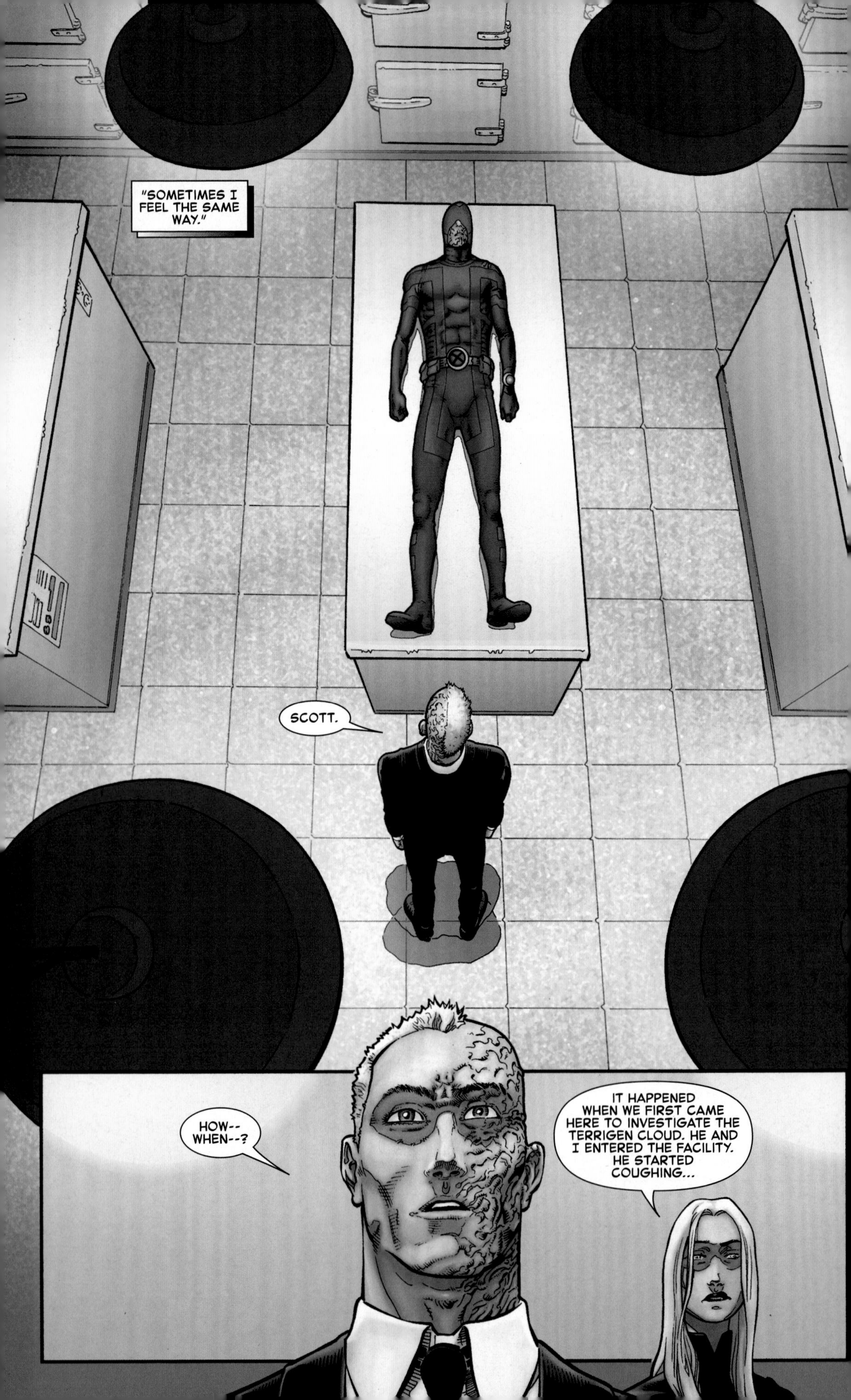
"SOMETIMES I FEEL THE SAME WAY."
SCOTT.
HOW-- WHEN--?
IT HAPPENED WHEN WE FIRST CAME HERE TO INVESTIGATE THE TERRIGEN CLOUD. HE AND I ENTERED THE FACILITY. HE STARTED COUGHING...

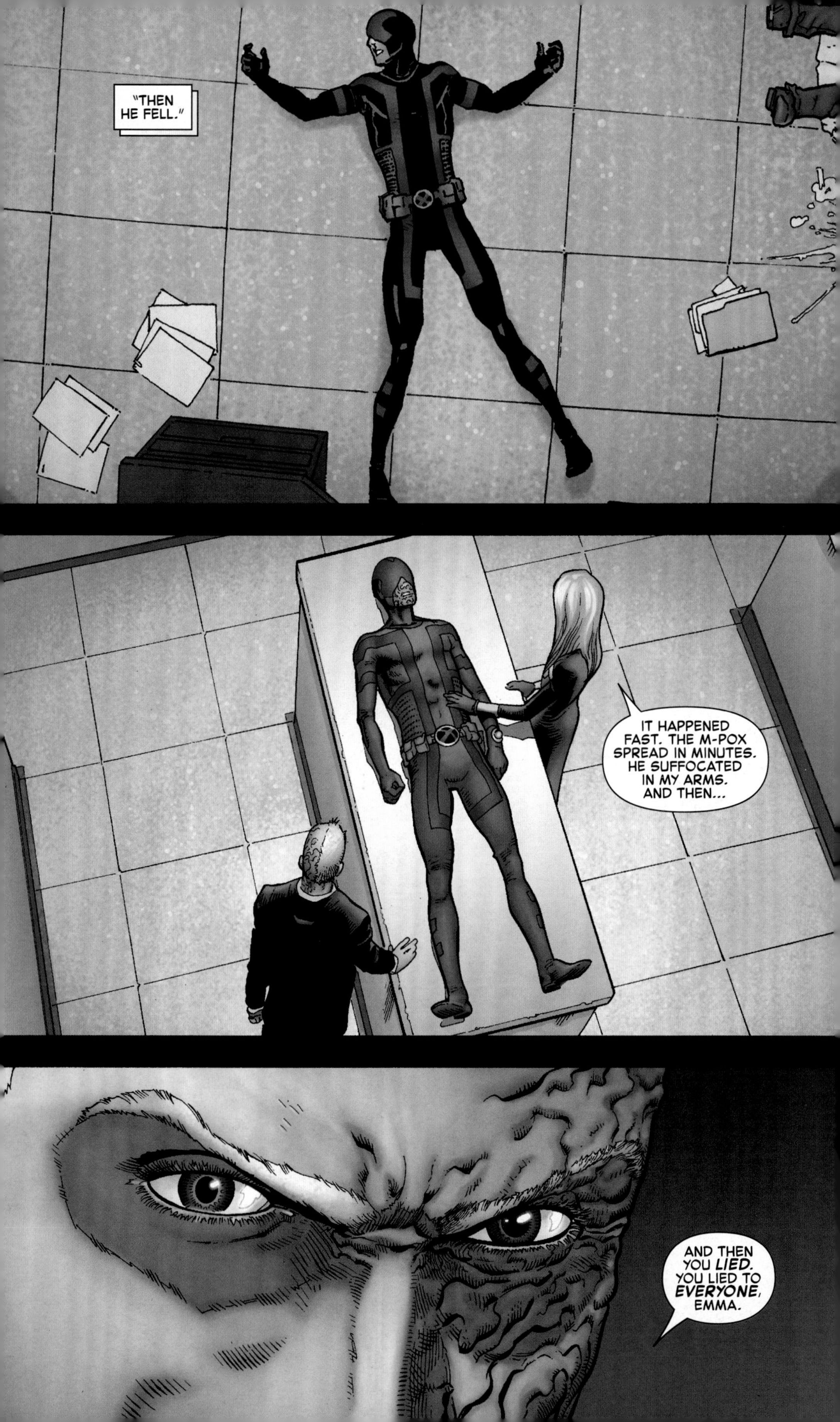
"THEN HE FELL."
IT HAPPENED FAST. THE M-POX SPREAD IN MINUTES. HE SUFFOCATED IN MY ARMS. AND THEN...
AND THEN YOU LIED. YOU LIED TO EVERYONE, EMMA.

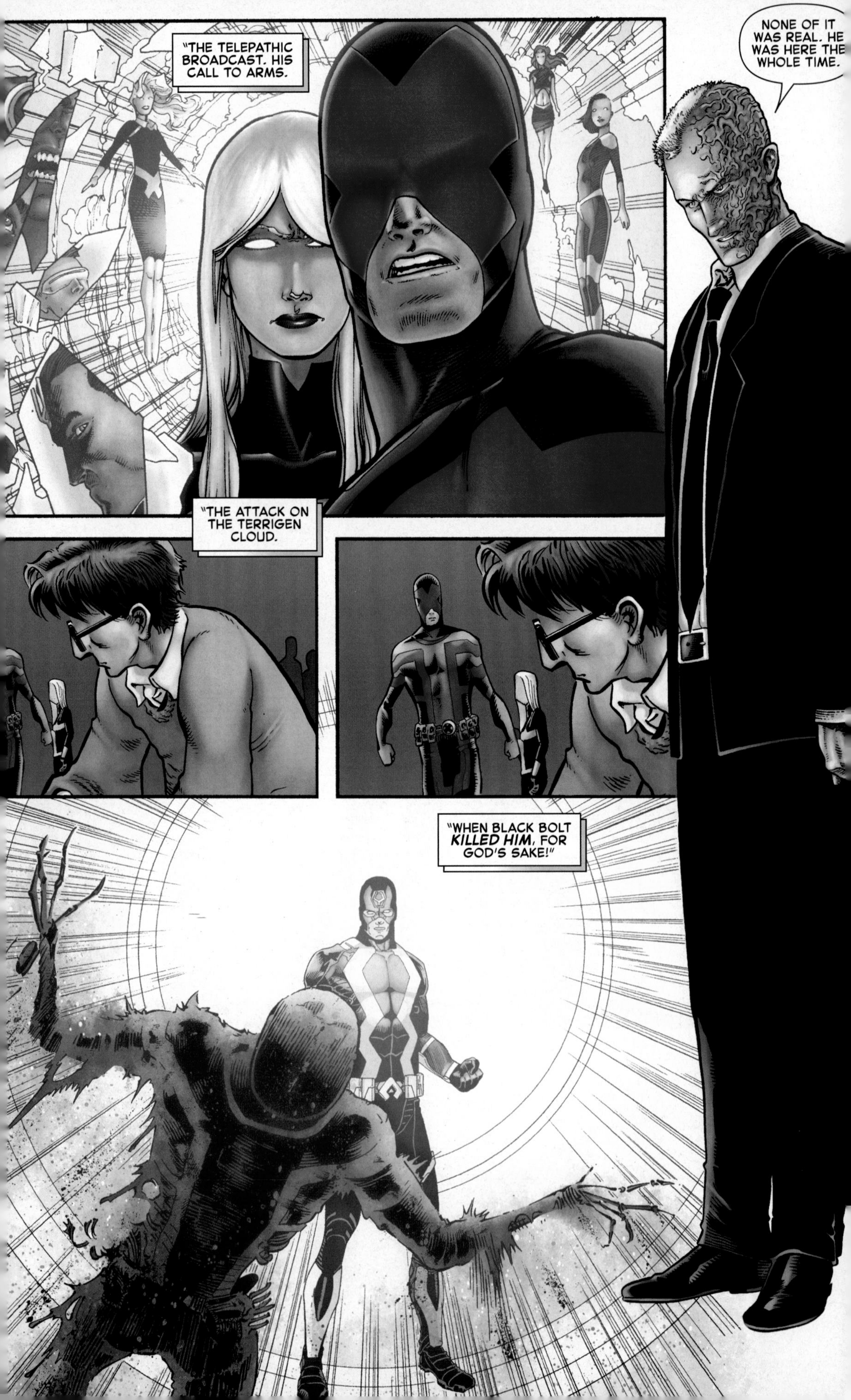
"THE TELEPATHIC BROADCAST. HIS CALL TO ARMS.
NONE OF IT WAS REAL. HE WAS HERE THE WHOLE TIME.
"THE ATTACK ON THE TERRIGEN CLOUD.
"WHEN BLACK BOLT *KILLED HIM*, FOR GOD'S SAKE!"

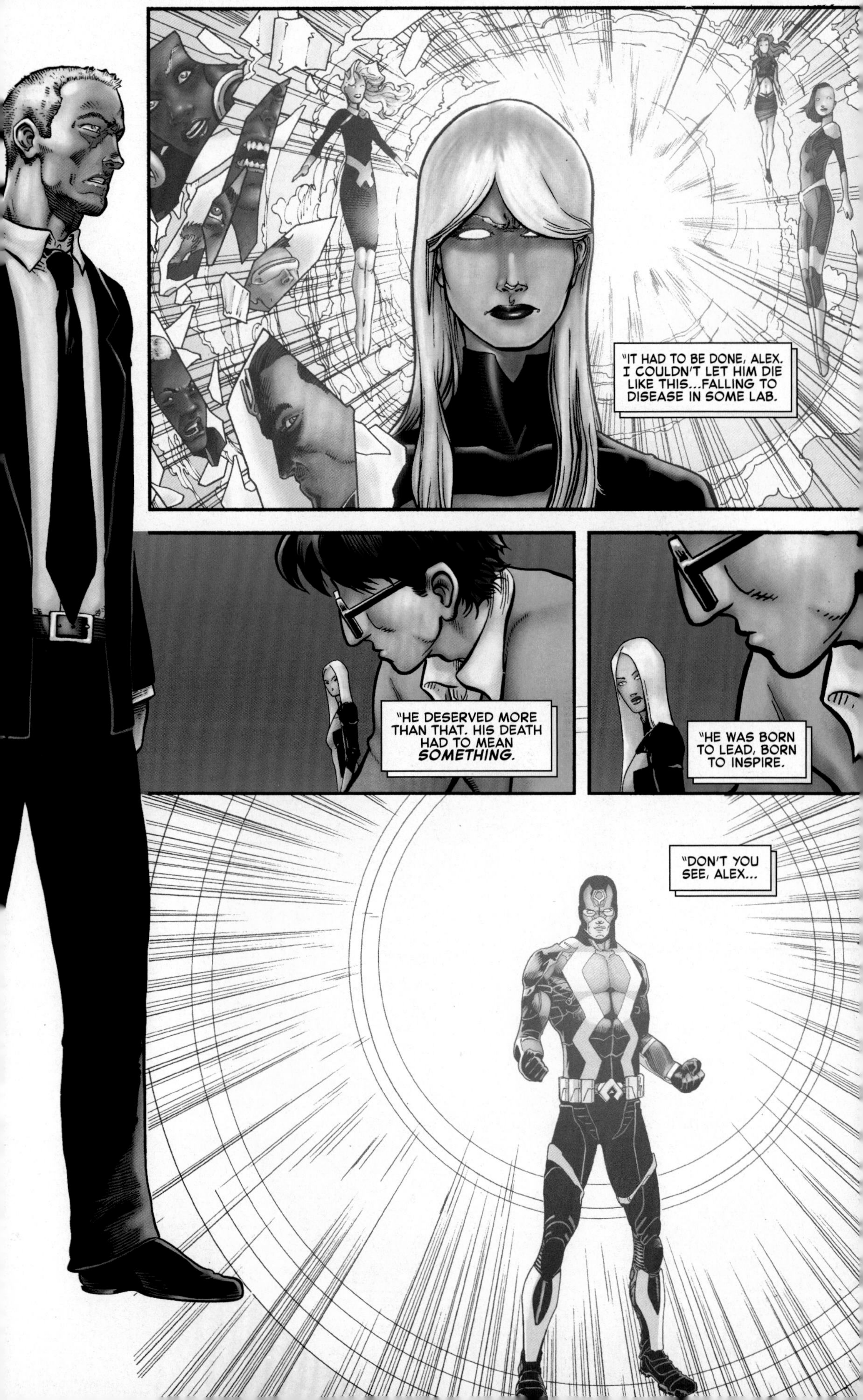
"IT HAD TO BE DONE, ALEX. I COULDN'T LET HIM DIE LIKE THIS...FALLING TO DISEASE IN SOME LAB.
"HE DESERVED MORE THAN THAT. HIS DEATH HAD TO MEAN *SOMETHING.*
"HE WAS BORN TO LEAD, BORN TO INSPIRE.
"DON'T YOU SEE, ALEX...

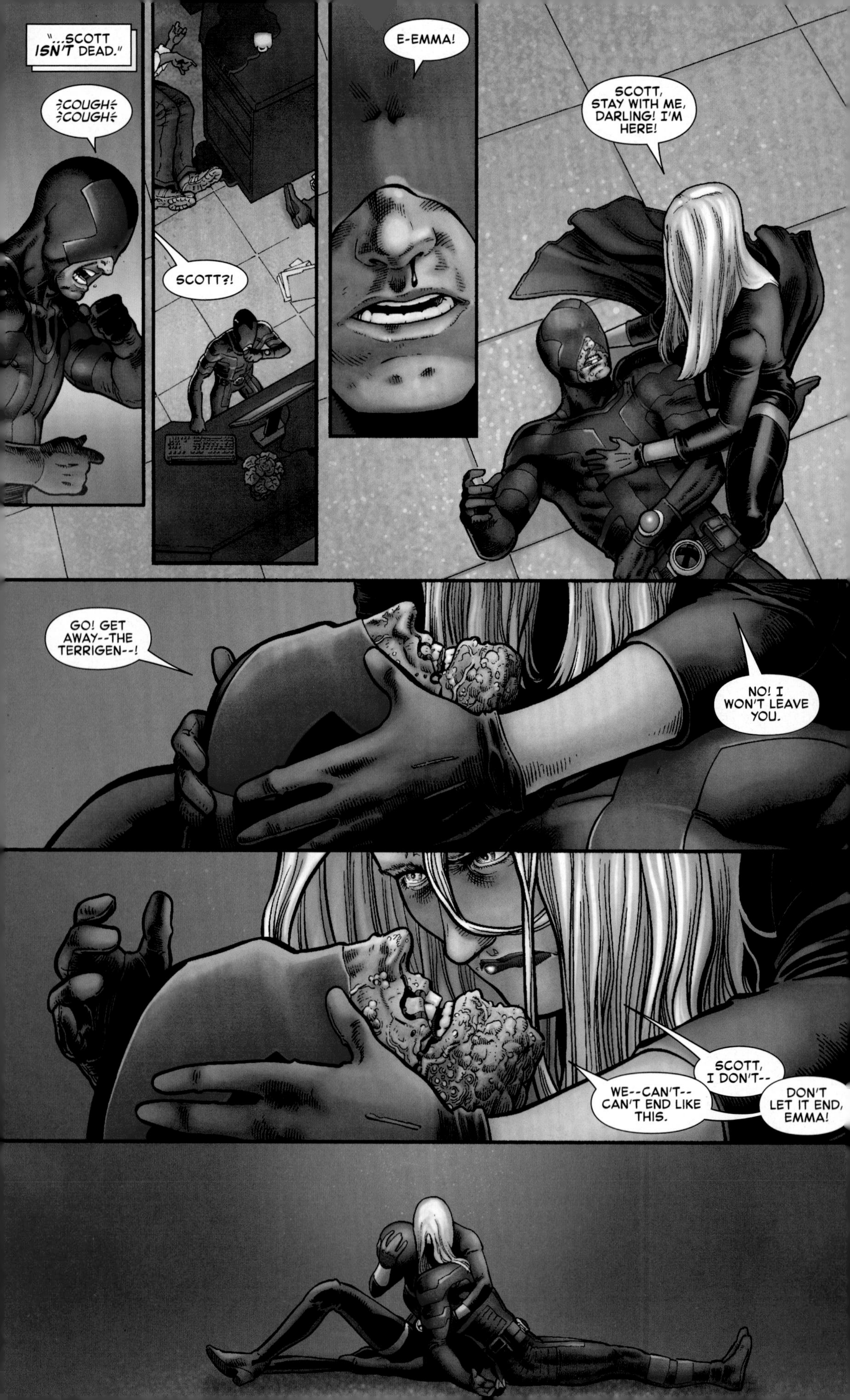
"...SCOTT ISN'T DEAD."
COUGH COUGH
SCOTT?!
E-EMMA!
SCOTT, STAY WITH ME, DARLING! I'M HERE!
GO! GET AWAY--THE TERRIGEN--!
NO! I WON'T LEAVE YOU.
SCOTT, I DON'T--
WE--CAN'T--CAN'T END LIKE THIS.
DON'T LET IT END, EMMA!

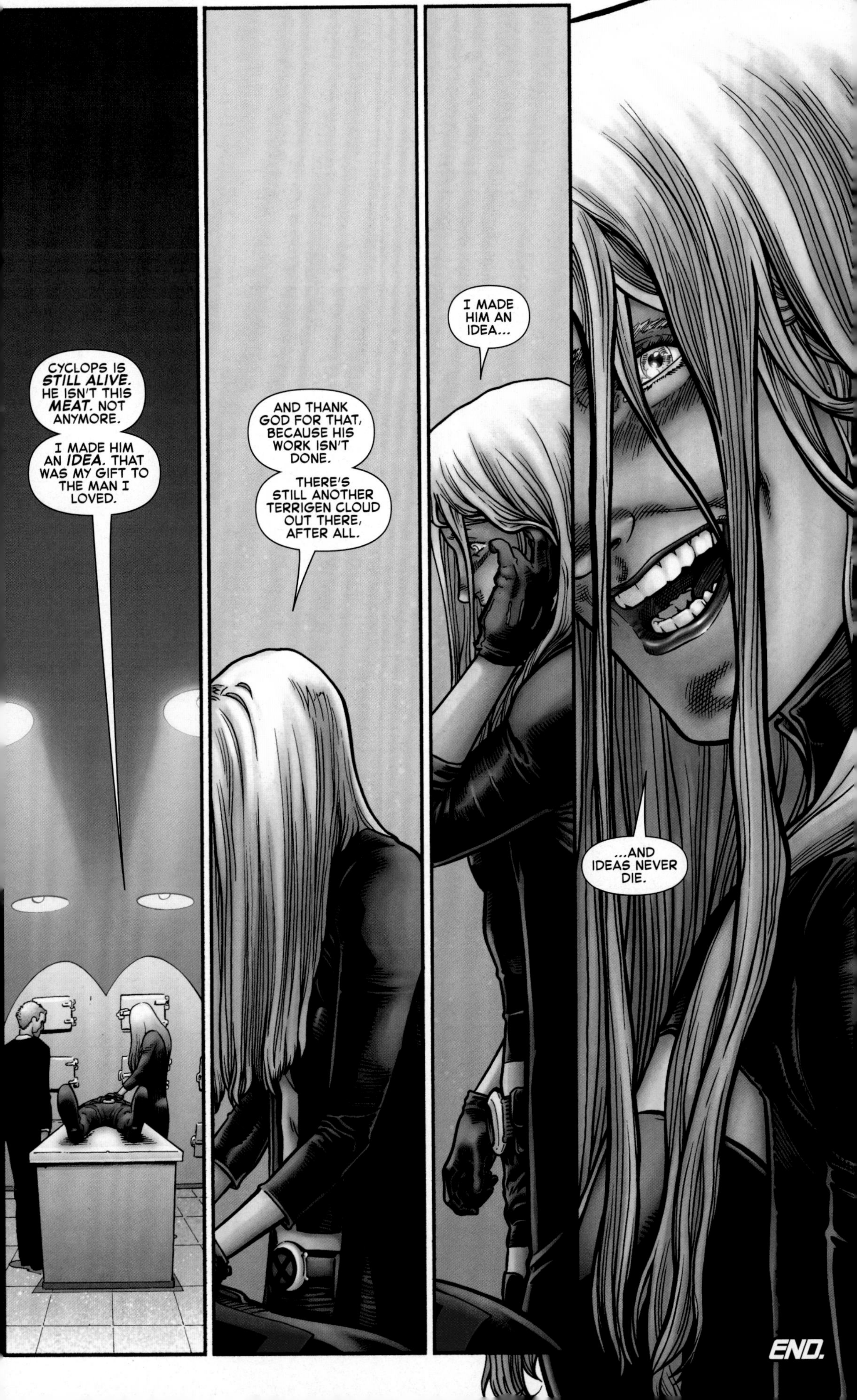
CYCLOPS IS STILL ALIVE. HE ISN'T THIS MEAT. NOT ANYMORE.
I MADE HIM AN IDEA. THAT WAS MY GIFT TO THE MAN I LOVED.
AND THANK GOD FOR THAT, BECAUSE HIS WORK ISN'T DONE.
THERE'S STILL ANOTHER TERRIGEN CLOUD OUT THERE, AFTER ALL.
I MADE HIM AN IDEA...
...AND IDEAS NEVER DIE.
END.

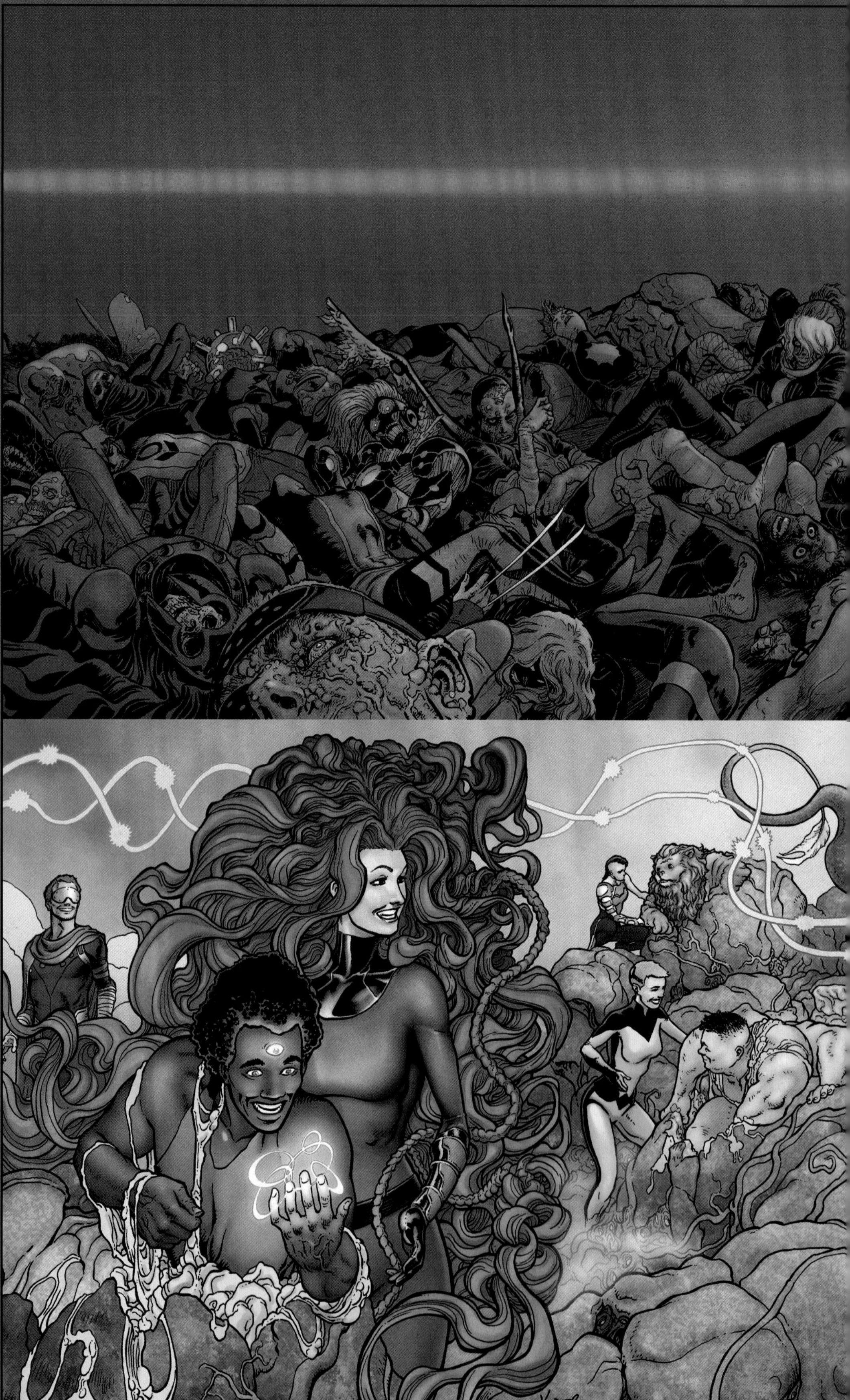
KUDER

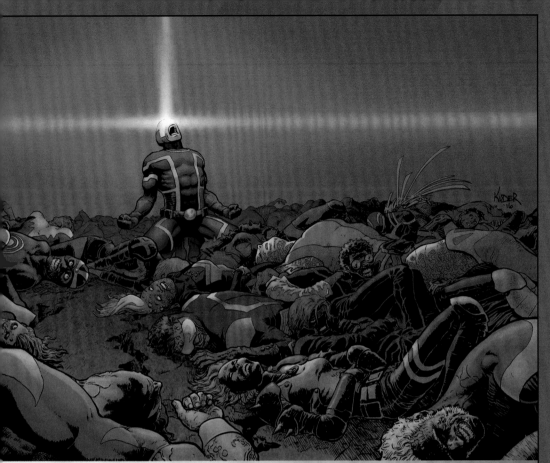

AARON KUDER & **MORRY HOLLOWELL**
1 variant

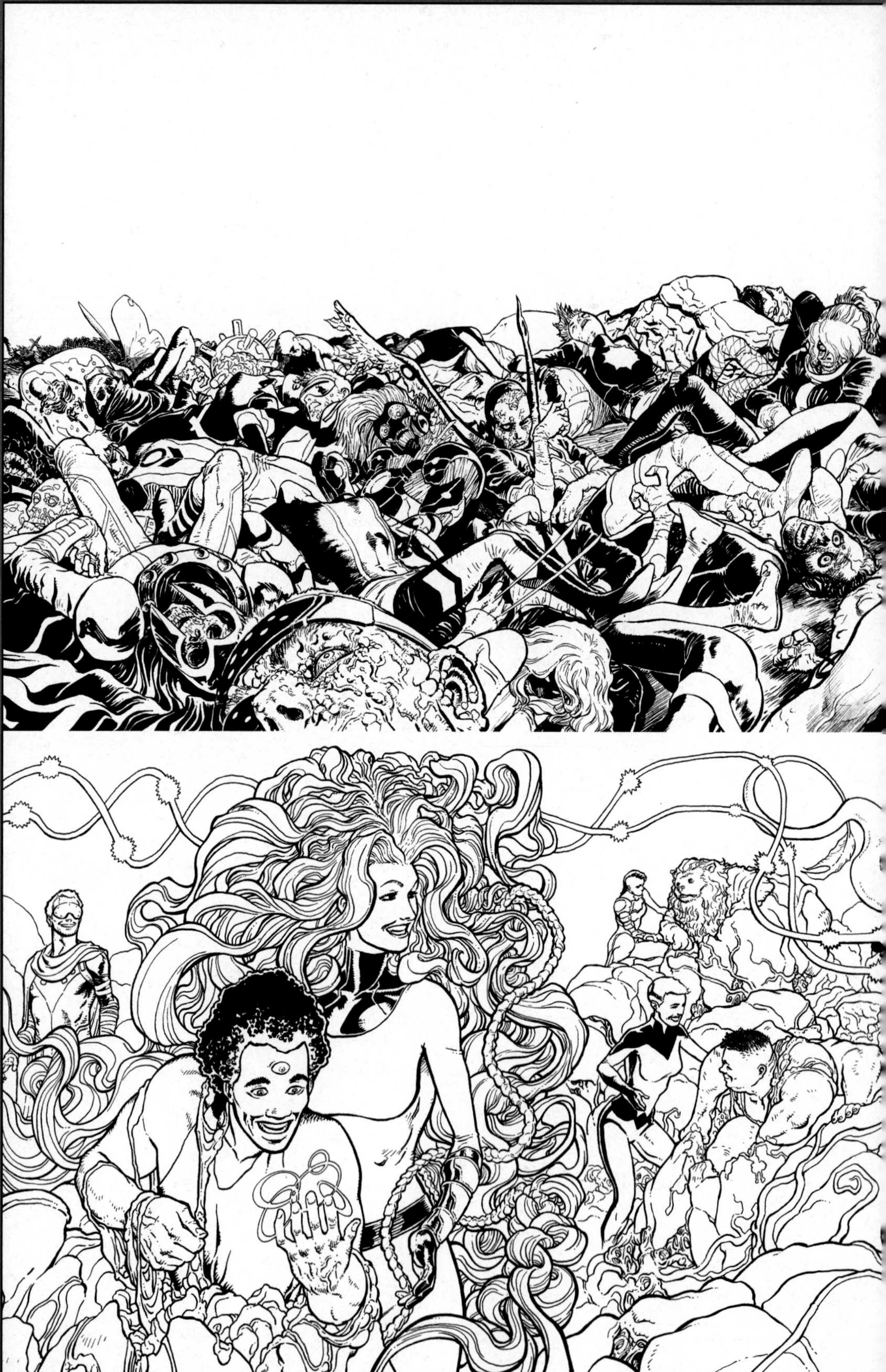

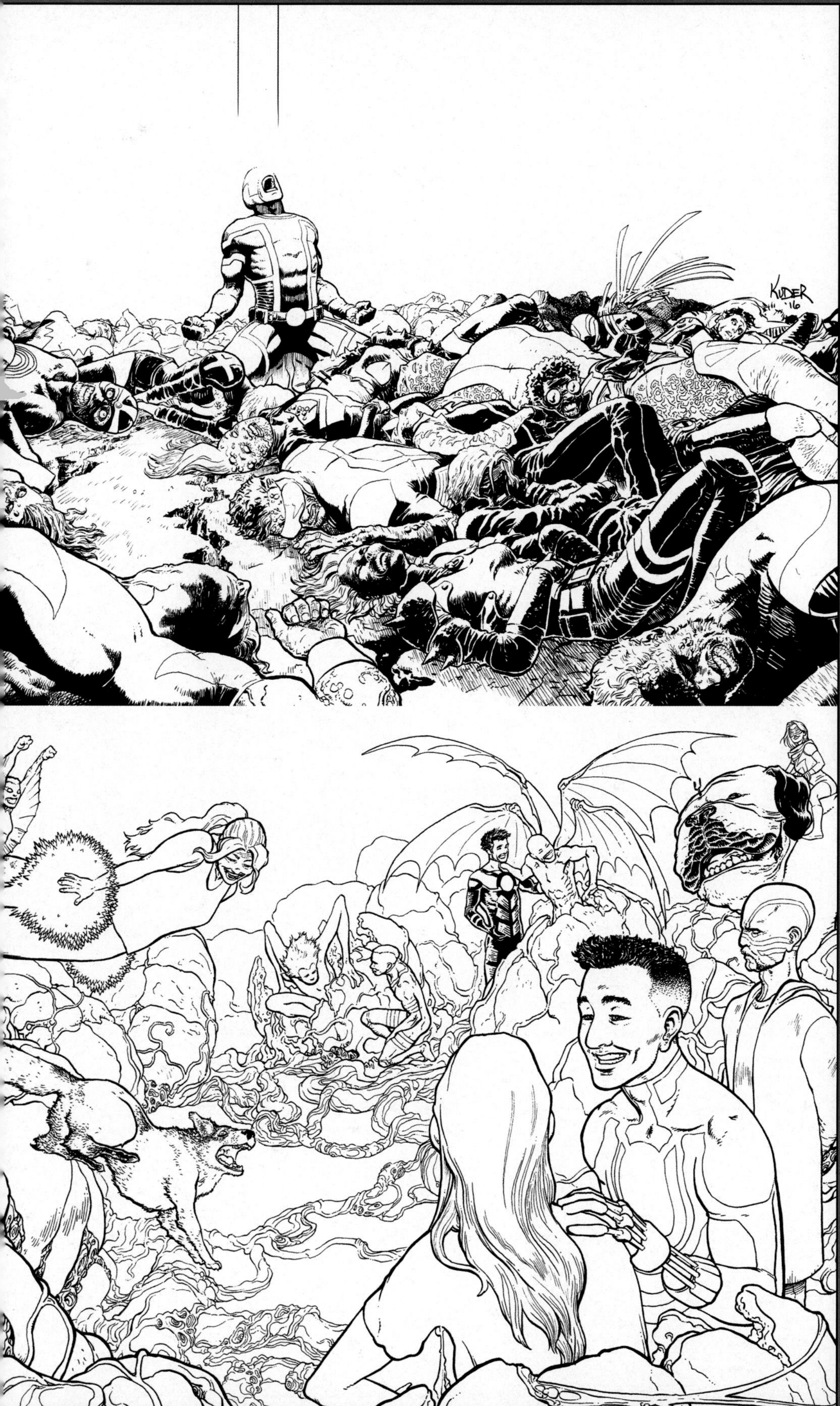
KUDER '16

AARON KUDER

1 black & white variant

MIKE CHOI & **DAN BROWN**
1-4 connecting variants

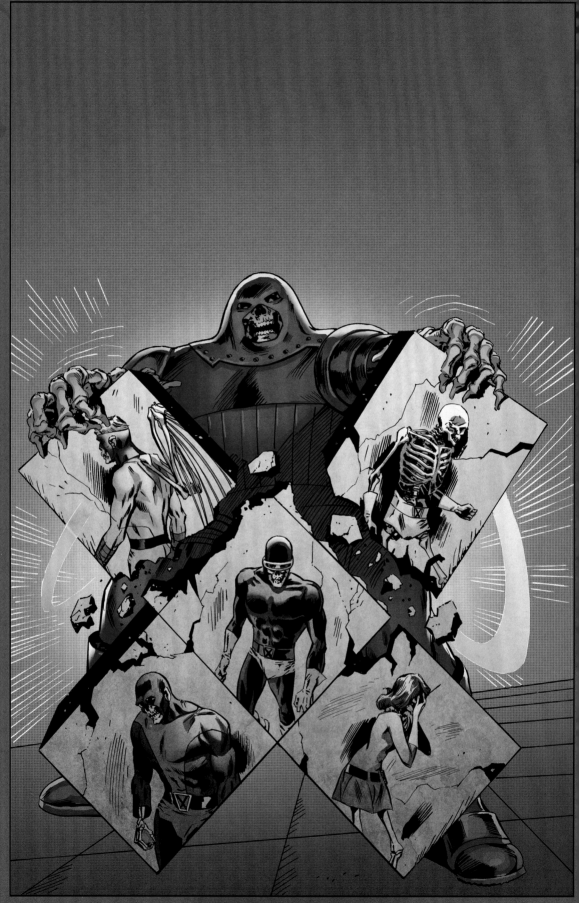

BUTCH GUICE & **RACHELLE ROSENBERG**
1 variant

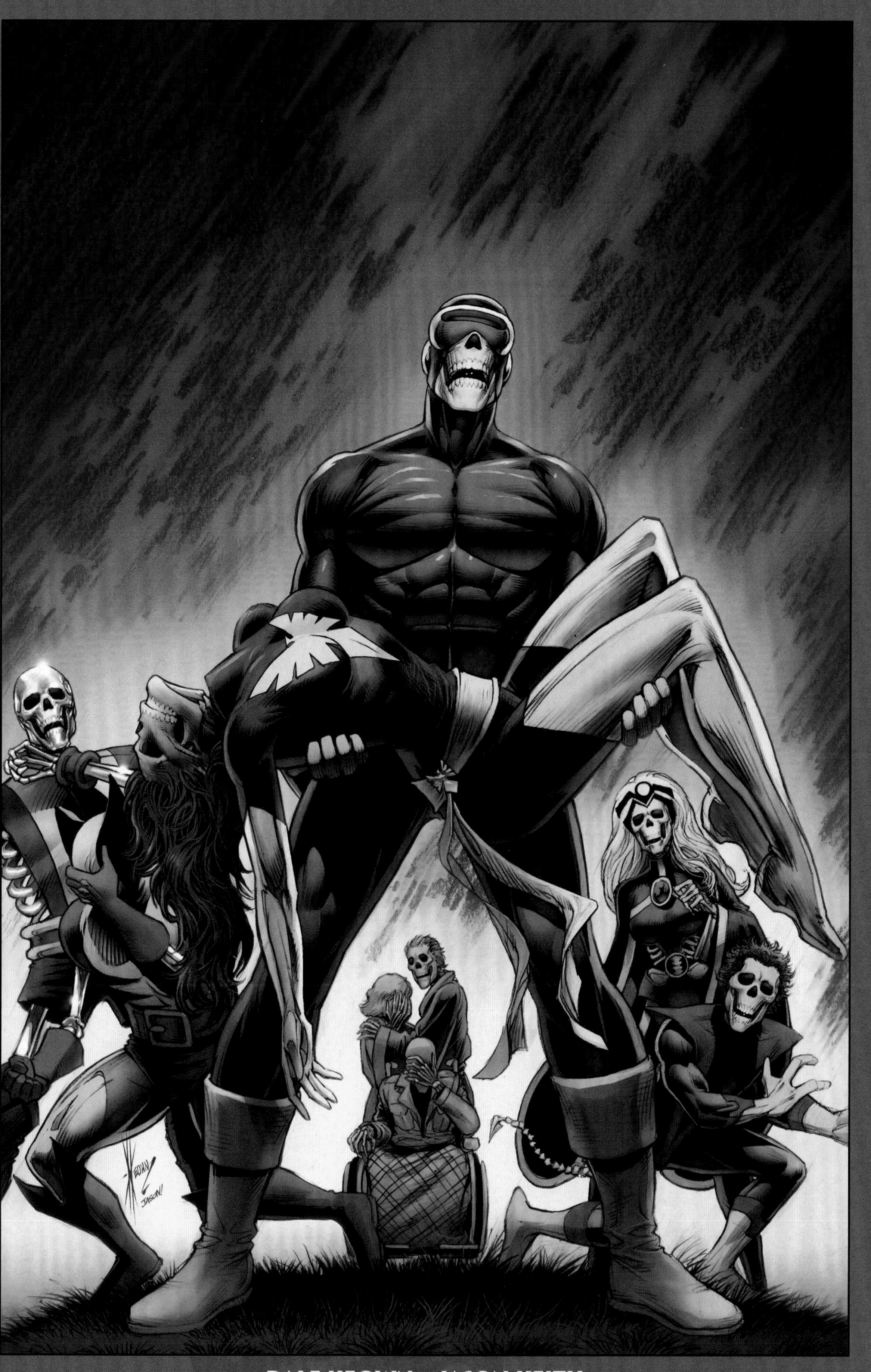

DALE KEOWN & JASON KEITH

2 variant

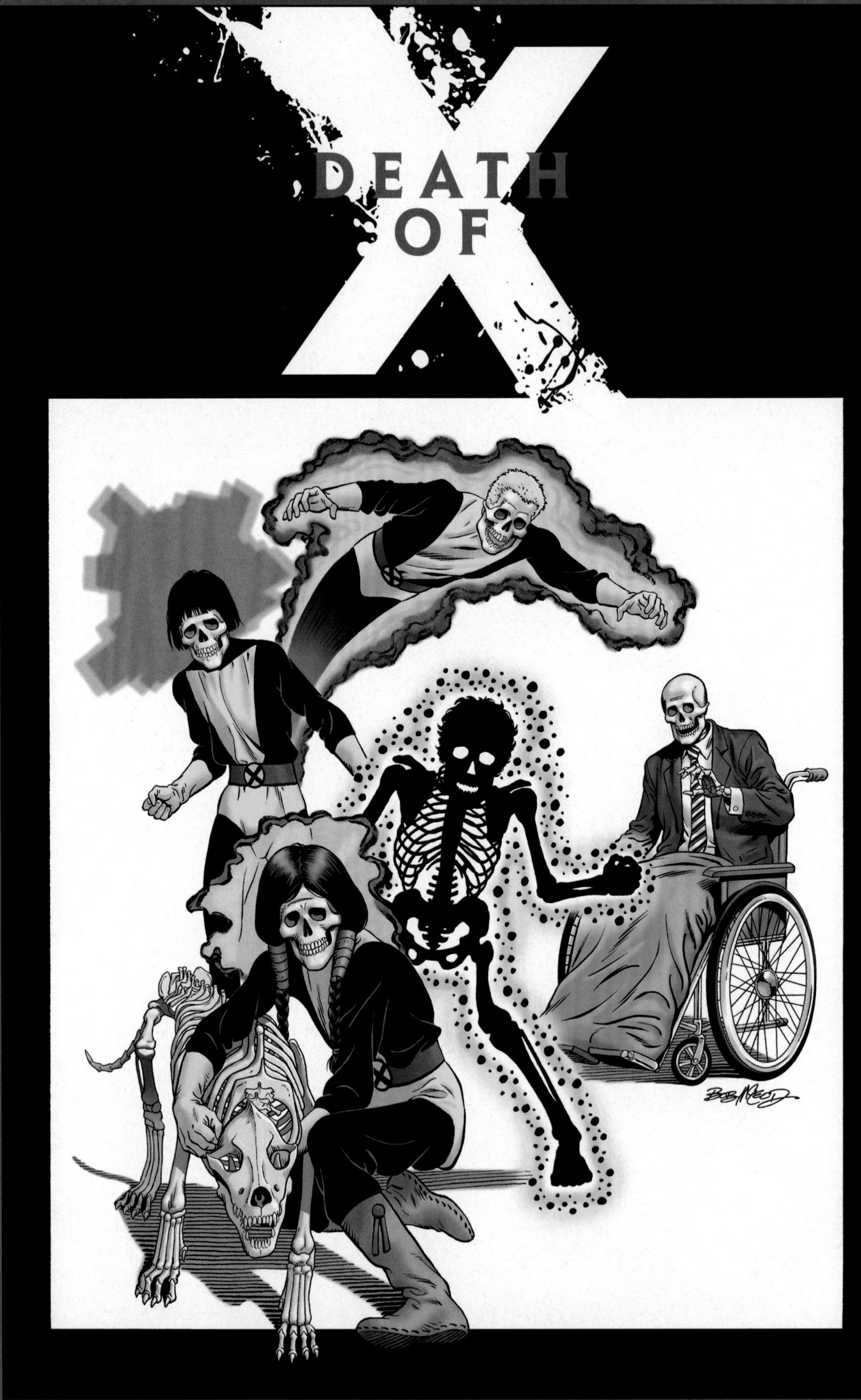
DEATH
OF
X
BOB McLEOD

BOB McLEOD

3 variant

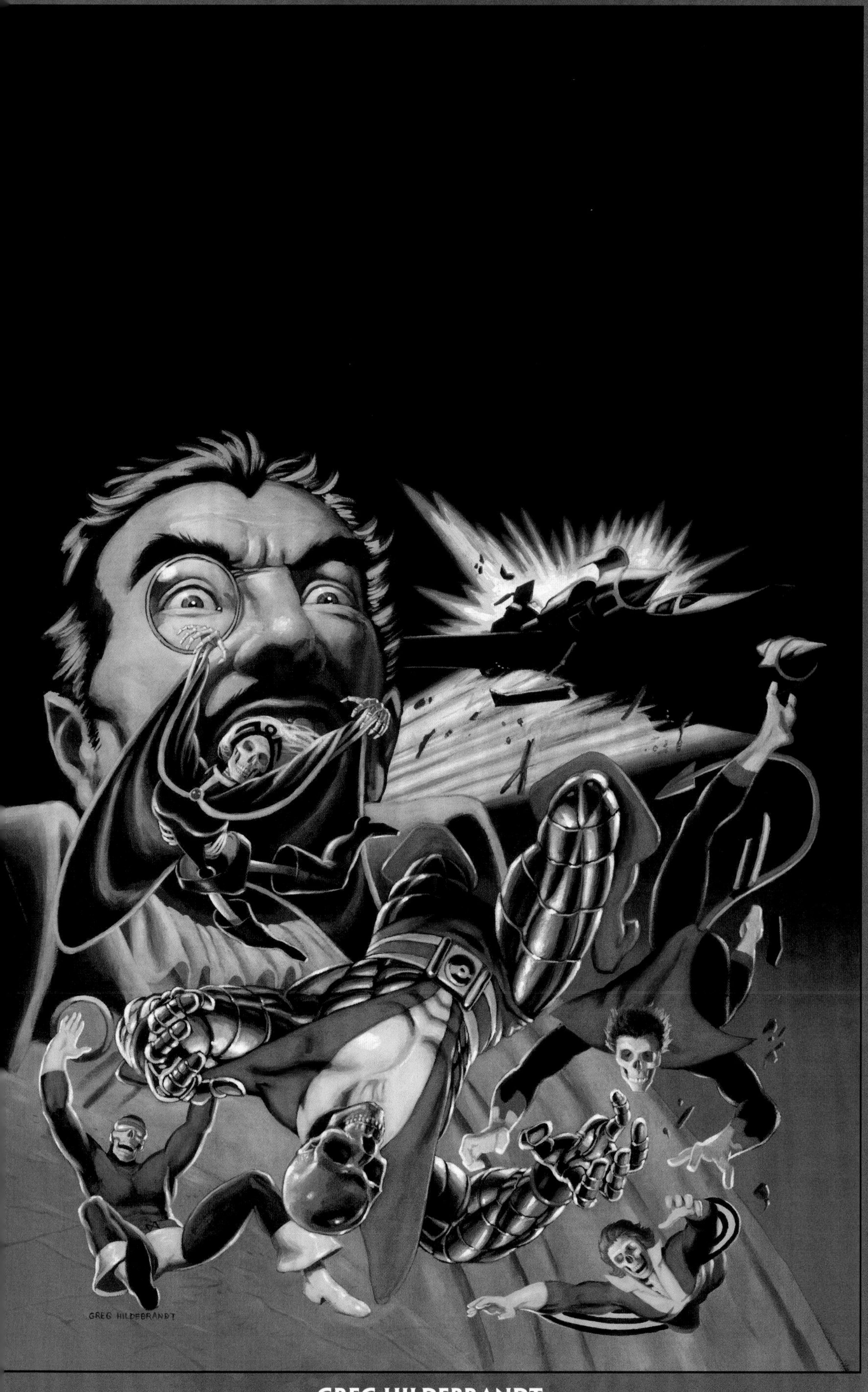
GREG HILDEBRANDT

GREG HILDEBRANDT

4 variant

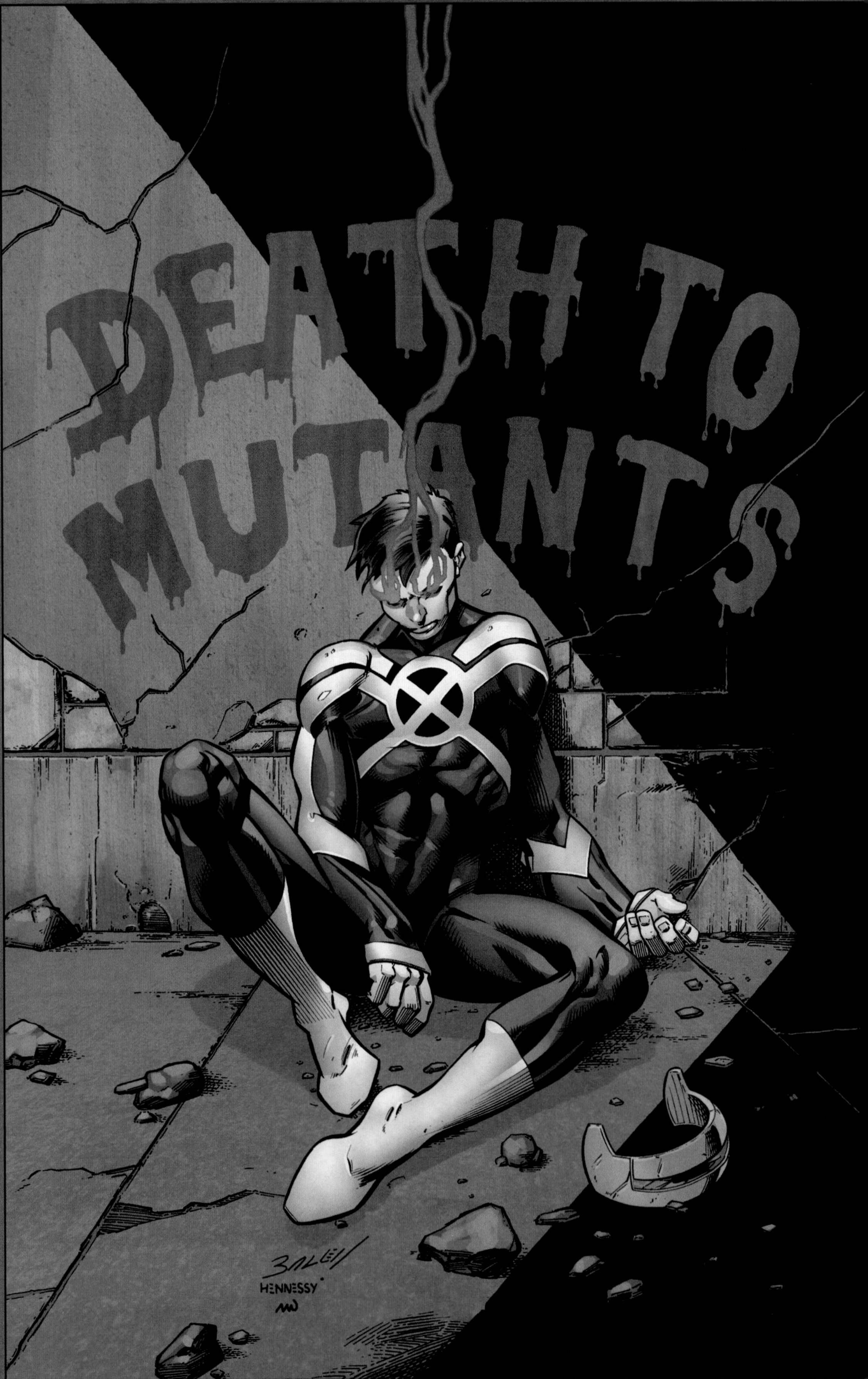
DEATH TO MUTANTS
BAGLEY
HENNESSY
NW

MARK BAGLEY, ANDREW HENNESSY & NOLAN WOODARD

All-New X-Men 11 Death of X variant

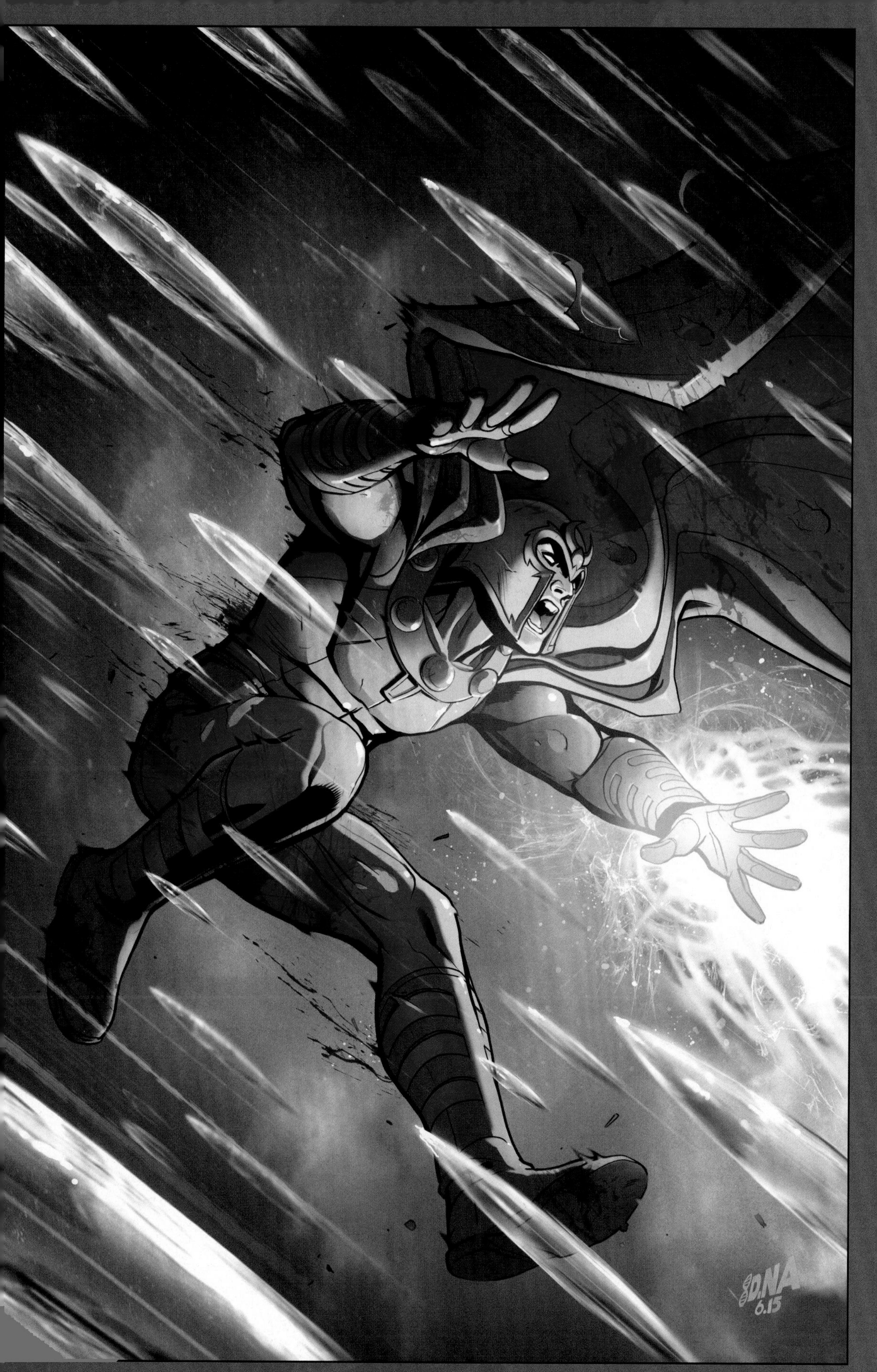
D.NA
6.15

DAVID NAKAYAMA

All-New All-Different Avengers 12 Death of X variant

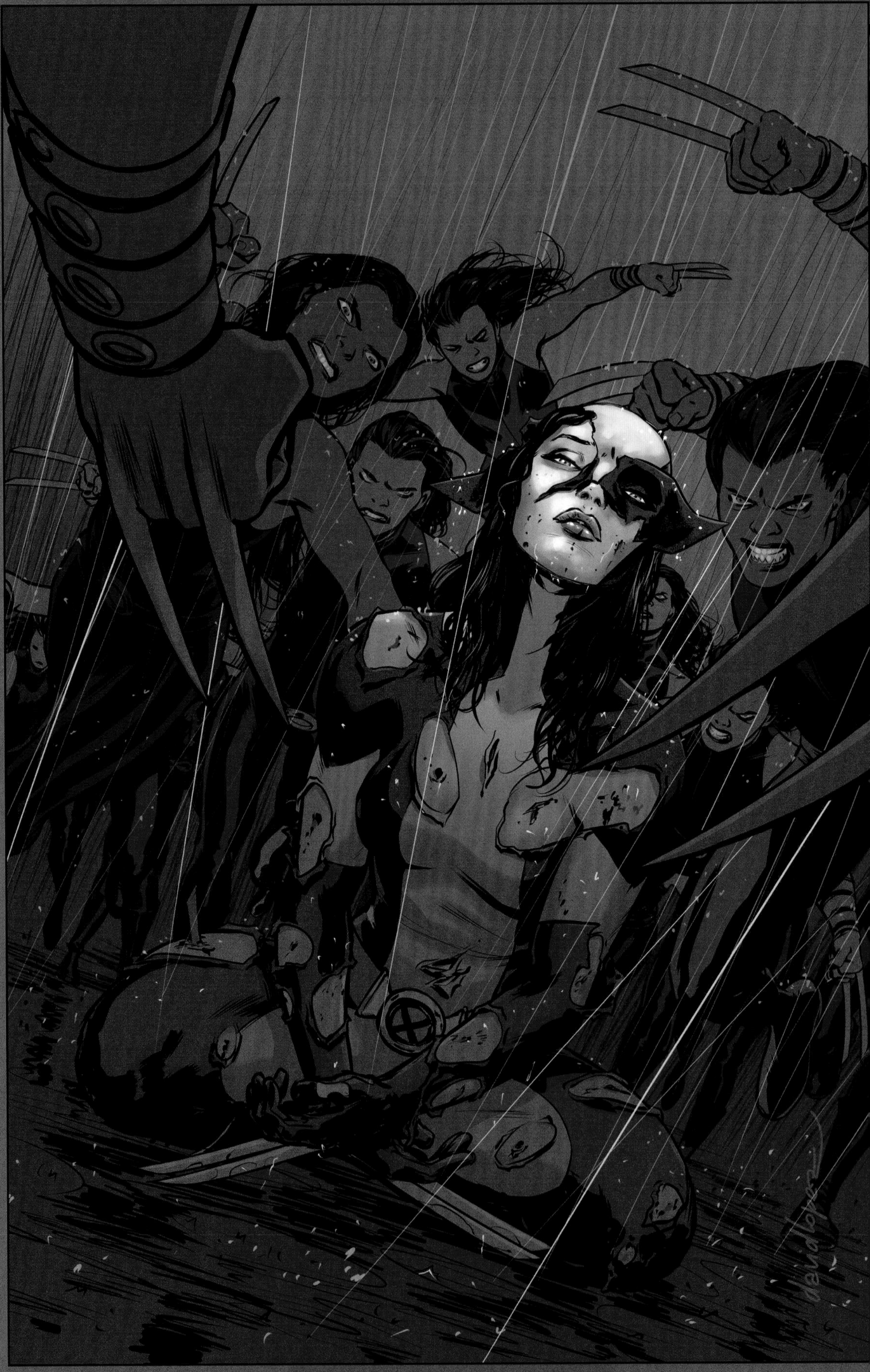

DAVID LOPEZ

Amazing Spider-Man 15 Death of X variant

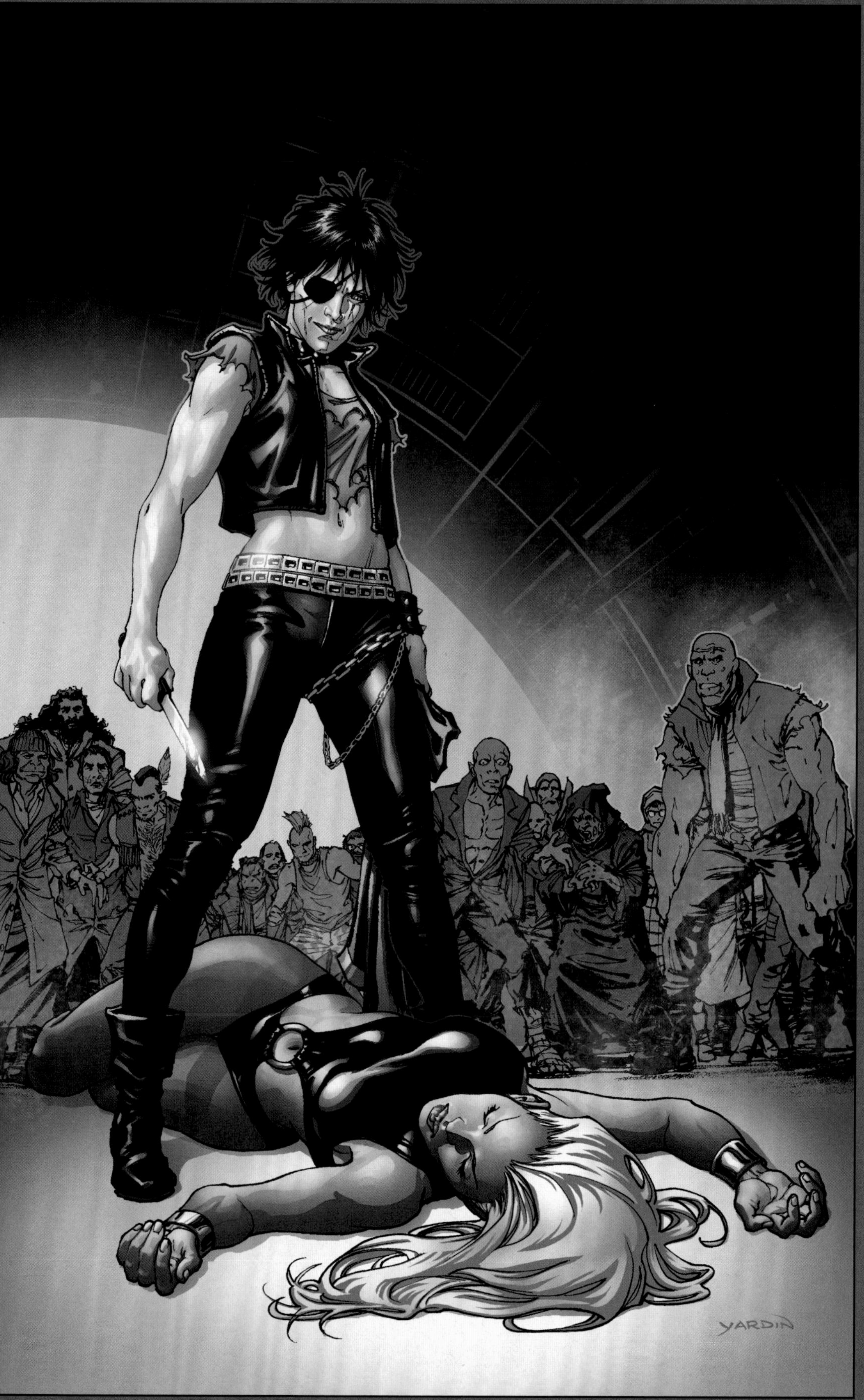
YARDIN

DAVID YARDIN

Black Panther 4 Death of X variant

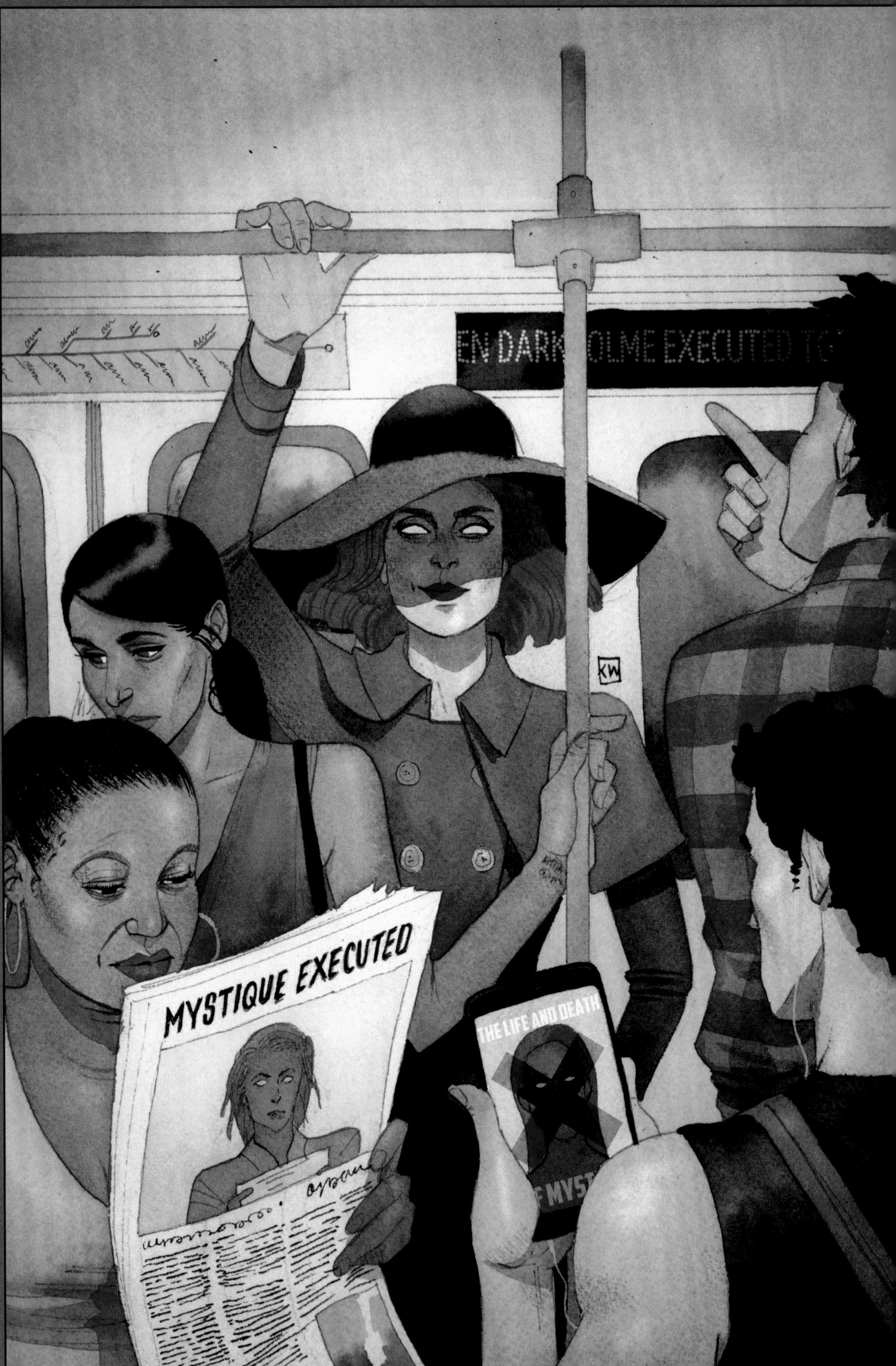
EN DARK OLME EXECUTED T
MYSTIQUE EXECUTED
THE LIFE AND DEATH
F MYST

KEVIN WADA

Steve Rogers: Captain America 3 Death of X variant

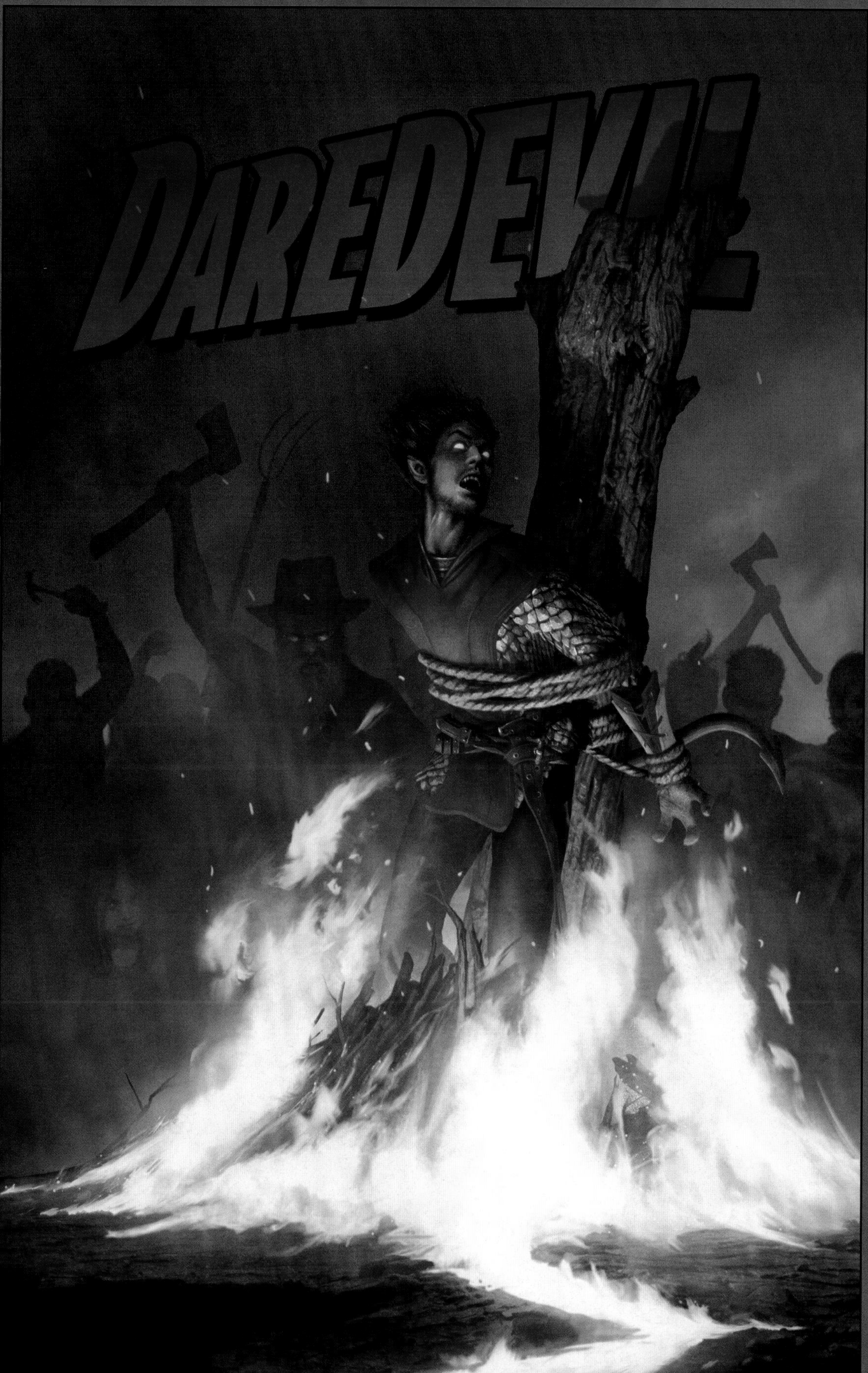
DAREDEVIL

RAHZZAH

Daredevil 9 Death of X variant

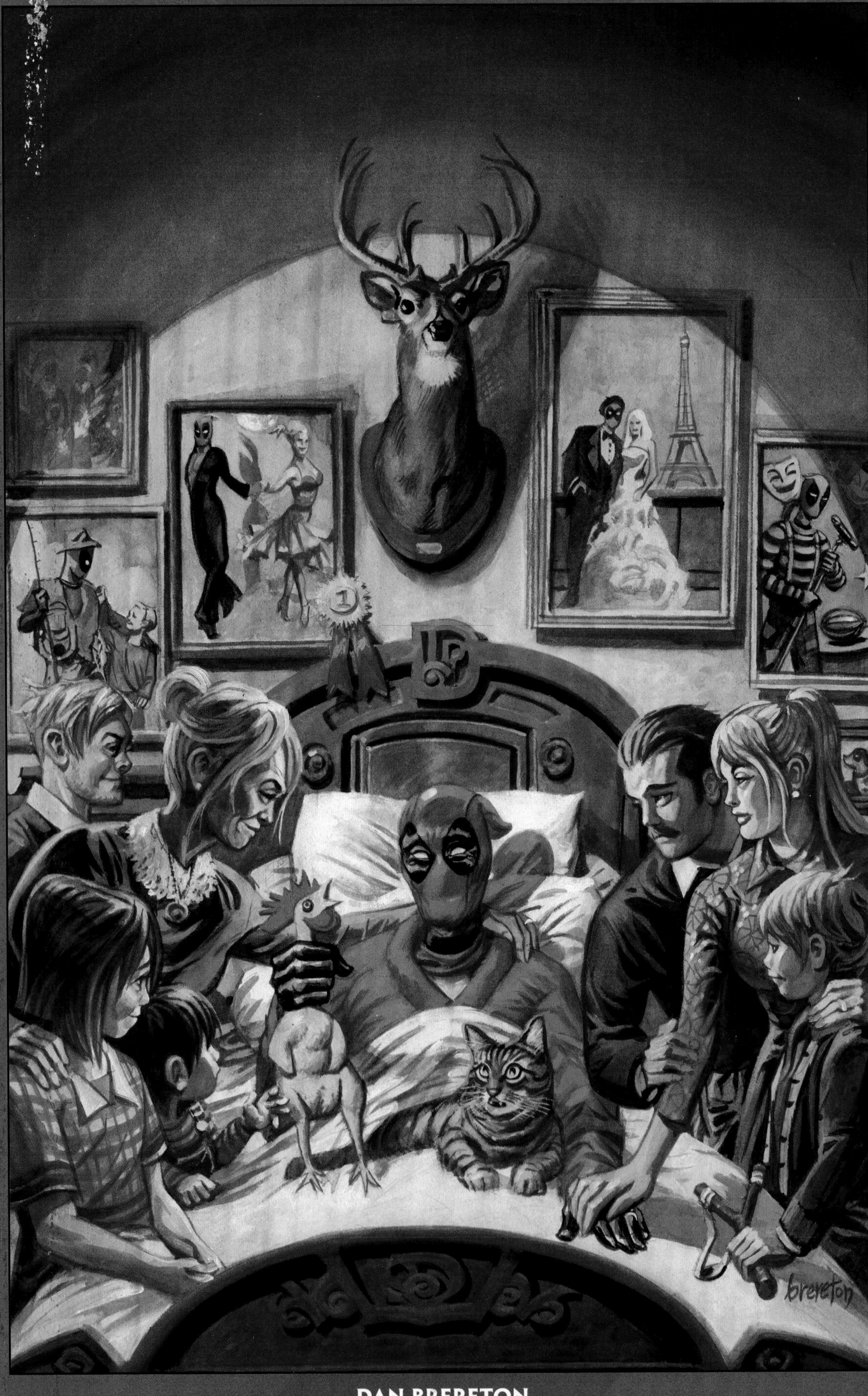

breretón

DAN BRERETON

Deadpool 15 Death of X variant

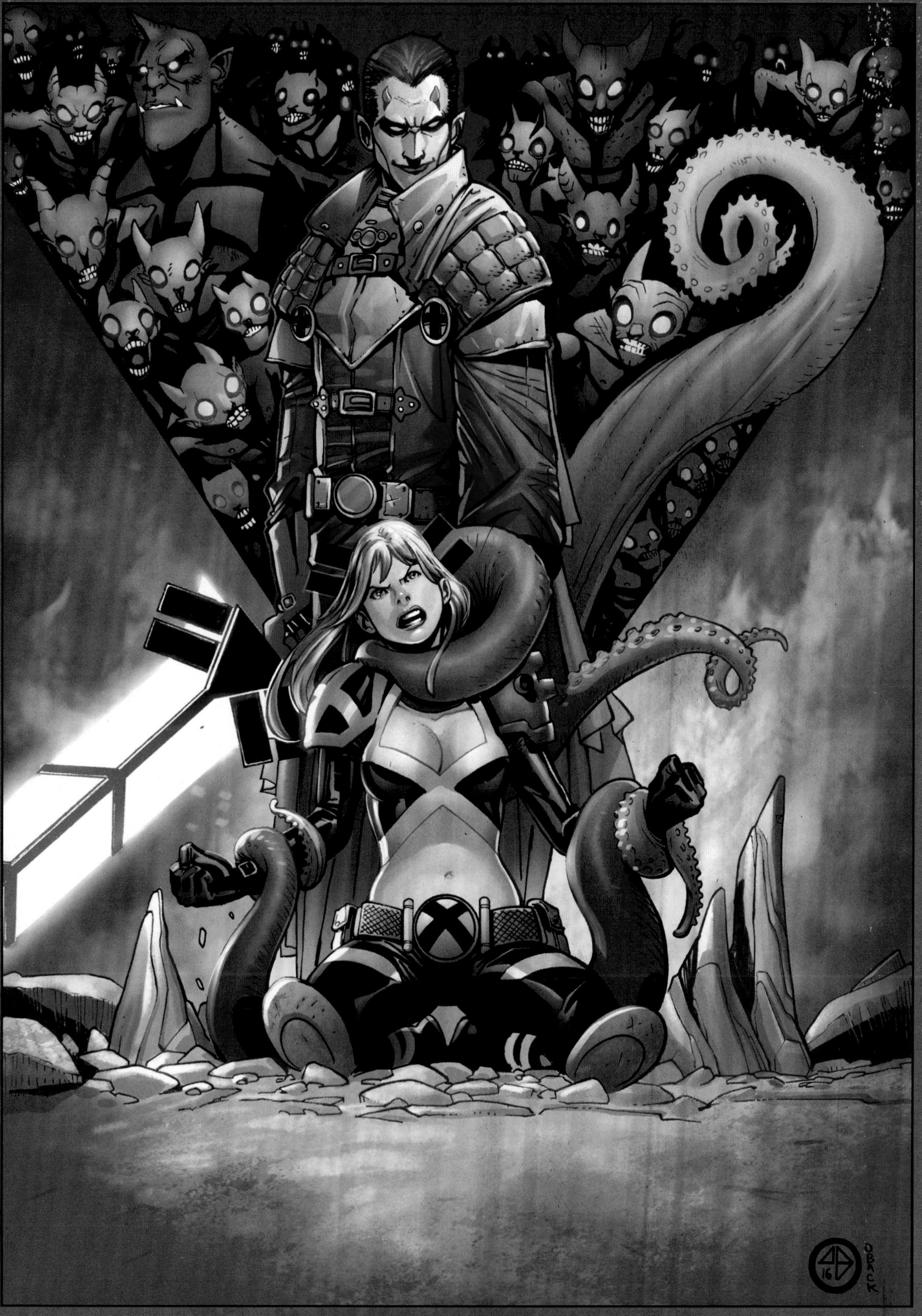

ANDREA BROCCARDO & **SONIA OBACK**

Doctor Strange 10 Death of X variant

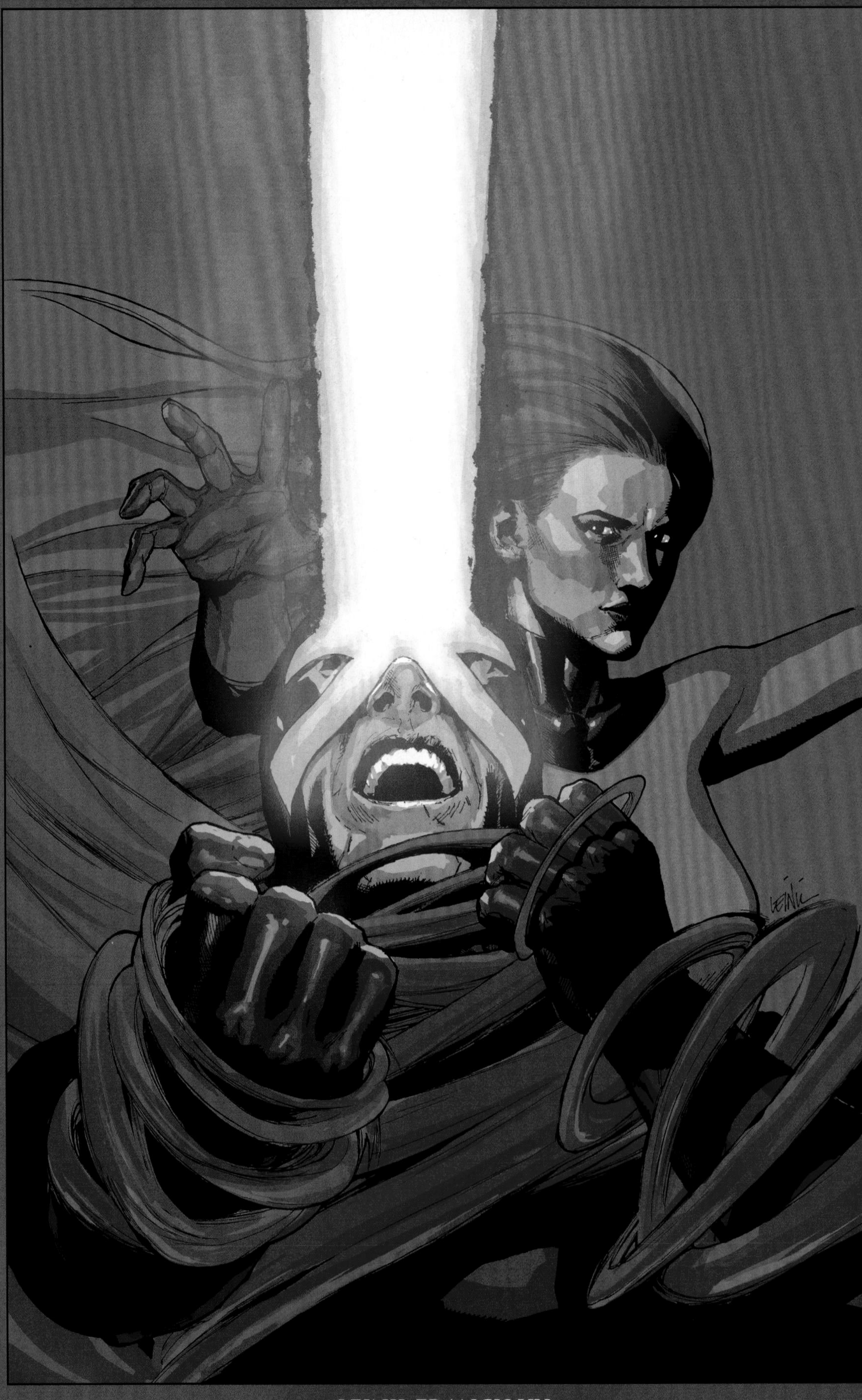

LEINIL FRANCIS YU

Extraordinary X-Men 12 Death of X variant

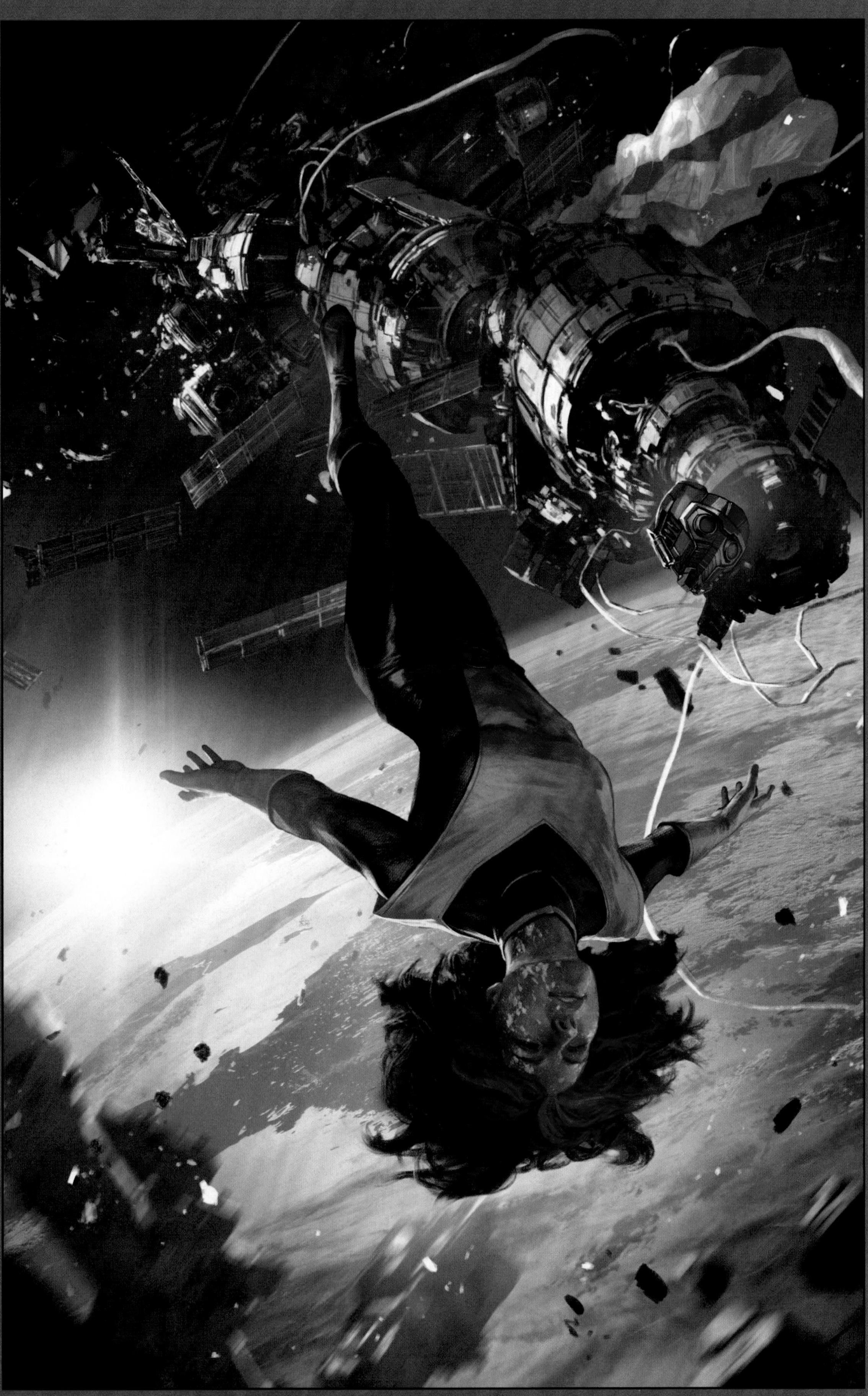

SKAN SRISUWAN

Guardians of the Galaxy 10 Death of X variant

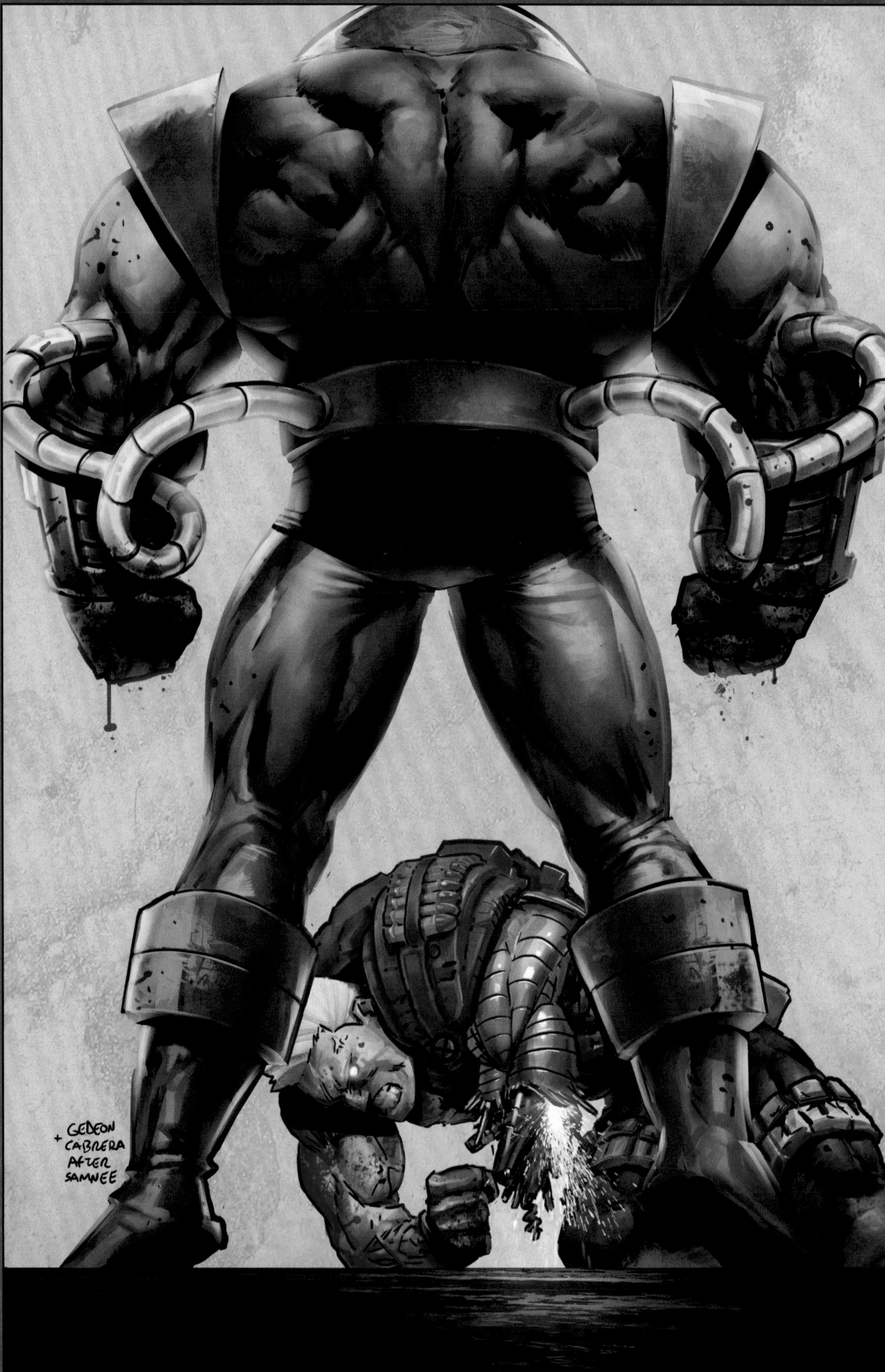
GEDEON
+ CABRERA
AFTER
SAMNEE

JUAN GEDEON & **CARLOS CABRERA**

Invincible Iron Man 11 Death of X variant

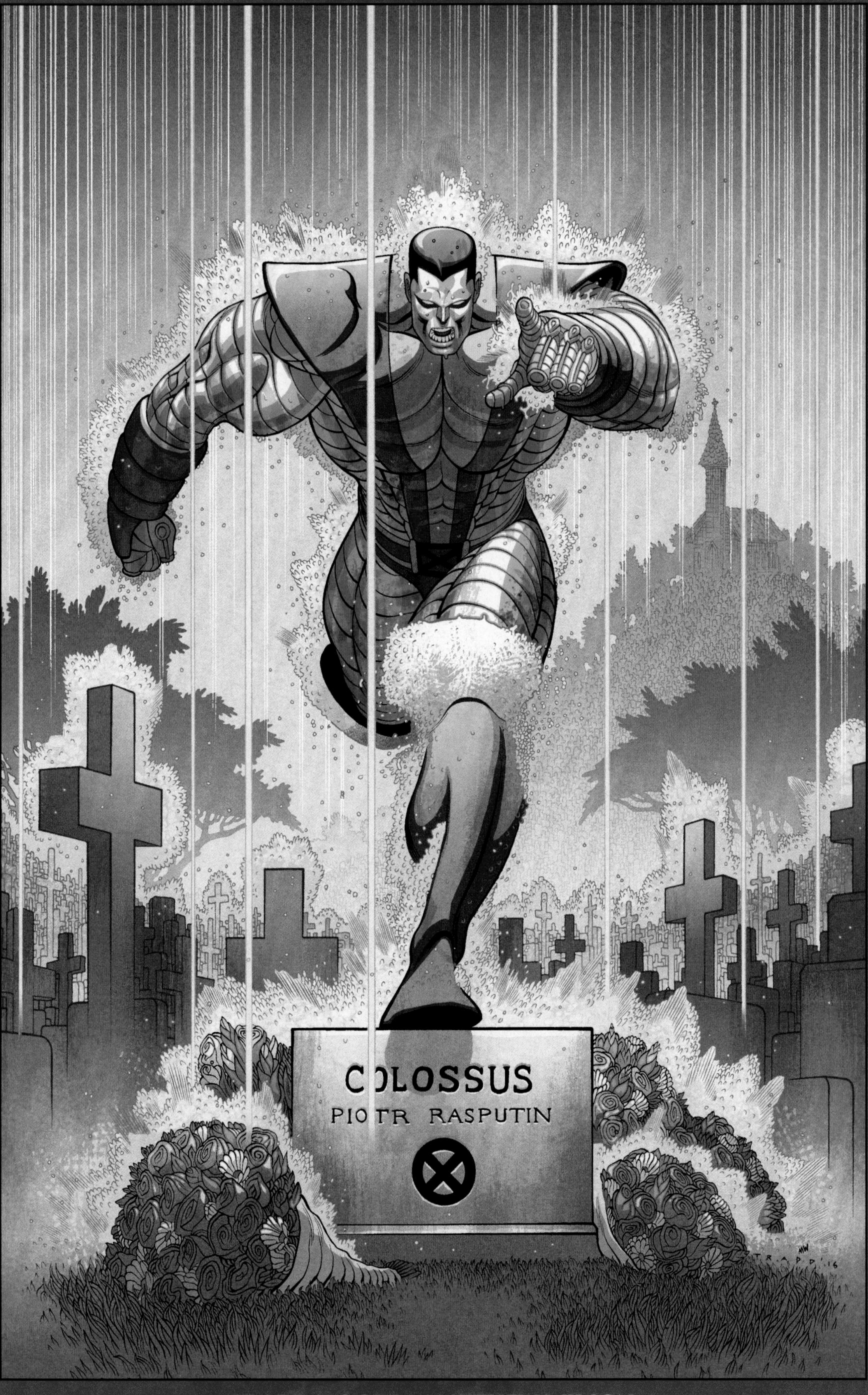
COLOSSUS
PIOTR RASPUTIN

TRADD MOORE & **MATTHEW WILSON**

Mighty Thor 9 Death of X variant

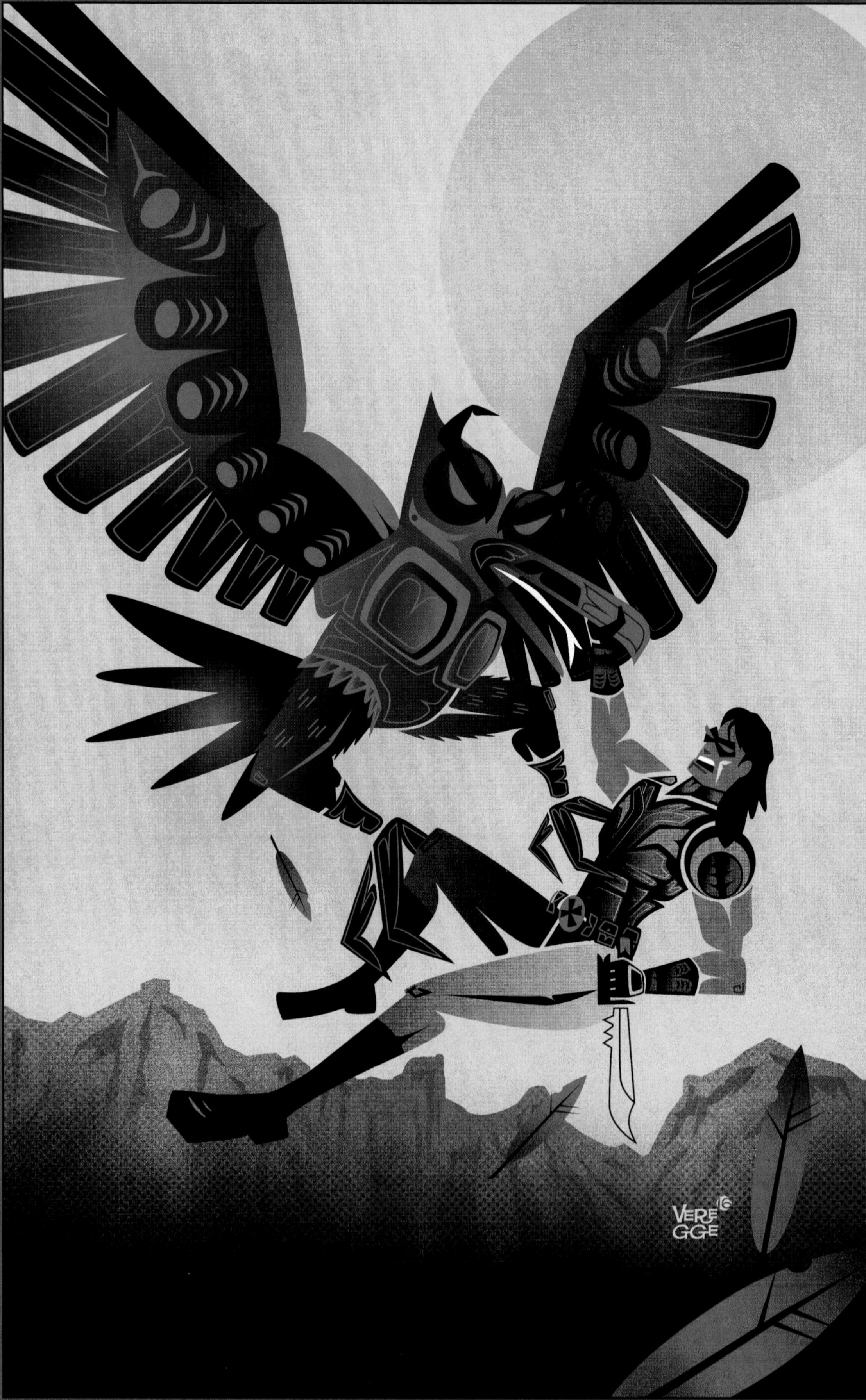
VEREGGE

JEFFREY VEREGGE

New Avengers 13 Death of X variant

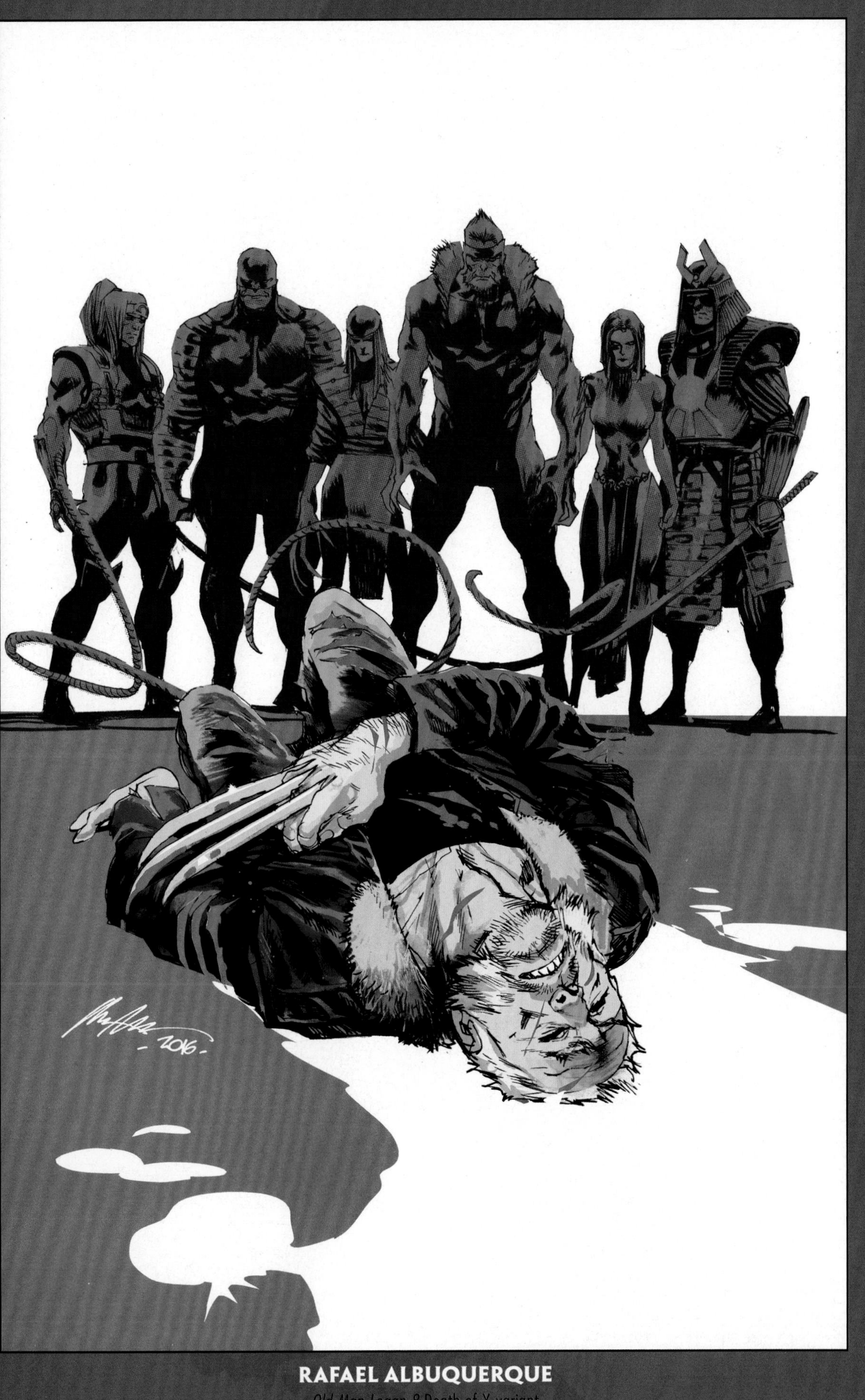
2016

RAFAEL ALBUQUERQUE

Old Man Logan 8 Death of X variant

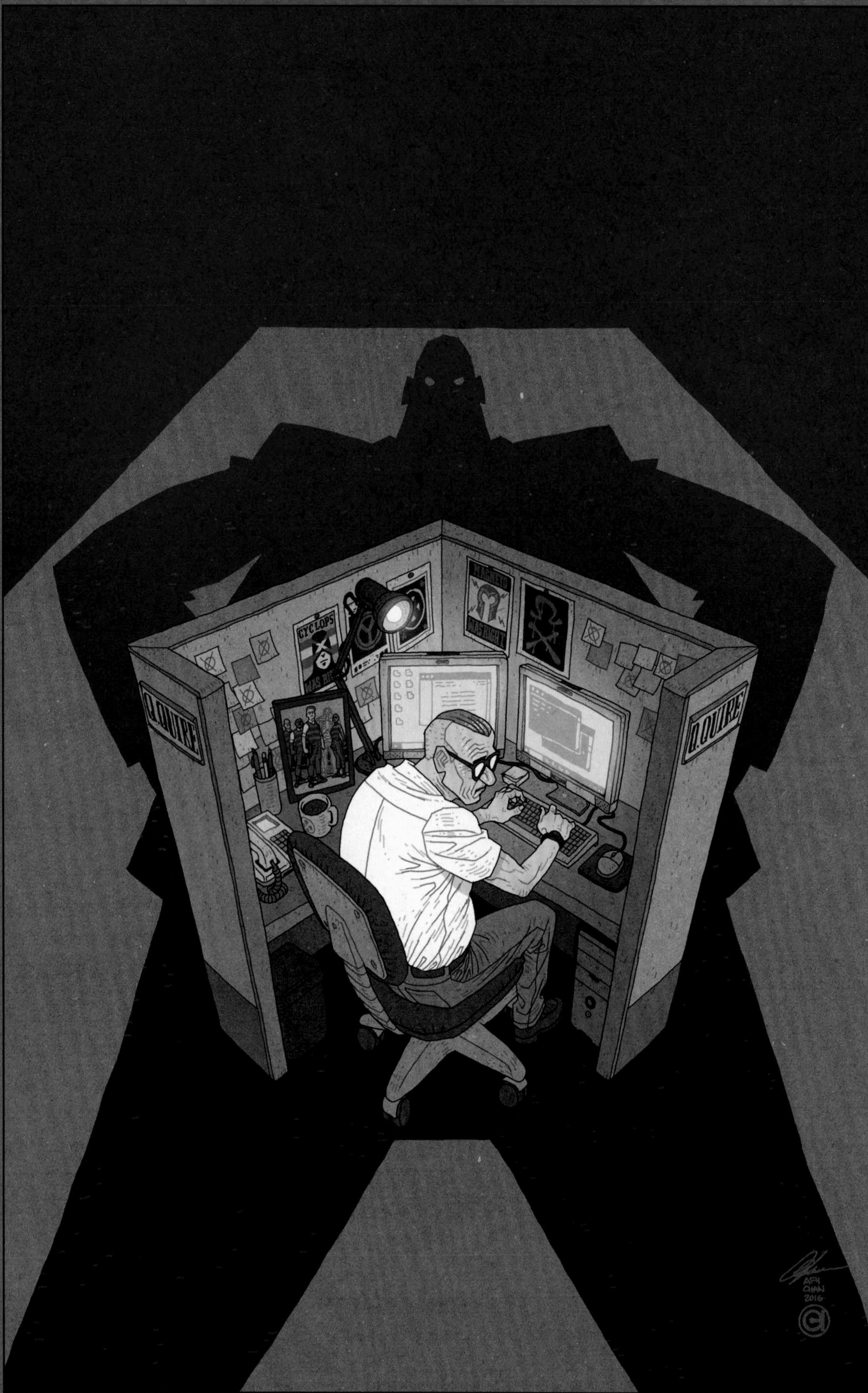
Q.QUIRE
CYCLOPS
MAGNETO
WAS RIGHT
Q.QUIRE
AFU CHAN 2016

AFU CHAN

Power Man and Iron Fist 6 Death of X variant

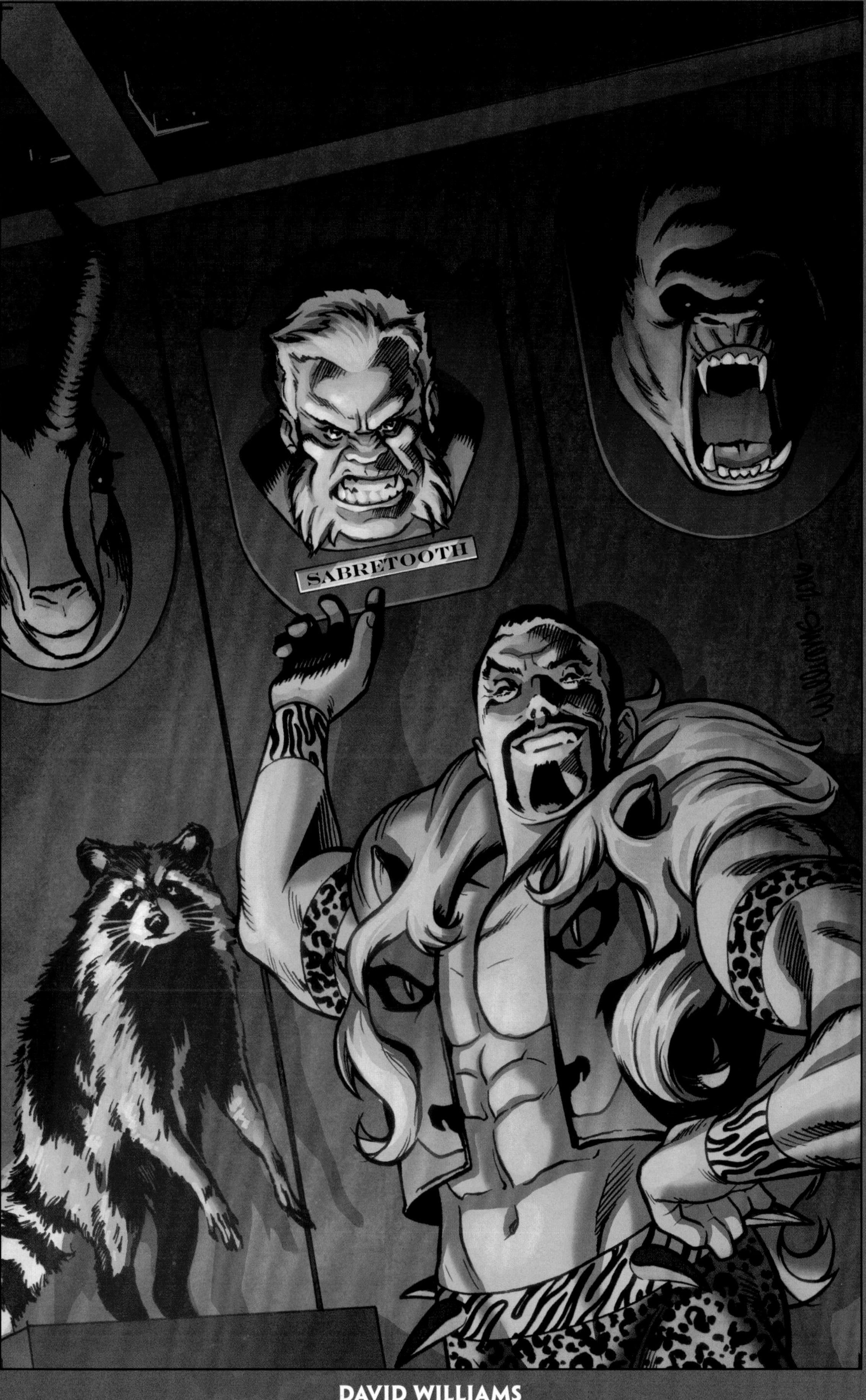
SABRETOOTH

DAVID WILLIAMS

Spider-Man 6 Death of X variant

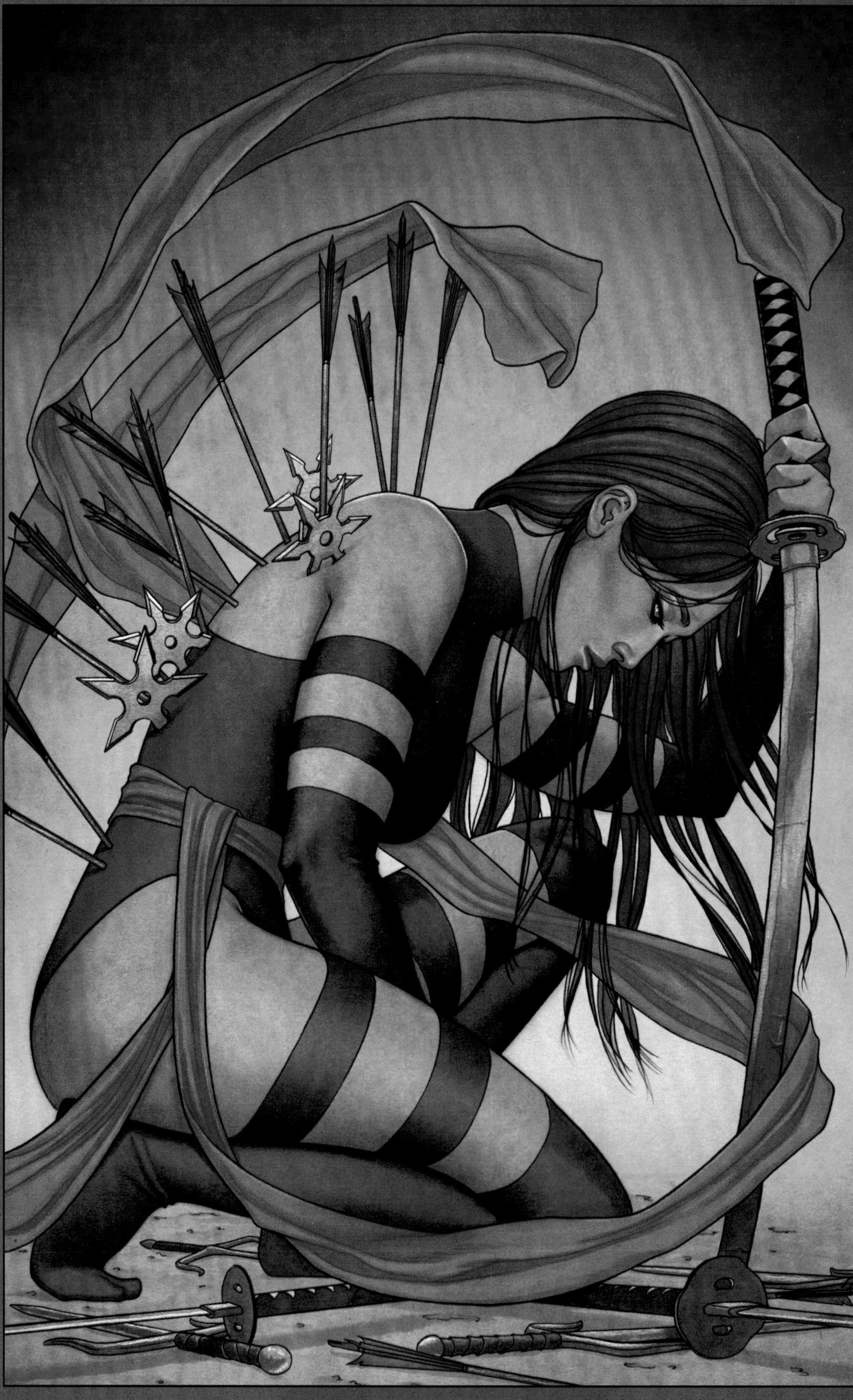

JENNY FRISON

The Astonishing Ant-Man 10 Death of X variant

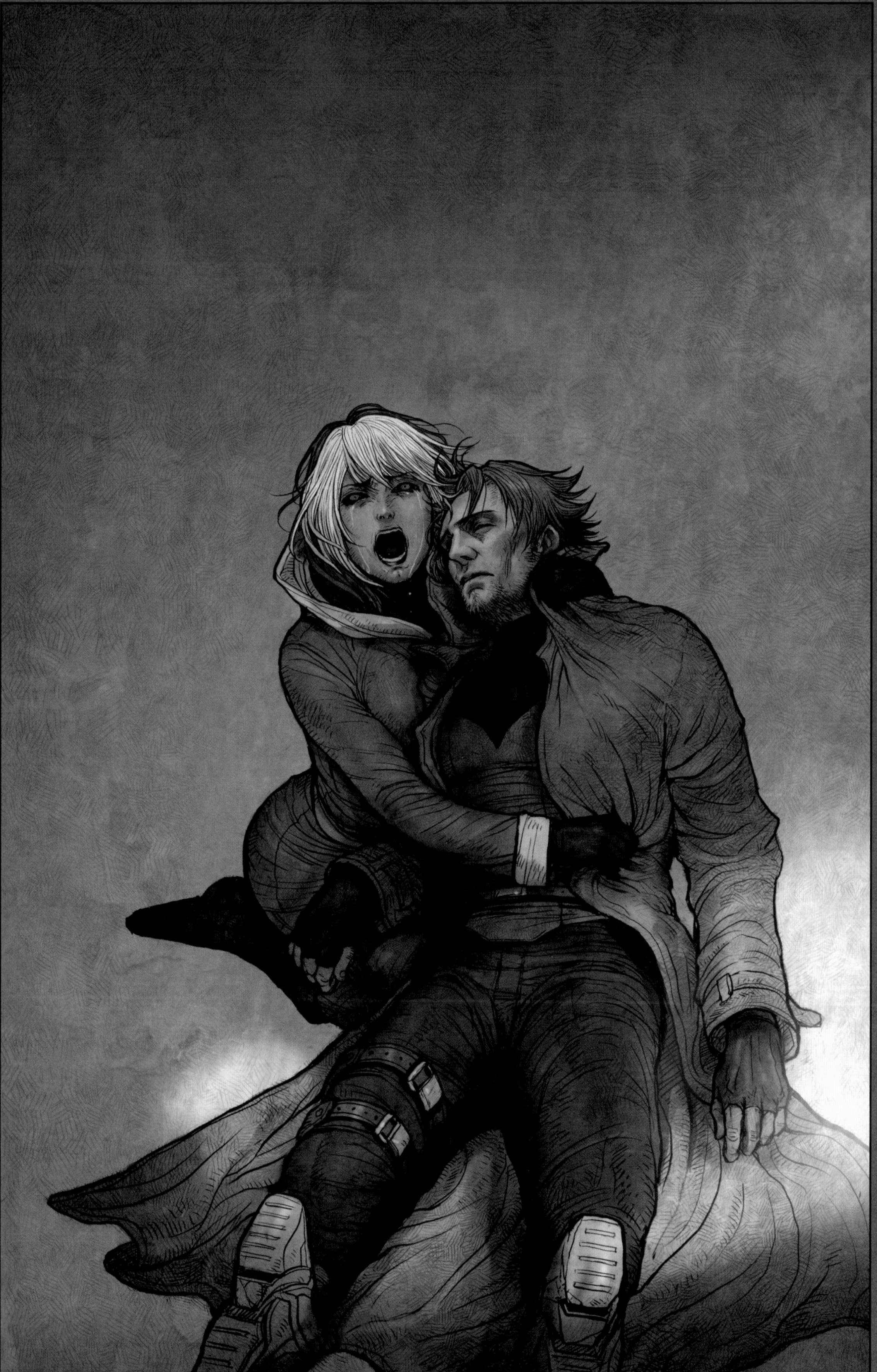

SANA TAKEDA

Uncanny Avengers 11 Death of X variant

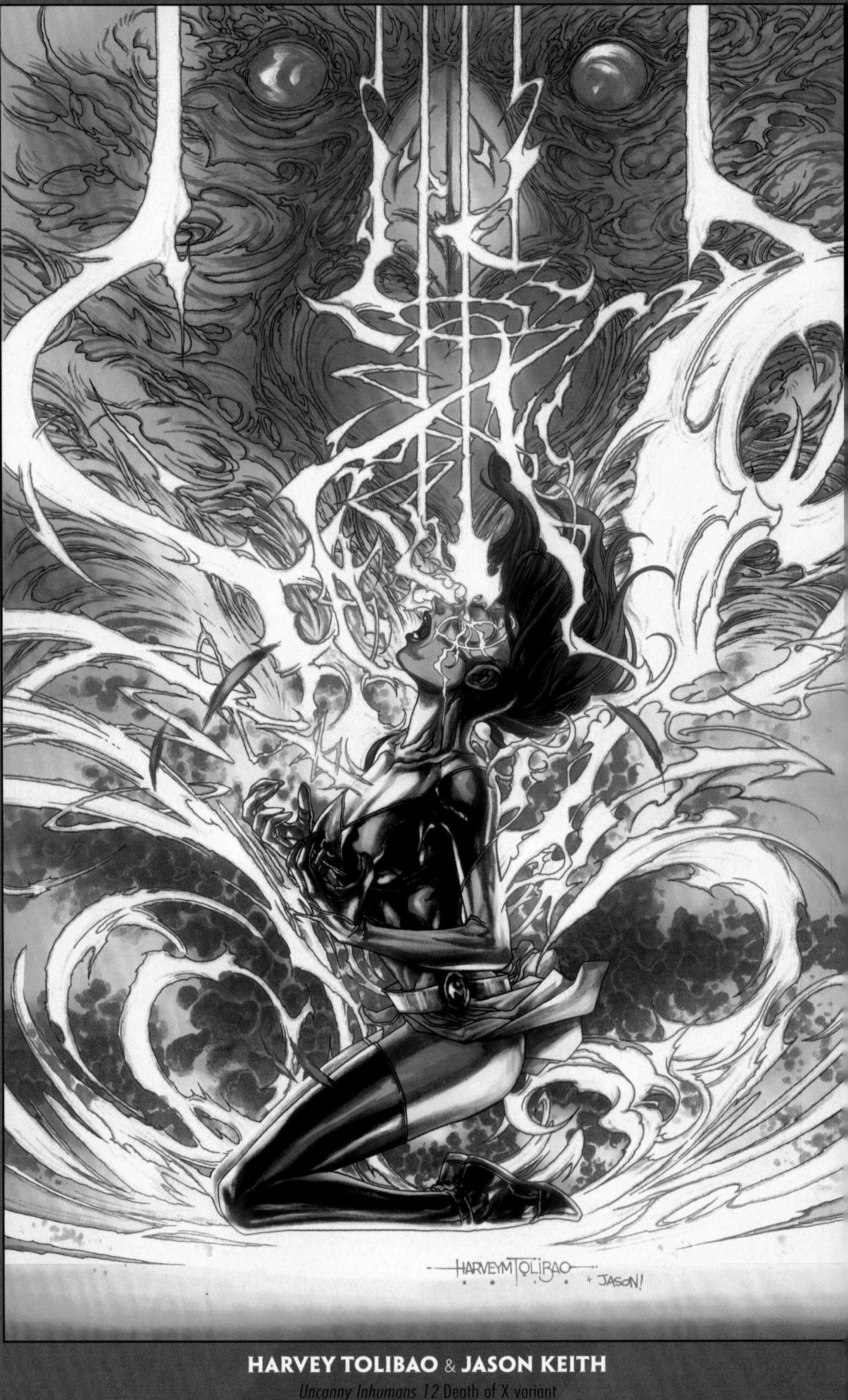
HARVEYM TOLIBAO
+ JASON!

HARVEY TOLIBAO & **JASON KEITH**

Uncanny Inhumans 12 Death of X variant

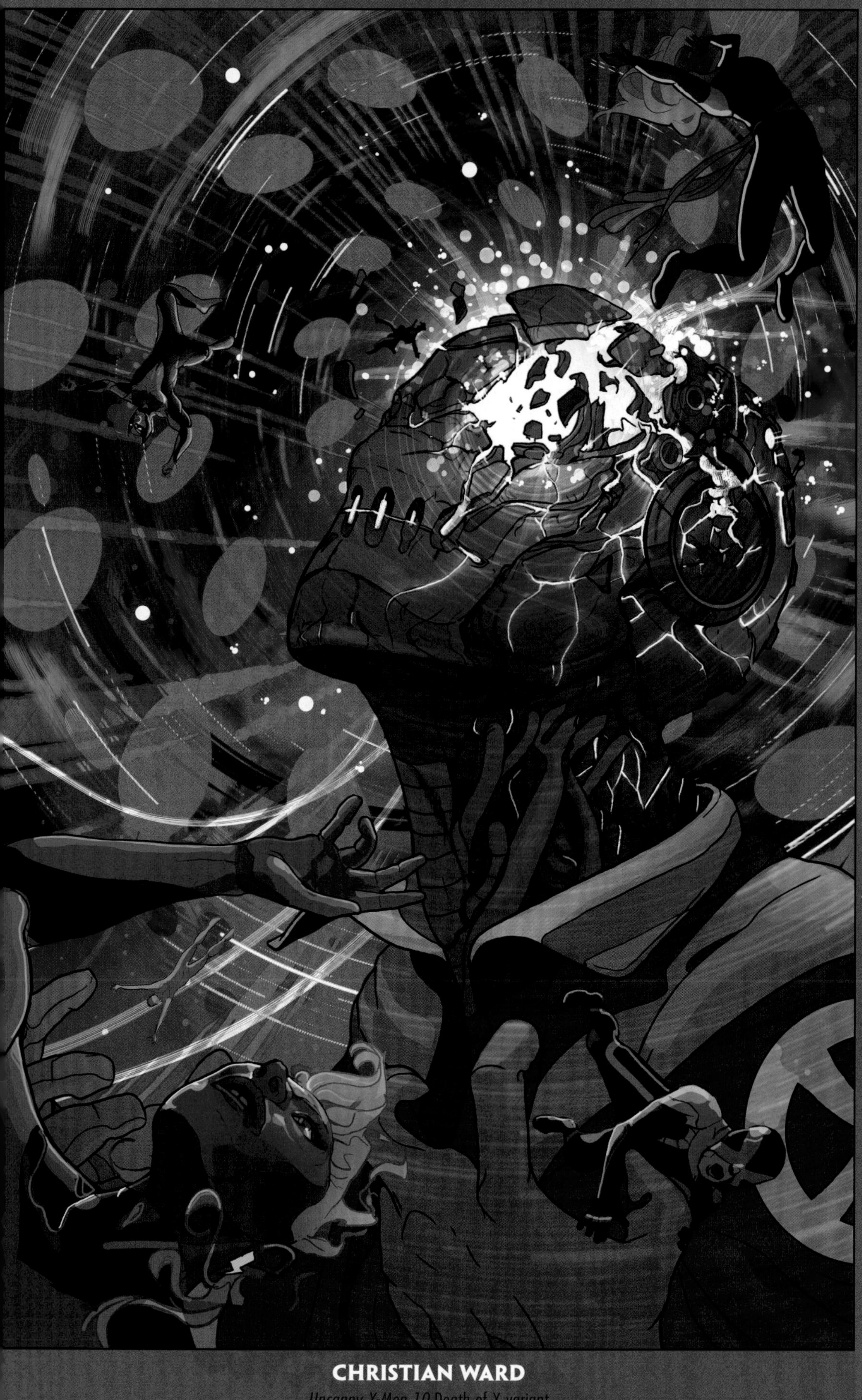

CHRISTIAN WARD
Uncanny X-Men 10 Death of X variant